ADVENTURES IN RUSSIAN HISTORICAL RESEARCH

ADVENTURES IN RUSSIAN HISTORICAL RESEARCH

REMINISCENCES OF AMERICAN SCHOLARS FROM THE COLD WAR TO THE PRESENT

EDITED BY

SAMUEL H. BARON AND CATHY A. FRIERSON

M.E.Sharpe
Armonk, New York
London, England

Library of Congress Cataloging-in-Publication Data

Adventures in Russian historical research : reminiscences of American scholars from the
Cold War to the present / edited by Samuel H. Baron and Cathy A. Frierson.
   p. cm.
Includes bibliographical references and index.
ISBN 0-7656-1196-1 (cloth: alk. paper) — ISBN 0-7656-1197-X (pbk.: alk. paper)
   1. Russia—History—Research—United States. 2. Soviet Union—History—Research—
United States. 3. Historians—United States—Biography. I. Baron, Samuel H.
II. Frierson, Cathy A.

DK38.8A35 2003
947′.007′202—dc21
   2003041559

Printed in the United States of America

The paper used in this publication meets the minimum requirements of
American National Standard for Information Sciences
Permanence of Paper for Printed Library Materials,
ANSI Z 39.48-1984.

BM (c) 10   9   8   7   6   5   4   3   2   1
BM (p) 10   9   8   7   6   5   4   3   2   1

Contents

About the Editors and Contributors

John T. (Jay) Alexander is Professor of History and Russian and East European Studies at the University of Kansas. His publications include four monographs, three book-length translations, some thirty articles, and forty-five encyclopedia articles. His *Bubonic Plague in Early Modern Russia* will be reissued by Oxford University Press in 2003.

Golfo Alexopoulos is Associate Professor of History at the University of South Florida in Tampa. Her publications include *Stalin's Outcasts: Aliens, Citizens, and the Soviet State, 1926–1936.* The focus of her current research is the practice of political amnesty from Stalin to Khrushchev.

Steven A. Barnes is a Ph.D. candidate at Stanford University. He is completing a dissertation on the Gulag in the Karaganda Region of Kazakhstan from the 1930s through the 1950s. He has published articles in *International Labor and Working Class History* and *Kritika.*

Samuel H. Baron, Distinguished Professor Emeritus at the University of North Carolina, Chapel Hill, is the author of *Plekhanov: The Father of Russian Marxism*; *Muscovite Russia: Collected Essays*; *Explorations in Muscovite History*; and *Bloody Saturday in the Soviet Union: Novocherkassk, 1962.*

James Cracraft is Professor of History and University Scholar at the University of Illinois at Chicago and a former fellow of the Davis Center for Russian, Eurasian and East European Research at Harvard University. He has published ten books in the field of modern Russian history. His *The Revolution of Peter the Great*, intended for students and general readers, will be published by Harvard University Press in 2003.

Laura Engelstein is Henry S. McNeil Professor of Russian History at Yale University. Her major publications include *Moscow, 1905: Working-Class*

Organization and Political Conflict; The Keys to Happiness: Sex and the Search for Modernity in Fin-de-Siècle Russia; and *Castration and the Heavenly Kingdom: A Russian Folktale.*

Cathy A. Frierson is Class of 1941 Professor of History at the University of New Hampshire. Her research has focused on the intersection between educated and peasant cultures in Russian history. Her most recent book-length study is *"All Russia is Burning!" A Cultural History of Fire and Arson in Late Imperial Russia.*

Paul R. Josephson is Associate Professor of History at Colby College, where he teaches the history of Russia and the history of science and technology. He has published five book-length studies on twentieth-century science and technology, of which the most recent is *Industrialized Nature.*

Nadieszda Kizenko is Associate Professor of History at the State University of New York at Albany. Her research focus is on Russian Orthodoxy. Her publications include *A Prodigal Saint: Father John of Kronstadt and the Russian People.* She is currently working on confession in imperial Russia.

Nancy Shields Kollmann is Professor of History and Director of the Center for Russian, East European and Eurasian Studies at Stanford University. Her research focuses on politics and society, gender relations, and legal culture in Russia through the eighteenth century.

Eve Levin is the author of *Sex and Society in the World of the Orthodox Slavs, 900–1700,* and many articles on pre-modern Russian and Balkan women's history, sexuality, popular religion, and medicine. She is also editor of *The Russian Review.* She has been a member of the faculty at Ohio State University since 1983.

Bruce W. Menning is Professor of Strategy at the U.S. Army Command and General Staff College in Fort Leavenworth, Kansas. He is the author of *Bayonets Before Bullets: The Imperial Russian Army, 1861–1914* and about thirty articles and chapters on Russian and Soviet military subjects. His current research focuses on Russian and Soviet military preparations for entry into the two world wars of the twentieth century.

Hugh Ragsdale, Professor Emeritus at the University of Alabama, lives in Charlottesville, Virginia. His research has focused on eighteenth-century Russian foreign policy, Paul I, and the Soviet role in the Sudeten crisis of

1938. His publications include *Imperial Russian Foreign Policy* and *The Russian Tragedy: The Burden of History.*

Donald J. Raleigh is Professor of History at the University of North Carolina, Chapel Hill. His most recent book is *Experiencing Russia's Civil War: Politics, Society, and Revolutionary Culture in Saratov, 1917–1922.* He is currently working on an oral history project tentatively entitled *Soviet Baby Boomers: Growing up in Khrushchev's and Brezhnev's Russia.*

Nicholas V. Riasanovsky, Sidney Hellman Professor of European History Emeritus at the University of California Berkeley, is the author of *A History of Russia* (sixth edition, 2000) and six other books on European and Russian history. His new study, *Identities: A Historical Survey*, will be published by Oxford University Press.

Priscilla Roosevelt is the author of a biography of the historian T.N. Granovskii and a book on Russia's prerevolutionary country estates. She currently heads a nonprofit organization assisting Russians in their efforts to preserve and enhance the utilization of surviving historic houses in rural Russia.

S. Frederick Starr, currently chairman of the Central Asia–Caucasus Institute at the Johns Hopkins School for Advanced International Studies (SAIS), was founding director of the Kennan Institute for Advanced Russian Studies. He is the author of nineteen books.

Richard Stites is Professor of History at the School of Foreign Service, Georgetown University. He has published extensively on Russian culture and Russian women's history. His has just completed a manuscript tentatively entitled *Serfdom, Society, and the Arts in Imperial Russia.*

Robert Weinberg teaches at Swarthmore College and has written books on the Revolution of 1905 in Odessa and the history of Birobidzhan. His current research focuses on anti-Semitism during the early years of the Soviet Union, particularly the efforts of the Kremlin to promote antireligious beliefs and secular values among Soviet Jews.

Elise Kimerling Wirtschafter is Professor of History at California State Polytechnic University in Pomona. She has published extensively on Russian social and cultural history. Her most recent book is *The Play of Ideas in Russian Enlightenment Theater.*

Acknowledgments

All the contributors of the following essays are indebted to the archivists and citizens of the USSR and the Russian Federation for their critical assistance to the success of our endeavors. Our sincere gratitude goes to Provost Robert Shelton and the Department of History at the University of North Carolina, Chapel Hill; to Dean Marilyn Hoskin, of the College of Arts and Sciences at the University of New Hampshire; and to Mr. and Mrs. Lee Marsh for support of the publication of this book.

Introduction

Samuel H. Baron and Cathy A. Frierson

Historical works are legion, but few works explore the varieties of experience involved in their production. The examination of the process rather than the product of historical research is especially germane with respect to U.S. scholars who have undertaken to research topics in Russian history since World War II, because the Soviet state was determined to "withhold the past." The contributors to this volume agreed with alacrity when we invited them to tell the stories of what one of their number has termed the "peculiar and confining experience" of being a U.S. historian of Russia, others have termed "adventures," and still others have referred to as a mix of agonies and ecstasies.

The contributors are a very diverse group, representing every generation of U.S. historians of Russia since the 1950s. In assembling the group, we sought to represent not only generations, but also genders, major doctorate-granting institutions, research approaches, and historical eras. These scholars have engaged in research on a wide spectrum of subject matters: diplomatic history and art history, military affairs and women's history, medical history and religion, biography, gentry culture and peasant life, intellectual history, Soviet science, and non-Russian regions. Their forays make for a panoramic view of the work accomplished across a multiplicity of areas of Russian life. The essays appear in the order of the authors' first research experience in Russia.

Each essay tells the story of author's experience, some over the full course of a career, others in a critical phase. The essays also provide studies in miniature of specific topics in Russian history through the author's description of how the research materials garnered through tenacity, *sitzfleisch*, and conspiring with rogue archival assistants or duping obstructionist ones shaped his or her interpretation. Each also displays a snapshot or series of snapshots of Soviet or Russian culture. As a whole, the essays constitute chronicles of both research and Russia itself since the late 1950s. We have organized the volume so as to make those chronicles most vivid. They are informative, insightful, engaging, sometimes moving, occasionally humorous, and always packed with human interest.

The adventures and agonies of Russian historical research resulted largely from the Soviet state's determination to keep a lock on its past. That determination may be considered the chronic condition of our professional lives. Several factors could worsen it. First among these was high politics, most acutely evident during the Cold War, with the Reagan era a period of particularly high tensions. Cold War politics always led the Soviet state to view us with suspicion. As several contributors to this volume intimate, our Soviet hosts (official and unofficial) generally assumed we were spies. S. Frederick Starr tells of being summoned and questioned about other foreign exchangees—an interrogation he deftly turned aside. Nicholas Riasanovsky offers evidence on a character with multiple identities who turned up periodically with the mission of obtaining information, and perhaps of entrapping him and a fellow traveler, the late Theodore Von Laue. Donald Raleigh gives an account of an experience with a security agent who cultivated him in Saratov.

Our status as participants in the U.S.-government-funded International Research and Exchanges Board (IREX) and Fulbright-Hays program added to suspicions about our mission. The vast majority of our research stays after 1968, when IREX took over management of exchanges previously run by the Inter-University Committee on Travel Grants (IUCTG) depended ultimately on inter-governmental agreements signed by the Soviet Ministry of Higher Education and the U.S. Department of State. U.S. scholars and graduate students who hoped to investigate topics in Russian history applied to participate, indicating the subject of interest and how they would research their topic. The Soviet side approved the applicants they found suitable from those whom IREX had nominated. As we will discuss more fully below, this power to approve or reject U.S. scholars generally rested on the perceived political or ideological sensitivity of each applicant's topic.

Our identity as U.S. historians of Russia, funded by the U.S. government, became acutely suspect when a Harvard historian of Russia, Richard Pipes, served as Special Advisor on Soviet and East European Affairs on Ronald Reagan's National Security Council. This was the point when our elected president dubbed the USSR the "evil empire." That label followed the Soviet invasion of Afghanistan, the U.S. withdrawal from the Moscow Olympics in 1980, and U.S. protests over the treatment of Andrei Sakharov. IREX's *Annual Report* for 1980–81 referred to the "deteriorating political relationship between Moscow and Washington" as exacerbating problems for U.S.–USSR academic exchanges that year.[1] These problems seemed especially jarring after the relatively good years of détente in the 1970s.

One can view our collective research experiences after 1968 as a story of decades. With the crisis of 1968 in Eastern Europe, IREX had to insist immediately on two cardinal principles of its programs: "to insulate intellectual exchange from the exigencies of international politics, and to establish its independence from any sources of influence other than those devoted to the advancement of knowledge."[2] With détente as the official U.S.–Soviet umbrella policy, the 1970s brought large numbers of U.S. applicants for the exchanges and special programs at IREX to attract social scientists to the field. The inter-governmental agreement increased the quota for the exchange of young scholars from forty to fifty per year.[3] As then IREX Associate Director Daniel Matuszewski acknowledged at the decade's end, "It may well be argued that these successes of the 1970s were due in large part to the then improving Soviet-American relationships."[4]

By 1980 he was predicting a new "time of troubles" in "the aftermath of Afghanistan and amidst the wreckage of 'détente.'"[5] All of the historians in this volume who attempted research in the early 1980s indicate that his predictions were correct when it came to access to materials and insulating programs from "outside political events and pressures."[6] One sign of those pressures was the number of U.S. exchange candidates nominated by IREX who were then rejected by the Ministry of Higher Education in Moscow. In 1969–70 and 1970–71, the rejections were 8 of 55 and 10 of 58 nominees, respectively. For the rest of the decade, rejections ranged from 2 of 71 in 1977–78 to 6 of 61 in 1979–80. In 1980–81, the number leapt to 22 rejections out of 50 nominees.[7] On the ground in the USSR, historians struggled against the most obdurate archival administrators of the Cold War era, making the early 1980s the thorniest patch of all in the quest for the Russian past.

If the "evil empire" years may be considered the low point for our access, the politics of the late Gorbachev and early Yeltsin years provided the high point. When Gorbachev decided to open the past to scrutiny by his own citizens to reinvigorate Soviet society through glasnost in 1987, he (perhaps unwittingly) threw the doors of research institutions wide open for U.S. scholars as well. In perhaps the most striking glasnost example in this volume, a military historian working with the Pentagon, Bruce Menning, found himself invited to go to Moscow as a guest of the Soviet Institute of Military History, doing "many things of which we had never dared to dream." As the essays in this volume reveal, many of us found this new condition disorienting, leading us to stumble before finding our way in our unprecedented research opportunities.

IREX records for the total number of U.S. scholars sent by IREX on research exchanges between 1968 and 1998 show that the peaks were clearly in the mid-1970s and glasnost years. Even at their highest, these numbers were under forty U.S. historians in the 1970s and only fifty in 1991–92. The numbers illustrate Riasanovsky's comment that few Americans ever received permission to do research in Russia in any year. Until the mid-1980s, these comprised exchangees of three types: senior scholars on the American Council of Learned Societies/USSR Academy of Sciences Exchange, graduate students/young scholars, and senior scholars. In the mid-1980s, IREX added Short-Term Research Exchanges, which contributed to an increase in the numbers of participants who were able to accomplish significant research in a relatively short time due to the new openness associated with glasnost.

Funding levels followed closely behind high politics as a constraining factor in our research experiences. Because our ability to do research in the USSR and post-Soviet Russia depended on official invitations and affiliations, we depended on IREX. That meant that we depended on IREX's funding, which, in turn, ebbed and flowed with the interests of U.S. legislators and foundations. IREX records for the 1980s support scholars' hunches that the more the Soviet Union was perceived as a threat and the more hard line the policies in the White House became, the more money flowed from the National Endowment for the Humanities, the Department of State, and the U.S. Information Agency. As Gorbachev's glasnost, democratization, and new thinking in foreign policy took hold in the late 1980s, U.S. funding of research in the USSR declined, just as archives became more open. Opportunities since the 1980s for citizens of the former Soviet Union to come to the United States have soared through IREX funding, but neither U.S. legislators nor major foundations have been willing to commit proportional funds to U.S. scholars seeking to do research in Russia.

The need for official status within the USSR also shaped our topics and methodologies. Both had to be approved by the Soviet research establishment. We may have designed our topics in New York, Berkeley, Cambridge, Bloomington, Palo Alto, or Chicago, but our U.S. advisors and colleagues reminded us that Soviet arbiters would ultimately decide whether or not we could do the research we envisioned. In the euphemistic language of annual reports, IREX noted the "tendency for our Soviet colleagues to react with a certain sensitivity to disciplines or research topics proposed by American candidates which may appear to them to be unorthodox,"[8] with rejection most likely to meet "those wishing to study post-revolutionary or contemporary topics."[9] Laura Engelstein describes it more directly as the "militant resistance to Western incursions into national themes." Several contributors to this volume allude to ways this reality influenced fundamental issues in their development as historians who had to adjust their research questions to the limitations of the Soviet historical establishment.

Much of the past (to say nothing of the present) was off-limits. For the modern period, approaches to or interpretations of the Great October Revolution of 1917, as well as developments across the nineteenth century that challenged the official Soviet version, certainly fell into the category of the "unorthodox." Topics and methodologies far beyond the expectations or comprehension of Soviet scholars would also meet with bemusement at best and obstruction at worst. In Starr's case in 1967, his two Soviet advisors could not contain themselves when he proposed the topic of local governance and decentralization in imperial Russia: "both of them . . . burst into uproarious laughter, which kept erupting anew during the waning minutes of the interview." Such sensitive topics as military and diplomatic history (even of the Napoleonic era, as Hugh Ragsdale's contribution illustrates) required almost blind optimism about access to the archives. Samuel Baron initially received approval to work in Plekhanov House in 1959 to further his biographical study of G.V. Plekhanov, only to be told soon thereafter that it would be fruitless to make the trip to Leningrad, where Plekhanov House is located. Richard Stites, who would write an excellent study of the women's liberation movement in Russia, reports that his advisor was puzzled by his interest in "the woman question," and others told him it was a subject suitable only for females. On the other hand, an archivist told Engelstein that her first research subject, the Revolution of 1905, was not "a woman's topic." John Alexander's Soviet supervisor initially advised him that the plague riot of 1771, the subject of an outstanding monograph now being reissued by Oxford University Press, "wasn't worth further investigation." Raleigh chose to do a dissertation on the Russian Revolution outside Moscow and St. Petersburg. Setting out to examine how events unfolded in the Volga River city of Saratov, he presently discovered to his chagrin that the city was closed to foreigners. Only years after he had published his book on the subject, and after an arduous struggle, was he permitted to visit and launch his inquiry into the Civil War that followed the revolution in that area. Those who chose such Soviet-sanctioned topics as popular movements in the revolution or subaltern groups in the imperial period could expect more generous treatment and usually got it, as Elise Kimerling Wirtschafter reports on the basis of her research into the social history of soldiers during the nineteenth century. Those who eschewed such topics did so at their peril, inviting more constant limitations than their fellows in any given year of the exchange. Many of us found that we were, as James Cracraft expresses it, "off on a lonely quest."

Once in the USSR or post-Soviet Russia, U.S. historians came up against still further research barriers. Archival regulations were onerous and potentially distorting. Before 1985, no U.S. scholars (and precious few Soviet ones) were permitted to see the catalogues of archives' holdings. Yet one's archival request had to include precise data on the fund (*fond*), file (*delo*), and page numbers. All such requests had to relate to the topic as each scholar had defined it on his or her application to IREX. Archivists could, and regularly did, refuse requests on the grounds that they did not match the approved topic. Most scholars relied on bibliographic references in previous scholarship (usually Soviet) as their guide to archival files. This meant that U.S. historians were potentially captive to the research of Soviet scholars. This system had the potential to limit inquiry to both acceptable topics and interpretations sanctioned by the Soviet establishment. Furthermore, scholars could request only a limited number of files a day. Because they had no access to the catalogue, they ordered without knowing the size of each file, which could range from one paragraph to hundreds of pages. Until the late 1980s, photoreproduction of archival materials was simply out of the question.

In this catch-22 world, U.S. scholars depended on their assigned Soviet advisors and archival assistants to break through into new research territories. Many of us were fortunate in such relationships, as the essays in this volume attest. It would have been impossible for Menning to achieve what he did without the help of General Dmitrii Volkogonov. Even with no official status beyond "spouse of a scholar" on his first trip to the Soviet Union, Paul Josephson found an activist patron in V. Ia. Frenkel. But such good fortune almost always was just that—luck rather than a variable that one could predict or manipulate in this critical sphere that determined one's career as a scholar in the United States as much as in the USSR.

Our "peculiar and confining experience" included not only obstacles in our research, but also personal sacrifices few U.S. historians of European or North American cultures have to make. The USSR was a third world country and police state with no environmental protection and a health care system few American citizens would willingly enter. To embark on an extended research stay meant embracing difficult living conditions always and health risks often, as the experience of Golfo Alexopoulos in an insular community in Siberia illustrates. Those of us who lived in Soviet dormitories found ourselves in a Soviet apartheid: citizens of capitalist countries (*kapstrany*) inhabited certain wings or floors; citizens of socialist countries (*sotsstrany*) inhabited others. This apartheid extended to libraries and archival reading rooms, where racial segregation also prevailed. Dark-skinned scholars (even from socialist countries and client states) were relegated to inferior facilities. And, of course, trustworthy Soviet citizens lived among us to report on our activities and relationships. For U.S. scholars with families, the choice has been between family separation on the one hand, and the logistics of securing a reasonably secure life for spouse and children in decidedly "iffy" settings. The need for fluency in the Russian language to manage daily life, as much as archival research further complicated such family choices.

Post-Soviet Russia is no longer a police state. Some of us are nostalgic for the KGB agents who shadowed and thereby protected us. The environmental situation has worsened. The public health situation is nothing short of catastrophic. And, as Nadieszda Kizenko's experience from the mid-1990s illustrates, prices for basics have risen so high as to make an IREX-funded research stay in Moscow or St. Petersburg the very antithesis of comfortable. In short, extended research stays in this culture were not and are not for the faint of heart.

Yet, as the publications of the scholars in this volume and the scores of others not included here show, neither Soviet nor post-Soviet leaders were able to withhold the past. On the contrary, U.S. historians have consistently breached or circumvented official barriers to enter it. For the scholar willing to embark on it, Russian historical research has proved to be a quest as replete with adventure as with roadblocks. Those who have chosen to study Russia have more strategic thinking, flexibility, tenacity, inventiveness, and sheer daring than the image of the historian typically suggests. While exercising these "heroic" or "individualistic" qualities, they have equally had to relinquish control over their fate and rely on—even trust—Russian officials, colleagues, friends, and acquaintances whose sometimes illegal assistance jeopardized their own careers and the future access to Russia for American students and scholars. The essays here explain why these American citizens chose to embark on such an intellectual odyssey, how they developed strategies in the face of constant obstruction, and how the Russian setting and Russian persons brought unanticipated discoveries and humane relationships.

Several contributors explain what first led them to Russia and kept them in its grasp. Engelstein credits "the imp of contradiction" and the *zeitgeist*; Wirtschafter explores her "privileged alienation" as a Jewish woman in Alabama, a southern woman at Columbia University, and a wife and mother practicing Russian social history in Beverly Hills; and Kizenko explores the "long series of misunderstandings" she encountered growing into adulthood in New York State as a daughter of a post-war émigré, Belorussian Orthodox priest during the Cold War.

Universally, the contributors testify to the importance of research *in situ*. Starr explores how his experiences belied images of a monolithic, totalitarian, even Soviet (as opposed to nineteenth-century) culture, which he calls "the pompous generalizations about the nature of the Soviet Union that had been concocted by political scientists in the West." His months of conversations with Leningraders in a public bathhouse would generate a few surprises in the steam, and even more later, when all the men met fully clothed for a farewell dinner. Cracraft observed that "a supposedly repressed people" hailed one of its heroes, Peter the Great, and "the authorities manifestly followed the popular lead" in celebrations marking the tercentenary of Peter's

accession to the throne. When he returned several times to view the exhibitions "Portraiture of the Petrine Period" and "Icon Painting of the Petrine
Period" in 1973, they "proved to be the turning point in [his] professional
life." Epiphanies of this sort were impossible to anticipate in any IREX application. They were also beyond the reach of Soviet authorities, no matter
their ambitions to monitor or control us.

The opportunities for U.S. historians to develop a "sense of place" by
visiting sites central to their research multiplied with glasnost and the collapse of the Soviet Union. Baron could travel to Novocherkassk to walk
the streets where in 1962 Soviet agents shot down workers' demonstra-
tions, which he was the first Western scholar to research. Steven Barnes
could make the journey to Kazakhstan to visit former prison camps of the
Gulag. Kizenko was able to reside in monks' quarters at the major monastery in St. Petersburg while writing her biography of the charismatic priest
Father Ioann of Kronstadt. Priscilla Roosevelt embarked on daily journeys
beyond paved roads to pick her way through the collapsed entry halls and
parlors of Russia's noble country estates. And Robert Weinberg could travel
even further beyond Moscow (5,000 miles) to Birobidzhan, capital city of
the Jewish Autonomous Region, to see that "national enclave of Soviet
Jewry" while writing its history.

Even the research topics most closely guarded prior to Gorbachev opened
up. Josephson had "the proverbial researcher's field day" in 1991, as he pored
over the papers of A.P. Ershov, a pioneer in the development of computer
science in the USSR. As a military historian, Menning reports that from the
spring of 1991 to mid-1994, "a new and heady atmosphere of freedom reigned
in the archives," as Soviet barriers to research were "melting away." In 1996,
Ragsdale was researching twentieth-century Soviet foreign policy and gained
access to "the richest collection of largely unexploited materials that [he]
had ever imagined to see in a Russian archive."

These essays also testify that *de visu* work with original documents was
as important as *in situ* explorations. Nancy Shields Kollmann describes here
how she chased down her most treasured research prize, a grand-princely
charter dating to the sixteenth century. Her description of this feat of detec-
tion and her steady campaign to secure the privilege of holding the charter in
her hands reveals much about the realities of research in the USSR while
providing a model for scholars in any field to emulate. If Kollmann resembles
a talented Sherlock Holmes, Cathy Frierson seems more like Alice in Won-
derland as she describes finding herself in a rabbit-hole world where the
director of a coveted archive sent word for her after months of being denied
access to any archive at all. Once inside the archive, she read provincial
correspondents' reports on village life in the 1890s that led her to question

long-standing conclusions about Russian rural society. For Eve Levin, a *de visu* thrill came in the form of a birchbark document from Novgorod, an artifact dating to the Kievan era and handed to her during her first meeting with her Soviet advisor, V.L. Ianin, in 1981. His generosity was especially noteworthy at this low point in U.S.–Soviet relations.

Ianin offered far more than a birchbark token of respect and welcome. He also offered Levin an introduction to her Soviet counterpart, Natalia Pushkareva, his graduate student, who was then also writing a history of medieval women in Muscovy. Levin's description of the lifelong partnership that ensued with Pushkareva is the most focused description of the research relationships with Soviet and post-Soviet/Russian colleagues that made our work possible, rich, and humane. Such assistance came not only in the distant history of Muscovy, but also in Baron's work on the sensitive topic of the Soviet slaughter of striking workers, Alexopoulos's probings into the Stalin period, and Josephson's forays into the Soviet nuclear program.

For the Soviet scholars, archivists, journalists, librarians, and designated research assistants who extended their help, risk was always present. They chose to abandon their official role as Cerberus to open the gates into often forbidden territories. Some contributors to this volume have named these guides and patrons with the goal of honoring and thanking them. Others have chosen to be vague in their descriptions of unnamed helpers and informants, explaining that their actions on our behalf may jeopardize them still. Their presence in our adventures points to the fact that Western scholars had no monopoly on dedication to unfettered scholarship or willingness to embrace special burdens, even hazards, in its pursuit. No matter how determined the state may have been to "withhold the past" or how many Soviet citizens were willing to comply with that goal, the persons who helped us ensured that, as Roosevelt writes, "The truths of the Soviet period came tumbling out. . . ."

The most senior of our contributors, Riasanovsky, frames our adventures with the question "Half-Empty or Half-Full?" As we move further into the twenty-first century, with the Cold War telescoping into the past, the historians in this volume concur that even the Cold War years were half-full. In the post-Gorbachev, Vladimir Putin era now in its third year, their appraisals display less agreement on how full our access is now or is likely to become. Cracraft sees recent and current research conditions as "normal," much like what prevails in the archives of other European countries. Frierson echoes this sentiment, noting that unrestricted access has become "standard" and "mundane." Weinberg goes so far as to say that he and some of his colleagues view the younger generation of Russia specialists as somewhat spoiled by how easy research has become, and confesses a certain nostalgia for the more demanding conditions of life and work in the Brezhnev era, when one had to figure out ways to penetrate the barriers to secure essential documents. But it would be a mistake to suppose that these judgments apply across the board. Menning notes the progressive closing down of various military archives in the second half of the 1990s. Archivists who assisted Ragsdale in the mid-1990s have urged him not to publish data they helped him extract from foreign policy documents. Baron was barred access to materials that would have allowed him to write a more circumstantial account than the one he published on the 1962 events in Novocherkassk. Barnes had to submit to old-style Soviet archival regulations in Kazakhstan a full decade after the collapse of the USSR. Current circumstances suggest that better than half-full aptly describes the situation, although the level seems to be falling. It remains to be seen whether the Russian Federation will relinquish the Soviet state's determination to keep a lock on its past. Russian officialdom will set the terms for current and future generations of U.S. historians of Russia and the research quests they undertake.

Notes

1. International Research and Exchanges Board, *Annual Report 1980–1981* (New York, 1981): 10.

2. International Research and Exchanges Board, *Annual Report for the Operational Year 1968–1969* (New York, 1969): 2.

3. International Research and Exchanges Board, *Annual Report 1973–1974* (New York, 1974): 2.

4. International Research and Exchanges Board, *Annual Report 1979–1980* (New York, 1980): 15.

5. Ibid.

6. Ibid.

7. These data can be found in IREX *Annual Reports* from those years.

8. International Research and Exchanges Board, *Annual Report 1969–1970* (New York, 1970): 10.

9. International Research and Exchanges Board, *Annual Report 1973–1974* (New York, 1974): 2.

ADVENTURES IN RUSSIAN HISTORICAL RESEARCH

1

My Historical Research in the Soviet Union
Half-Empty or Half-Full?

Nicholas V. Riasanovsky

The Merriam-Webster Dictionary defines "adventure" as follows:

> 1 a: an undertaking usually involving danger and unknown risks; b: the encountering of risks (the spirit of adventure); 2: an exciting or remarkable experience (an adventure in exotic dining); 3: an enterprise involving financial risk.

For several generations we students of Russia and the Soviet Union have had peculiar and confining experiences. Our colleagues in European history as a matter of course did extensive research, occasionally for years at a time, in the countries of their choosing, and easily studied and even obtained advanced degrees there. We were generally banned from the archives and frequently from the country of our specialty, except for painfully established and extremely limited scholarly exchanges and conferences. Whereas no one counted the foreign men and women who studied or engaged in research in Paris, London, or Rome, we were glad to obtain our dozen or two dozen slots and had to hope that nothing untoward would happen during a given year to spoil our chances for the next. When one of the Soviet exchange students went into a drunken stupor and was failed at Columbia University, one of our students was promptly sent home from Moscow. One of my Ph.D. candidates, a Canadian from a Russian family, was accused, resoundingly, of wrecking, but fortunately was allowed to leave the Soviet Union promptly though with his research materials (he was writing a dissertation on the Slavophiles) lost. Throughout, Russian and especially Soviet studies remained at a high level of political tension and vituperation, comparable to such subjects as the Holocaust and the Vietnam War. On the one hand, during the Cold War politics helped to provide our field with U.S. government and foundation subsidies, nostalgically remembered at present. On the other hand, that

3

circumstance added to the partisan and combative nature of our area of interest and its relative isolation from other areas. A few of our very best scholars, such as professors Father Georges Florovsky and Gleb Struve, refused on principle to set foot in the Soviet Union or to have anything to do with it.[1]

Perhaps even more significant in their negativity toward Soviet learning have been the reactions of many scholars outside our field when for the first time they encountered Marxist–Leninist or Marxist–Leninist–Stalinist historiography. My Berkeley colleague Henry May, a splendid American intellectual historian, went unprepared to a joint American–Soviet conference dealing with the eighteenth-century Enlightenment in the two countries. He was horrified by the encounter. What shook him most in the Soviet papers and discussion was the crudeness and the simplicity of the approach to the subject, and especially the totally irrelevant quotes from the classics of Marxism as well as from Lenin and Stalin. Poor Henry, so upset that everything had to be treated in a crass Marxist manner in the Soviet intellectual world, did not know that many subjects could not be treated there at all.

Still, without challenging the moral stance of Georges Florovsky and Gleb Struve or dismissing the just criticisms of Henry May, I must admit that I have been an enthusiastic supporter of the regular cultural exchange between the two countries from its inception in the late 1950s to the present. It has proved to be of enormous help to us and to our students, many of them now professors contributing to this volume. Russian history is based overwhelmingly on Russian sources, Russian publications, and Russian historiography, just as France is indispensable for French history and Germany for German history. In addition to what Russia could contribute to almost every scholarly project in our field, the very perception of the general context is of great significance. In isolation, too many of our graduate students have come to think of topics in Russian history in terms of two or three books available in English. And exchange, together with the general easing of travel and communication, has already improved knowledge of the Russian language on the part of most of our researchers beyond the point that Professor Maurice Friedberg, a wit in our midst, designates "intermediate Russian."

Even Soviet historical scholarship itself is a rich and many-faceted subject with strong as well as weak characteristics. In discussing it, I often used the image of a glass half-empty or half-full. I remember, for example, talking with a former student of ours, now a fine professor, a man of the left, by the way, not of the right—historical opinion was never divided simply into left and right. His topic was the Revolution of 1905 and its interpretation by scholars, including Soviet historians. My companion said: "Oh, I dismiss Soviet writings." "All right," I said, "if you dismiss Soviet writings"—I had just finished reading his manuscript on 1905—"why then do you mention historian A so often?" He replied: "Well, historian A is an exception. He is fine." I asked: "How about Historian B?" He replied: "You must know what I think of historian B, but he is the only person to use these documents." "And historian C?" "Historian C is in a class by himself, he is so good. Don't even mention him with the others." Well, it was not necessary to continue. One usually finds historians A, B, and C, as well as others, as one studies one's Russian topic.

Good history could be and was written in the Soviet Union. Several considerations help to explain this rather rare happy outcome. To begin with, the Soviet system as we knew it became fully formed only with the Stalinization of the country in the early 1930s. The preceding period may be called transitional, but it was strongly linked to the past. Also, even after it had been fully formed, the Stalinist system had its more permissive as well as its restrictive phases. Different aspects of history were treated differently. Thus, it was much easier to do serious work in economic than in religious history. Besides, the audience mattered. Especially in the Brezhnev era, highly specialized and advanced studies usually suffered little from censorship, while historical works for mass readership had to deal in black and white, present their heroes as paragons of every virtue, and so on. Most importantly, as I shall explain later in more detail, the imposed fundamental historical framework usually allowed genuine historical investigation in at least some directions that would not endanger that framework.

All of these circumstances and still others permitted the writing of some good history in the Soviet Union, and all of it was in the open, so to speak, above board. But Soviet writers, historians included, also specialized in beating the system—in a sense, it even became a great game. Perhaps the most common way to do this was to include programmatic Marxist statements in the introduction and the conclusion and to ignore them in the body of the text. I did not know whether to laugh or cry when one of the best, perhaps the best, Russian historian of the nineteenth century told me, "Nikolai Valentinovich, note that I mention that view in the introduction and the conclusion, but not a word of it in the text." Other messages, intended or not, can also be obtained from Soviet books. One of my favorite such studies—people in our field often have favorites—is a volume on the revolutionary movement in Russia in the second quarter of the nineteenth century. The point is that there was no such movement. In fact, this book is a fine example of negative evidence. The author, a fully qualified scholar, had gone through the archives as I had not. Thanks to him, I know that there was nothing on the subject to find. His laudatory tone merely emphasizes the lack of serious evidence.

One of the joys of visits to the Soviet Union turned out to be its people. I must say that almost all of my Soviet colleagues, professors, librarians, archivists, and researchers of various kinds did all they could, within the allowable limits, to help me and my work. Surprisingly, in addition to books and other materials I had asked for, still other items were often brought, which apparently someone deemed useful for my research. And the selection of these extra items was usually very good. My papers and research presentations were well attended and well received. Some of them led to long and interesting discussions. The advantages ranged from occasionally getting a thorough and able critique of what I was doing from a different perspective, to obtaining a wealth of factual and bibliographical information I would not have obtained otherwise. Although at times hesitant, most Soviet academics seemed glad to talk to me. Especially in the earlier years of the exchange, the presence of a foreign scholar appeared to be an event. I remember having dinner in the apartment of Professor Petr Andreevich Zaionchkovskii when he answered a telephone call informing him that he was permitted to invite me.

Moreover, I found the same friendly and admiring attitude toward foreigners, in particular Americans, outside academic circles. I remember a chauffeur for the Academy of Sciences telling me that he knew there was no race problem in the United States. When, somewhat taken aback, I asked him how he knew this, he answered that it was because the Soviet media kept insisting there was one. Many such examples could be cited, but I remember a certain episode above all others. In the course of several sabbatical years, my wife Arlene and our children would remain in Paris while I worked several weeks or even several months in the Soviet Union. Arlene would come to Moscow or to Leningrad for a week or ten days of wonderful sightseeing and general celebration sponsored by our Soviet hosts. This time it was Leningrad, and we were trying to have dinner in a good restaurant on Nevsky Prospect. We managed to get in with the help of a strange character who claimed that he was soon to emigrate to the United States. At a recent medical convention he had asked two American doctors unknown to him to sign papers certifying that he was their nephew, and they had done so. We sat at a long table with perhaps ten or twelve naval officers. I spoke Russian with them, English with Arlene. Suddenly, one officer asked: "What is your wife speaking, Finnish?" "No, English." "Why English, who is she?" "An American." "What a fine fellow!" he exclaimed. "Married an American." I shall never forget his look of approval and fascination.

The positive Russian attitude toward foreigners was all the more remarkable because, in a sense, we had everything and they had almost nothing. Once, I found something to buy in a *berezka* store (these shops were established to attract hard currencies), namely, a wooden toy of a peasant and a bear jointly chopping a log, like the one my father had when growing up in

Kostroma. But the Academy car was waiting impatiently. I explained the situation to the vendor in Russian, of course, and promised to pick up the toy and pay for it in the afternoon. She responded: "This is not for such as you, this is only for foreigners."[2]

It was the people in the Soviet Union who were kind, not the system. I have already referred to the "allowable limits," and they were tight. Only after the collapse of the Soviet Union did the wife of a Soviet colleague, and by then a friend of mine, tell me that when Arlene came to Moscow, she had petitioned the Institute of History of the Academy of Sciences to be allowed to invite us for dinner. She received the reply: "They are already being given one dinner. Enough." More seriously, when Arlene suddenly had to have major surgery in Paris, the bureaucrats arranged for my report to be given immediately rather than several weeks later as scheduled. But instead of expediting my flight to Paris, they had me fill out paper after paper affirming that my early departure was voluntary and I had no claims against the Soviet Union; and they encouraged me by saying that, according to their government's information, surgeons in Paris were excellent and I had nothing to worry about. One bureaucrat added: "If she dies, she dies; if she lives, she lives." She lived.

Scholars had many opportunities and advantages when part of an exchange. Most of our participants were preoccupied with their own research, although that usually included at least some consultation with Soviet colleagues, occasional presentations of the results of their research, and other means of participation in Soviet intellectual life. For example, I was invited to attend Professor Militsa Vasilevna Nechkina's seminar, as well as some meetings at the Institute examining the research projects of its members.

As a theme for one of my research trips to the Soviet Union, I sought a better acquaintance with Russian and Soviet historiography, one of my lifetime interests. I asked in particular for interviews with a number of leading Soviet historians. I had selected major figures whom I had never met, or had met only very briefly, rather than Boris Aleksandrovich Rybakov, who had been my brother Alexander's mentor during the first graduate student exchange between the two countries and with whom I had maintained relations ever since, or a friend such as Petr Andreevich Zaionchkovskii. Although all of those to be interviewed were prominent scholars who had presented their historical views richly in books and had no reason to impart revelations to me, my expected gain was obvious: the details should fit into the pictures I already had of them, and the men themselves would become closer and somehow more human. And, indeed, I learned something about Soviet historiography and perhaps even about historiography in general, although not always as I had planned.

The first meeting, with Academician Lev Viktorovich Cherepnin, was in certain ways a disaster. I began awkwardly by noting that my host was both a continuer of the mainline Russian historical tradition and a leader of Soviet scholarship, and asked him to comment on the relationship between the two. He answered: "Nikolai Valentinovich, one must know how to renounce the old world and live one's way [*vzhitsia*] into the new." And so it went. Only at one point, when he realized that my father had been a student of Vasilii Osipovich Kliuchevskii, probably the most famous historian of Russia of all time, he became somehow less formal and more accessible. But that didn't last long. And Cherepnin concluded loudly in praise of Marxism and Soviet historiography. Whatever my interest in the interview, he clearly used it only to reaffirm his Marxist credentials. And what could I expect from someone with Cherepnin's painful past—he had been arrested and exiled, and was now addressing for the first time a foreigner he did not know? (Despite the earlier unpleasantness, he along with Rybakov and a very few others had risen to the highest levels of the Soviet historical guild.)

The problems with Aleksandr Aleksandrovich Zimin were quite different. He surprised and almost disconcerted me by having read some of my books in preparation for the interview, and by offering respectful and helpful advice. I, in turn, wanted to discuss his important work on the sixteenth century, but we never got to that. Once my topics were out of the way, Zimin could talk only about *The Lay of the Host of Igor.* I knew, to be sure, that the situation was a very tense one. A few days earlier, I had been advised by a Soviet colleague not even to mention Zimin's name when I came to visit Rybakov. Zimin had denied the authenticity of *The Lay of the Host of Igor*, the pearl of ancient Russian literature. Rybakov was one of its most ferocious defenders. But, although I could not plead ignorance, I kept missing something. Thus, when Zimin said that he had been accused of a lack of patriotism, and even of treason, I commented that we were, after all, historians and had to go with the evidence. He replied: "You do not understand me. I am more patriotic than all of them." Zimin went on and on, and the climax came when he charged me with a mission. I, an American, a Russian, and a Russian scholar, must tell the world about the behavior of another American, Russian, and Russian scholar, Roman Osipovich Jakobson, in the crisis over *The Lay.* I am now discharging my mission. Jakobson, a leading proponent of the authenticity of *The Lay*, came to a conference on the subject in Moscow. He telephoned Zimin and, according to Zimin, the conversation went as follows: "Jakobson speaking, give me quickly your manuscript—there is not much time left before the conference." "Roman Osipovich, we have not even been introduced to one other." "You are not giving it! Alright. I shall tear it apart [*raznesu*] just the same." I obtained from my interview with Zimin the most complete list as of that time of his published writings related to *The Lay of the Host of Igor.* In his case, as in a number of others, the Soviet authorities did not simply ban his publishing on the subject, but limited it in effect to short pieces in out-of-the-way periodicals.

I shall not proceed interview after interview, but I should mention one more, the most memorable, although it was not part of the series I have been dealing with, and not even in Russian history. At that time, I was writing my book on Charles Fourier[3] and was briefly in Moscow for another reason, but I decided to seek out the best Soviet specialist on Fourier, Ioganson Isaakovich Zilberfarb. I found him easily at an historical institute of the Academy, and he received permission to have lunch with me. We went through the line in a nearby cafeteria and sat down at a table for two. Zilberfarb then got up from the table and brought me a big apple. The rapport was immediate because Zilberfarb was a kindly, well-mannered, and soft-spoken Russian intellectual like many of the people with whom I had been brought up. I concentrated on the bibliography of our subject, which he had probably mastered better than anyone else in the world.[4] I hurried because I did not know how long we could be together. Still, when the apple was gone, I found time to ask Zilberfarb about his letter to a prominent periodical. That periodical had published a scholarly article about Fourier's anti-Semitism. Fourier had, in fact, been anti-Semitic along the lines common in his time, namely, in believing that the Jews were always middlemen and did not themselves produce anything of value to society. Zilberfarb had exploded with a letter denouncing the author of the article for slandering Fourier, one of the brightest lights of humanity. I asked: "Ioganson Isaakovich, how could you, who know Fourier perhaps better than anyone else, state that he was not anti-Semitic?" He answered: "But, Nikolai Valentinovich, he did not want to exterminate us, did he?"[5]

Of course, it was not always necessary to request formal interviews to become acquainted with Soviet scholars. Our graduate students were assigned to appropriate specialists who were to supervise their research. Faculty members received help from "companions" or "facilitators," usually scholars in the same or an adjacent field. Also, it was assumed that foreign scholars would meet at least some of their Soviet counterparts in a given area of knowledge. Yet even these strictly limited and regulated contacts seemed to strain the Soviet system to the limit, with the police never far behind. Although I was generally treated very well by the Soviet authorities, I could cite many personal examples to support the above statement. Take, for instance, my contacts or noncontacts with Academician Dimitrii Sergeevich Likhachev. We established reasonably close relations when I was president of the American Association for the Advancement of Slavic Studies from 1973 to 1976, while he, as usual, headed at least half a dozen important Soviet organizations. For a number of years, our relations were normal. Then Likhachev stopped answering my letters. Moreover, when I came to Leningrad, he twice invited me to meet him, but never showed up. The explanation came only in the spring of 1990 at a lunch for Likhachev arranged by James Billington, director of the Library of Congress. Likhachev told me that he had never received my unanswered letters and had never invited me to a meeting. He added that I was relatively fortunate because I merely drew blanks, whereas in several other cases the letters were answered in his name by the police and he was still dealing with the resulting problems.

Nevertheless, like other foreign scholars in the Soviet Union, I made friends. In Moscow, I would list first the already-mentioned Petr Andreevich Zaionchkovskii, a wonderful gentleman as well as a leading historian, who was especially helpful and kind to foreign visitors. Most of his books, as well as most of mine, were on nineteenth-century Russian history, and we had countless interests in common. In addition to helping me with libraries and archives, he took me on a trip to the field of Borodino, a battle fought during Napoleon's invasion of Russia, which he knew down to the last detail. He also accompanied me to churches, telling outsiders that it was necessary for my research. (Actually, it was he who in that manner could safely go to church services.) I remember begging him to tell me what I could send him (in general, books and medicines were favorite gifts) or how I could otherwise help him. He asked for only one thing: a funeral service when he died. I remember when the Red Arrow train was about to carry me off to Leningrad and I shouted to Zaionchkovskii, who had come to see me off: "St. Peter the Apostle?" And he shouted back: "No, St. Peter the Metropolitan of Moscow!" We had the service in Berkeley after Zaionchkovskii's death in the spring of 1983, with his closest American student and fellow-scholar, Terence Emmons, also in attendance.

I probably spent even more time in Moscow with another fine historian, a specialist on populism, Zaionchkovskii's former student Boris Samuilovich Itenberg, who had been appointed as my "facilitator." Given time and opportunity, we became as much friends as colleagues. Incidentally, it was Itenberg's wife whose petition to give Arlene and me a dinner was rejected by the Soviet authorities.

In Leningrad, my best friend was the late Vadim Borisovich Vilinbakhov, an historian and a descendant of an imperial elite family. His father, if I remember correctly, sided with General A.A. Brusilov and continued serving in the Red Army (although he lost his palatial residence). Vadim Borisovich himself had a military career in World War II, as well as the requisite training and publications as an historian. At university, he had been acquainted with some members of the so-called "Leningrad conspiracy," but he escaped serious trouble partly because he was an outspoken atheist, while the "conspiracy" was religious in character. Still, he remained a marginal intellectual, allowed to publish, but not in the main periodicals, without a regular teaching position; and he was visited regularly by the police. It was perhaps this "loose" status that enabled him to approach me, and the reader can find my thanks to him for critically examining my work already in the second edition of *A History of Russia*, published in 1969. Perceptive, critical, imaginative, at times original, but uneven and occasionally going beyond his evidence, Vilinbakhov was a wonderful historical and general companion. We especially visited cemeteries, but much else besides. Vilinbakhov's wife had a steady position as a biologist. I remember their son, Georgii Vadimovich Vilinbakhov, presently associated with the Hermitage Museum and a leading authority in Russia on heraldry, military uniforms, and related matters. The police apparently tolerated as well as supervised my relationship with the family. After one of my visits to Leningrad, the police commented to Vadim Borisovich that I had come to him only three times, while on the preceding visit it had been five, and asked whether our friendship had been cooling.

Vilinbakhov came to know my *A History of Russia* exceptionally well, but in general it remained a "non-book" in the Soviet Union. In contrast to my volumes on the Slavophiles, on Nicholas I and Official Nationality, and on the image of Peter the Great—the last item to be discussed later in this essay—it never entered official or semi-official Soviet historical discourse. The first Russian review of the book, a long and excellent one to be sure, appeared in *Voprosy istorii* (Problems of History) in 1994, thirty-one years after the publication of the first edition. Yet a few copies apparently circulated in the country, and several Soviet intellectuals told me that they had read it and even that they based their knowledge of Russian history on it—needless to say, a huge exaggeration. On a different level, I was informed that certain parties relished my *History* because of its picture of Stalin's funeral with Khrushchev, Beria, Chou En-lai, Malenkov, Voroshilov, Kaganovich, Bulganin, and Molotov all in the first row of marchers. When asked how I managed to obtain such a photograph—of course, several of these individuals later were purged or deprived of their exalted status—I could only answer that it was the official Soviet release at the time of the event.

I had many advantages on my visits to the Soviet Union and I doubt that I made the most of them. My family, especially my father, was reasonably well known, and my following in his footsteps as an American professor seemed entirely appropriate. Besides, I did research and published books. The point is that the Soviet authorities, in my opinion, were especially concerned with people they could not fully identify and they had no difficulty identifying me.

Being of the Orthodox faith opened additional possibilities. I remember on one occasion my Western colleagues complained that they could find no sign of Orthodoxy alive anywhere. I discovered, probably because I had brought with me a small icon of St. Nicholas, that the entire service personnel at the hotel, except for the supervisors, was Orthodox. I was told the schedule of church services, the location of the "good" and "bad" priests, and even of alleged miracles. In general, I attended services often, but avoided all other contact with the clergy and other church-affiliated people in order not to harm them.

Whenever I spoke Russian, I was taken for a Russian unless it had been previously explained that I was an American. As already indicated, my knowledge of the language helped my scholarly work, but of course it was with me at all times. Perhaps my most interesting unscheduled participation in Soviet life occurred during my first visit to Moscow in the summer of 1958. In a post office I came upon a group of ragged and befuddled people, who turned out to be illiterates, waiting for a social worker or Party worker to write letters for them to their relatives in villages across Russia. (Illiteracy practically disappeared by the end of the Soviet era, but it was still present in 1958.) The writer never came, so I offered myself as a substitute and spent an afternoon writing letters. I shall never forget that experience. Possibly the greatest single impression I obtained was of grinding poverty—so-and-so is going into hospital, please bring him two eggs.

There were also interesting meetings in restaurants. I have already mentioned the naval officers in Leningrad. Perhaps more risky was a certain dinner and discussion in Moscow. In line with my continuous effort to eat well by going to the best restaurants at the least-frequented times (for instance, before alcohol could be served), I found myself at a table for two with a well-dressed man who struck me immediately, in spite of his civilian clothes, as a military figure. We began to talk, and I discovered that my companion was a Soviet military adviser to the Egyptian government. (Our meeting happened shortly before Egypt broke off its close relationship with the Soviet Union.) Therefore, I was careful not to ask any specific questions, but still tried to profit from my unexpected contact. I inquired, for example, why Egyptians were such poor soldiers. He answered: "I shall tell you why. They have no respect for man. How often I would tell officers, 'Let me address the soldiers.' They would say, 'Discuss things with us. Why would you want to speak to them?'" I finished the meal first, and as I was leaving my companion asked: "Comrade, you, of course, must also be doing important work?" I said: "Of course," and went back to the Lenin Library.

I allegedly "saved the life" of a French colleague who claimed that he was dying because he could not find real coffee. After a long search, coffee was discovered on the top floor of the Metropol Hotel (we were staying in a different hotel). As we started on our first cup, the supervisor appeared and told me in Russian (I had been speaking Russian to the waiter): "You realize, comrade, that coffee is only for foreigners." I said: "Yes." Then we each ordered a second cup. Again the supervisor appeared, anger in her voice: "I told you, didn't I make it clear, that it's only for foreigners?" I said: "You made it perfectly clear. Could not be clearer." And we proceeded to order a third cup each. Eventually, I had to tell the supervisor that I was an American.

Visitors to the Soviet Union have countless stories to relate about the country, ranging from reactions to the Holocaust to reactions to the third cup of coffee. Space being limited, I shall comment briefly on only two more items: my last research visit to the Soviet Union before its collapse and my very first visit to that country. The former is a fairly representative example of scholarly exchange at the time of "high Brezhnevism." The latter comes closest to the title of this volume, which refers, after all, to adventures.

My project, which presently became a book, dealt with the image of Peter the Great.[6] I wanted to obtain two things in particular from my Soviet visit: first, much material on the subject, especially from the eighteenth century, for, roughly speaking, only 25 percent of such material was obtainable in the West as against 75 percent for the nineteenth century; second, opportunities to discuss the subject with Soviet specialists, many of them shapers of the Soviet image of Peter. With Stalinization, that image had acquired a remarkably bifocal character. Peter the Great had been enormously important, great and good for Russia as the modernizer of the Russian army and the creator of the Russian navy, as an admiral and a general, as a builder of war industries, as a diplomat, as the driving force in education and culture, and as the overall director and inspirer of the tremendous effort mounted by the Russians during his reign. Yet at the same time, he was said to have strengthened the "feudal" state, compelling the peasants, that is, 90 percent of the people, to pay three times as much dues and taxes as previously. Besides, masses of them died in wars or in the building of St. Petersburg, which proved more costly in terms of corpses than any battle. Good books could be written and sometimes were written within this framework, provided they treated appropriate aspects of the reign in the accepted manner. One could, for example, expertly study the rise of the military and naval might of Russia or demonstrate the decline, even devastation, of whole areas of the country because of the government's impossible demands.

On some issues, especially the economic dimension, there was no single dominant view and various scholars advanced different claims. The basic contradiction between the good and bad impacts of the reign could not, of course, be resolved. I asked probably the best known Soviet student of the reign which he really preferred, the victory over Sweden or the success of Bulavin's popular rebellion against what was in Soviet terminology the feudal order, because he could not have both. He promised a long letter explaining his position, but the letter never came.

As usual, I was received cordially and given much help. However, it soon became clear that my Soviet colleagues, even my friends among them, did not want me to write about the Soviet image. They suggested that a fine historian such as I would do best to forget contemporary subjects. At the very least, I could publish on the Soviet part separately. Some of my Oxford teachers might have agreed, but for different reasons. As one Soviet scholar whom I regard very highly put it: "Suppose you discuss the views of an Ivanov and then he recants his views. How will you know whether it was Ivanov himself who wrote the recantation?" I answered that perhaps I could not know for certain but might have to refer to the appearance of a recantation allegedly signed by Ivanov. Gradually, I came to realize how horribly painful the years of purges and Stalinism were in the sphere of Soviet historiography as well as in the Soviet world in general. The overwhelming desire of scholars who had lived through that era was not to delve into it. Significantly, the extremely rich and valuable multi-volume history of Russian and Soviet historiography *Ocherki istorii istoricheskoi nauki v SSSR* could not be completed for those dreadful years until the fall of the Soviet Union. Not surprisingly, many of the same specialists who objected to my writing of contemporary history encouraged my study of the Petrine theme in pre-revolutionary Russian historiography and, indeed, in Soviet historiography prior to Stalinization or in the works of Russian émigré scholars.

During a part of my visit, I was anchored in Pushkinskii Dom in Leningrad, the Institute of Russian Literature of the Soviet Academy of Sciences. I was asked to present the results of my research. I made a point of my sincere gratitude for having been invited to state my views on the history of the image of Peter the Great in the emperor's own city to a magnificent group of experts. I could not claim any important factual discoveries, but the overall structure and the main arguments of my study might seem different and of some interest to the audience. In fact, without declaring my intention, I wanted to include the Soviet segment of my work and have it discussed as thoroughly as possible. I had some success. To be sure, I was told that the two groups within the Institute that had invited me and requested special attention were the eighteenth-century group and the one devoted to Pushkin and his age (not exactly the Soviet period). But I spent much time on the projected book in general, including the Soviet period, and that helped to animate the discussion. My presentation was followed by a formal critique and after that a general discussion. The entire session lasted almost five hours. It went on and on, but few people left the crowded hall before the end.

Once the discussion started, one man in particular kept cutting in. Some of his remarks were good, others less so, but he seemed eager to continue for several more hours. He was next to me when I finally stepped into the street. It was five o'clock and rather dark. The man said: "You know, you may not find your way to the metro. Could I show you the way?" Well, I had been finding it for the last three months; it was about a block distant. Nevertheless, I said: "Yes, show me." We wound up walking up and down the Nevsky Prospect, talking continuously. He told me a strange story of how a leading Soviet scholar, once his great patron, had become his great enemy, and how that scholar was terrorizing him. At one point, the former patron had even invaded the printing press and torn up my companion's composition, which was in the publication process. It all sounded vaguely familiar, except that in our society one man would be unlikely to have such power. At the University of California, at least things would be done by committees.

The fellow stopped talking for a moment and that gave me an opening. I said that I also had a question to pose.

> I shall never forget this day. To speak about Peter the Great and his image in the center of St. Petersburg with people who know so much. . . . It was really a wonderful experience, and so was my entire visit, studying with the Hermitage materials, working in Moscow, and so forth. But one thing bothers me. So many people, my colleagues, your colleagues, tell me not to write on the Soviet image of Peter the Great. Or some advise me to write a separate article and publish it in some obscure journal. What do you think? Should I write on the Soviet image of Peter the Great or not?

He replied: "Write. By all means, write. Don't listen to them. Do what your government tells you."

My most memorable visit to Russia was the very first, only a month in the summer of 1958, in Leningrad, Kiev, and Moscow. The stunning beauty of Leningrad, the inexhaustible artistic and historic riches in Moscow, and the charm of Kiev in summertime remain fresh in my memory. I had an excellent traveling companion, another historian, the late Theodore Von Laue, along with his custom-made-in-Berlin camera (I still show his slides to my students in preference to other illustrations). We also had excellent accommodations, a car, a chauffeur, and very good tickets to plays, operas, and concerts. Our most extraordinary contact was with the Academy of Sciences, of which Theo's father, Max Von Laue, one of the German creators of modern physics and a Nobel prize winner, remained, ironically, a foreign member. I remember especially the great Russian scientist Mendeleev's last secretary and Mendeleev's papers behind a glass, which the secretary said would never be published because they dealt with the "yellow peril."

Not that the USSR was a paradise. People were poor, and even on the main streets in Moscow and Leningrad one could see that rooms were partitioned probably to accommodate more than a single family. I could not help but note that the very first Soviet professor I met said one thing in public and the opposite when he took me alone to see some of the Moscow University lecture halls that my father would have remembered. And the police, in one form or another, were ever present. In fact, even before I arrived in Leningrad by train from Finland, Theo had been arrested for photographing "unsanitary backyards." That episode ended peacefully, with only the film and not the camera confiscated. Afterwards, Theo did the photographing, I did the talking, and we ran into no more trouble. Still, Theo's departure provided another memorable episode. He was returning to Warsaw by train, while I was to fly to Finland the following day. So we were at the railroad station perhaps forty-five minutes before the train's departure; but forty-five minutes was not much in Soviet time. Because of what followed, I wish I could reconstruct the tone of my voice and my entire manner. Anyhow, I saw someone with a cap indicating that he worked at the station and told him: "Kindly help this gentleman; he is leaving on the Warsaw train." Suddenly, the man snapped to attention, took Von Laue to the train, returned, and said: "I beg to report"— this must be a new style of speaking, I thought—"I beg to report: the gentleman is in his compartment; his suitcases are with him; he is comfortable; he is alone and will do no talking." As I walked out of the station, I wondered: "To whom do I report?" And suddenly, I was very happy to realize that I was returning to Finland the next day. As luck would have it, as I reentered my hotel, I heard an American woman loudly declare: "What is all this talk about a police state? I see no policemen around."

Our most interesting as well as most problematic acquaintance during that first visit to the Soviet Union turned out to be a certain Krasovskii. The second or perhaps the third night of our stay in Leningrad, as we were led to the front of one of the great imperial, later Soviet, theaters, with people whispering that we must be very important foreign comrades, we noticed that one seat next to our own was already occupied. The occupant introduced himself as Boris Nikolaevich Krasovskii, an electrical engineer, and he spoke decent English. He even produced a pencil with an inscription on it in English which read something like "World Electrical Engineering Convention, Milan, 1955." He also explained to us that the Soviet government had changed its policy and was now encouraging foreign contacts. As we switched to Russian, our conversation became faster and more intimate. After the performance, he took us on a night ride through Leningrad and some of its palatial suburbs. He repeated these night rides several times that week.

The white nights had just ended, but much brightness and freshness remained. I remember Krasovskii's car standing alone in huge squares or great parks as we also toured the magnificent city and its environs on foot. Meanwhile Krasovskii kept asking questions. He proposed, for example, to compare the standards of living in the Soviet Union and the United States, and when I tried to dodge the issue by claiming that the societies were too different, he insisted that the comparison could indeed be made. One had only to state one's income, the costs of different kinds of products and services, and then those costs as percentages of the income. He never told us the result of his calculations. But for me, the glories of St. Petersburg will forever remain tied to the price of white potatoes or yellow onions in Berkeley. One question was different from all the others. Suddenly, Krasovskii reminded us that he was an electrical engineer, and asked whether we wanted him to take us to his factory. The offer was so strange and unreal in that summer of 1958 that we simply said nothing, and Krasovskii returned to his usual talk. I was glad, however, that Theo also heard the offer, because that proved that I had not been dreaming. After Krasovskii brought us back each night, or rather morning, to the Hotel Astoria, Theo would ask me: "Do you think he's a spy?" and I would answer: "What's the difference? We have nothing to hide." "But do you think we can trust him?" "Who can trust anyone in this world? Theo, go to sleep."

On our last night in Leningrad, Krasovskii invited us to his apartment, our first visit to a Soviet "home." It was an old and unsightly apartment building, and it took three keys to open two doors. Krasovskii explained that he lived with his mother, but she was away on a summer vacation. The apartment consisted of at least two rooms and a kitchen, and contained many works of French literature, some in French and others in Russian. We had vodka and herring, and we talked. Krasovskii remarked that "that business in Hungary" (the revolution of 1956) must have done serious damage to the Soviet Union. I agreed and added that in Great Britain, the Communist Party had lost half its membership, while in the United States, where there was almost no party to speak of, it had become even more isolated. Then I asked: "What was the impact of the Hungarian events here in the Soviet Union?" Krasovskii answered me with a story, which apparently came from Anatole France. Pontius Pilate returned to Rome from Judea; when his friends asked whether anything special had happened there during his tour of duty, Pilate declared, "Nothing; yes, someone was crucified, but really nothing." Krasovskii concluded: "That is how we missed the events in Hungary." Back at the Astoria, Theo kept demanding my opinion of Krasovskii and I kept telling him to go to sleep.

We parted as dear friends, and Krasovskii promised to visit us in Moscow, but he did not appear again. Theo tried to correspond with him, but received no replies. At one convention of the American Historical Association, he proposed that we write a joint letter, but I declined. Still, the Krasovskii story has an ending. As exchanges multiplied, the famous French firm Coty mounted an exhibit in Leningrad. One of the employees traveling with the exhibit was a friend of mine, a Parisian beauty from a Russian family. Lo and behold, Krasovskii appeared at the exhibit, this time with his mother, and they invited my friend to their apartment. He presented himself as Krasovskii, professor of French literature, and he spoke perfect French. To be sure, even perfect French might have been insufficient to identify him as a university professor to Theo and me, both professors from academic families. I told Theo the latest news about Krasovskii, after which my friend stopped trying to reach him.

The reader of this piece will now fully appreciate the dedication in one of Von Laue's well-known books, *Why Lenin? Why Stalin?*[7]

To the students and faculty of the University of California, Riverside, and, with a heavier heart, to Boris Nikolaevich Krasovskii.

Notes

As I remember my "adventures" in the Soviet Union, I am grateful to my parents, Professors Valentin A. and Antonina F. Riasanovsky (also known as a writer under the pen name Nina Fedorova), from whom I obtained the Eastern Orthodox faith, a native fluency in Russian, and a general knowledge of Russian history and culture, which I have proceeded to study throughout my life. I also appreciate the generosity of many individuals, organizations, and grants that made my visits to the Soviet Union possible, as well as the work of the organizers of this volume and their invitation to me to contribute to it.

1. I remember that as president of the American Association for the Advancement of Slavic Studies, I deleted from our application for funds the well-meaning but ridiculous statement that one had to visit the Soviet Union at least once every several years to be considered a specialist in the field.

2. Purchasing in the Soviet Union deserves a book, or rather books, and they should be written by experts. I bought very little, except for historical material. My triumph, however, urged upon me by my wife, was the acquisition of a *samovar.* The process involved a ministry, an appeal to the manager of the GUM department store, whom I caught roaring at his subordinate because of theft in the latter's section of the store, and a verbal battle in the only post office allowed to mail things abroad at that time. At the post office I was told that there were no cardboard boxes for packing left. I shouted that there must be a cardboard box in Moscow, the capital of the USSR. The poor clerk ran off, and I heard her repeating my words to someone behind a screen. A cardboard box appeared.

3. Nicholas V. Riasanovsky, *The Teachings of Charles Fourier.* Berkeley and Los Angeles: University of California Press, 1969.

4. Cf: I. Zilberfarb, *Sotsial'naia filosofiia Sharlia Fure i ee mesto v istorii sotsialisticheskoi mysli pervoi poloviny XIX veka* (Moscow, 1964).

5. Hitler, no doubt, deserves the chief credit for Zilberfarb's remarkable answer. But there was anti-Semitism in the Soviet Union, too. One Soviet colleague mentioned several times that he was married to a Russian wife. A Russian scholar in Moscow married to a Russian woman seemed right and proper, and hardly in need of comment. Then one day he said: "You know I am married to a Russian wife; we are a mixed family." For once I exclaimed on an impulse before thinking: "But then who in the world are you?" He answered: "I am a Jew." I came to appreciate a "Jewish" joke that I now tell in class. The Soviet police check on relatives abroad and obtain the answer from a man that he has none. The man receives a letter from his brother in Tel Aviv. The police demand: "How is that possible?" The man responds: "You don't understand: he is at home, I am abroad." And, indeed, the Soviet Union did much to make Jews feel "abroad."

6. Nicholas V. Riasanovsky, *The Image of Peter the Great in Russian History and Thought.* New York: Oxford University Press, 1985.

7. Theodore H. Von Laue, *Why Lenin? Why Stalin? A Reappraisal of the Russian Revolution, 1900–1930.* Philadelphia and New York: Lippincott Williams and Wilkins, 1964.

2

A Tale of Two Inquiries

Samuel H. Baron

Plekhanoviana

My adventures in Russian historical research began in 1946, with my enrollment in the first class of Columbia University's Russian (now Harriman)
Institute. Two years later, having been awarded an M.A.—my thesis dealt
with Lenin's views on the peasant commune—I was admitted to the doctoral
program. My supervising professor was Geroid T. Robinson, author of the
excellent *Rural Russia under the Old Regime,* and, as I learned, a formidable
taskmaster.[1] Rather than pursue a dead-end subject for my dissertation, such
as Lenin's views on the trade unions or Zinoviev's views on world revolution, which Robinson pressed on fellow students, I elected to study the initial
decade of G.V. Plekhanov's career as a leader of Russia's first Marxist revolutionary organization, the Emancipation of Labor Group. In 1952, the Ph.D.
in hand, I undertook to produce a much more comprehensive work, a project
which terminated eleven years later with the publication of *Plekhanov: The
Father of Russian Marxism.* Although these years were not without tedium,
grappling with Plekhanov's learned and insightful excursions into politics,
economics and history; philosophy; and literary and art criticism was intellectually illuminating and richly rewarding. Nevertheless, having spent fifteen years in his company, I was eager to write *finis* to my association with
Plekhanov. Wishing to investigate subjects of a different era and kind, I translated and edited *The Travels of Olearius in Seventeenth-Century Russia.* This
was the point of departure for many another research on the Muscovite (sixteenth and seventeenth century) period of Russian history, but my adventures in Muscovitica will not be addressed here.

After a hiatus of a dozen years or so, however, I was impelled in the
1970s and 1980s to return to Plekhanov, to explore in a number of articles
facets of his life and thought, which I then recognized had not been treated
in sufficient depth in the biography. As I entered further into his historical
thought, and revisited his position in the 1905 and 1917 revolutions, I could

not but be struck by the revival of my intense interest in Plekhanov. In 1981, thirty-three years after I had first become engaged with him, I reflected on certain psychological dimensions of this enduring relationship in a piece entitled "My Life with G.V. Plekhanov."[2] Perhaps the most arresting discovery in this exploration was that most of the problems I had been investigating since 1963—the Westernization of Russia, the nondevelopment of capitalism, and the evolution of Marxist historiography in Russia—were all related, either directly or indirectly, to matters of concern to Plekhanov. Although I had been only vaguely or not at all aware of it, my protracted involvement with Plekhanov had profoundly affected me and, unwittingly, concerns of his had become concerns of mine too. This article might have brought closure to the relationship, but in fact it did not. A decade later I composed another article on the man, this time for a Russian journal. And fifty-one years after I began work on Plekhanov, a Russian edition of the biography— in whose preparation I became deeply involved—was published in St. Petersburg by the Russian National Library (1999). Mine has been a truly extraordinary, lifelong engagement with this figure.

Over the years my concern with Plekhanov brought me into contact with many an individual and organization, but none over so long a time—though sporadically—as with the Dom Plekhanova (Plekhanov House). This institution, established in Leningrad in 1928, houses Plekhanov's papers and library. In the decade following his death in 1918, the Soviet government tried to persuade his widow, then living in Paris, to transfer these valued materials to Russia. Its efforts at last succeeded when an agreement was struck to create an independent institution to preserve the materials, with Plekhanov's wife as the first curator. I learned of this archive early in my research, but had no hope of working there prior to the late 1950s, when a limited cultural exchange program was initiated by the American and Soviet governments.

I had by then almost completed my research on Plekhanov and had begun writing the book. In drafting the first few chapters, I found myself lacking some data on my subject's early life and wrote to the Dom Plekhanova to solicit assistance, mentioning by the way that I should very much like to work in the archive. I was pleased to receive helpful answers, and simply overjoyed to be advised by the archive's then director, Mme. Ukhmylova, that she would "be pleased to see [me] within the walls" of the institution. On the strength of this invitation, I applied to the Social Science Research Council (SSRC) for a grant. I was disconcerted to say the least when, after the award had been made, I received a second letter from Ukhmylova, disingenuously stating "as an addendum" to the previous communication that it would be wise not to plan a visit to Leningrad. Evidently, she had indiscreetly extended the invitation on her own and had been reined in by her superior, the head of the Saltykov-Shchedrin (formerly St. Petersburg Public) Library. Nevertheless, the SSRC agreed to my proposal to try in person to secure access. Thrilled to be going to Russia for the first time, I arrived June 1, 1959, to witness the white nights.

The following day I found my way to the Dom Plekhanova. My appearance without advance notice took Ukhmylova by surprise, but when she recovered, she and her assistants treated me cordially enough. On the matter of access, however, she was immovable, explaining (transparently falsely) that all the materials were being used in preparation of a new edition of Plekhanov's works. I asked to see her superior, determined to vent my spleen, and was granted an interview. I think I'm a mild-mannered person, but the frustrations I've experienced in the Soviet Union have provoked me a number of times to unrestrained anger. On this occasion I complained bitterly, expressed disbelief in the excuse given me, and warned of future retaliation against Soviet investigators who wished to do research in the United States. The official calmly absorbed my verbal blows and yielded not an inch. Still, my effort to advance my research in Russia was not entirely fruitless. One of the Dom Plekhanova workers who sympathized with my plight privately facilitated my purchase of a set of Plekhanov's *Sochineniia.* The precious twenty-four volumes of the collected works—they greatly facilitated my work thereafter—went for twenty-four rubles!

Following my month in the Soviet Union, I proceeded to Paris where I had arranged to meet Plekhanov's two daughters. They had both been born and lived their entire lives in Switzerland and France. Eugenia had married a man of letters, Georges Batault, and Lydia, a psychiatrist named Savoureux, but each proudly bore the family name (Plekhanova) along with her spouse's. The two gracious ladies shared with me their reminiscences and put unpublished material at my disposal, as well as a copy of *God na Rodine* (*A Year in the Homeland*), a rare two-volume collection of Plekhanov's writings in 1917–18, which their mother had brought out in Paris in 1921. They also entertained me on more than one occasion; at one dinner a fellow guest was Boris Souvarine, author of the first significant biography of Stalin. These informative and stimulating encounters were supplemented by an engaging meeting at his apartment with Nikolai Vol'skii (Valentinov), a remarkably vivacious old man who had once known Plekhanov rather intimately but was definitely no partisan of his. The women were anxious to counter the image of their father as a cold and arrogant person although, contrariwise, Eugenia quoted with some relish Trotsky's memorable phrase that Plekhanov was "un maître de toutes les nuances de froideur." They told me feelingly of his love and concern for them and urged me to read his heartfelt letter to their mother, expressing sympathy for his foe, Tsar Alexander III, who had just lost his wife.

In 1963–64, shortly after the appearance of my biography of Plekhanov, I spent an academic year in the Soviet Union under the auspices of the Inter-University Committee on Travel Grants (IUCTG), the predecessor of the International Research and Exchanges Board (IREX). My research time was spent mostly in Moscow, and it related to seventeenth-century Russia. However, I took the opportunity to distribute copies of my book to several scholars and also donated one to the renowned Lenin Library. I had noticed that copies of new books were conspicuously displayed just outside the reading room where foreign visitors were privileged to work along with high-level Soviet scholars. When I suggested to the reading-room attendant to whom I had handed my book that I hoped it too would be exhibited, she replied, with a knowing look, that this was unlikely to occur. Obviously, the barriers I had run up against in Leningrad in 1959 were no more passable in Moscow in 1963, and they would continue to frustrate me for a long time.

In the course of the academic year, I spent a few weeks in Leningrad and contrived to visit the Dom Plekhanova again. Ukhmylova had by then been replaced by I.N. Kurbatova, a younger, better-educated woman and a specialist in the history of medieval Europe. I believe that she was unaware of the publication of my book, and she accepted with interest and gratitude the copy I presented to her. Whether or not she read English is uncertain, but she clearly wished to acquaint herself with the book's content, and invited me to return some days later. When I did, she indicated her respect for my opus, asserting that it was obviously a "serious" piece of work. Although I sensed that Kurbatova was not a dogmatist, nevertheless she felt obliged to add the ritual reservation: "But, of course, *we* view things differently." (I later received the same response from a historian of early modern Russia, A.M. Sakharov, to whom I had given a copy of *Windows on the Russian Past: Soviet Historiography since Stalin.*[3]) In the 1970s, while preparing an article on Plekhanov and World War, I wrote to Kurbatova, asking whether in this connection I might have access to the archive. Instead of replying directly, she sent me a photocopy of a relevant article.

My *Plekhanov* was reviewed, generally favorably, in more than two dozen journals and newspapers in several countries, but so far as I am aware there was only one notice of it in the USSR. It came in 1965 in a volume entitled *Plekhanov and Russian Economic Thought* by F. Ia. Polianskii, who evidently had been commissioned to do a hatchet job. In the book's last chapter, labeled "Bourgeois Falsifiers of the History of Marxism in Russia," Polianskii devoted no fewer than twenty-seven pages to my opus. He sounded the theme of his review at the outset: "The work is written from the position of bourgeois liberalism [and] malicious anti-communism, given to a tendentious interpretation of the history of Marxism in Russia [and] crammed with falsification." There followed a summary of the book rendered so distortedly as to be hardly recognizable. The force of his overall position may be retrospectively gauged by the final sentences of the review. Whereas he simplistically attributes to me the view that "in the West reformism could not eliminate capitalism and in Russia the proletarian revolution came about only unlawfully," in fact, he proclaims, "capitalism collapsed in many West European countries and socialism triumphed on Russian soil."

Times have changed, of course, and judging by the opinions expressed recently by S.V. Tiutiukin, the reigning Plekhanov specialist in post-Soviet Russia, this former "falsifier of history" is now evaluated rather more positively. In reviewing the historiography of the subject in a recent comprehensive study, Tiutiukin observes that Baron's book is "universally recognized as the best intellectual biography of Plekhanov and [when it appeared] was in many ways a revelation for Soviet historians." Moreover, he approvingly quotes at length my summary conclusion in a recent article (published in a journal he now edits) that Plekhanov and Lenin each grasped part of the truth and neither the whole truth about the Russian Revolution.[4]

In March 1991, I learned via Daniela Steila, an Italian colleague who had written a book on Plekhanov's philosophical views, that she would be participating in a conference on "the father of Russian Marxism" at the Dom Plekhanova at the end of May. I had had no knowledge whatever of such a conference, my interest was piqued and, in the hope that I might attend, I dispatched an express letter to Leningrad asking if I might be invited. Anticipating a positive response, I meanwhile requested and received from our Dean of Arts and Sciences the promise of a travel subsidy. As days and weeks went by, I eventually despaired of receiving a response and made alternative arrangements for the use of my time. As a consequence of the maddeningly inefficient postal system in the Soviet Union, a letter of invitation reached me only on April 24, too late to enable me to attend the conference. I then faxed a note to the conference organizer, which reached her only on May 18, when, she subsequently responded, "we already had lost any hope of seeing you among the conference participants." This was another episode in the history of my unproductive relations with the Dom Plekhanova, but it was about to end.

In the fall the new curator of the Dom Plekhanova, T.I. Filimonova, advised me that another conference would be held in 1993 and she hoped that I might find it possible to present a paper. Filimonova read, wrote, and spoke English well, was familiar with my work on Plekhanov and felt free to speak her mind about it. Indicative of the radical changes that had occurred in Russia in the preceding few years was her gratifying assertion: "I wish we could meet some day to discuss so many problems the Plekhanov House is facing now. Your profound knowledge of the subject might be of great help in solving them. We would be very glad to welcome you among the scholars regularly visiting Dom Plekhanova." I had been advised long before that I would be welcome within the walls of the institution, but this time there would be no equivocation.

I attended the conference at the end of May 1993—the meeting was scheduled to coincide with the date of Plekhanov's death and serve as a commemorative event. I had submitted a paper entitled "Plekhanov, Utopianism and the Russian Revolution," which was subsequently printed in *Otechestvennaia istoriia*, and I read an abstract to the assemblage. I deliberately preceded the abstract with an acerbic review of my relations and experience with the Dom Plekhanova over the years. My participation in the conference, I exulted, was a token of the new freedom in Russia, adding that Plekhanov would certainly have shared my celebratory sentiment. My remarks were well received, as they harmonized with the reflections of other participants on the damaging constraints on historical investigation that had long prevailed and were now giving way.

One of the most enduring consequences of my involvement in the conference was the establishment of a strong professional relationship with Filimonova. We conversed a good deal during the conference; afterward she invited me to tea in the kitchen Plekhanov's wife had used and we discussed possible future collaboration. My observation that my work had appeared in Spanish and Japanese editions but not in the country to which it was most relevant suggested to her the idea of correcting this omission, and she presently raised the matter with her superiors in the Russian National Library (the city's principal library had recently been renamed). More immediately, as a result of work on her doctoral dissertation, she was interested in bringing out a selection of Plekhanov's articles written in the years 1914–18 and she invited me to collaborate. Because they were so at odds with the Leninist line on the war and the revolution, these materials had been banned from the twenty-four-volume *Sochineniia*. By way of correspondence, we worked for some time on the choice of writings to be included and each embarked upon the production of a prefatory article. To advance the project more efficiently, I went to St. Petersburg for a month in 1994 and at last gained an opportunity to work at the Dom Plekhanova. I was given absolutely free access to everything in the archive and, to boot, the wholehearted cooperation of its staff members. Of course, I appreciated the situation, but I could not suppress the ironical thought that it had come to pass at a time when I had no further interest in basic research on Plekhanov. Although considerable effort went into this endeavor, it had to be shelved for want of funding to bring it to fruition.

In contrast, the idea of bringing out a Russian edition of the biography caught fire with the responsible officials of the Russian National Library (RNB). As an unmistakable token of their interest, a highly qualified employee of the library was assigned to do the translation and spent many months at the task. I was distinctly impressed with the quality of the translation although I detected not a few turns of phrase that did not ring quite true. A Russian friend in Chapel Hill rendered invaluable service in straightening out these flaws, and Filimonova, who was designated editor, did a good deal of further redacting. I composed a preface to the new edition, but the troublesome question of financing held up the book's publication for what seemed like an interminable period. Be that as it may, in my wildest imagination I had never entertained the idea that my work on Plekhanov would appear in Russia. Therefore, words cannot convey how exciting was its appearance. At the same time, it is sobering to reflect that it required a world-historical event, the collapse of the Soviet Union, to make my opus publishable there.

Tracking the Novocherkassk Story

I first heard something of the June 1962 massacre of workers on strike in Novocherkassk in 1963–64, an academic year I spent in Moscow under the auspices of IREX. A student at the residence hall where I was housed once confided to me in a hushed voice that something awful had happened in that south Russian city, whose name was unfamiliar to me. The informant was vague about the circumstances, and my research was focused on the travels of Olearius at the time, so the rumor made little impression on me. So far as I can remember, I never encountered anything in print on the Novocherkassk events until about thirty years later, when serendipity happily came into play. At the conference on Plekhanov that I attended in St. Petersburg in 1993, the commentator on my paper was A.A. Chernobaev, the editor of the journal *Istoricheskii arkhiv*. At some point, he handed me a copy of the most recently published number of the journal. I accepted it with thanks, supposing that it would wind up on a shelf together with other piles of books and journals I had not examined. I couldn't have been more mistaken. On the flight home, having run out of other reading material, I perused the table of contents and was drawn to a collection of documents entitled "Novocherkasskaia tragediia, 1962." It was the first installment of a two-part collection of top-secret KGB documents produced contemporaneously with the events and addressed to the Central Committee of the CPSU and the Council of Ministers. The documents were based upon virtually round-the-clock observations of a multitude of agents who had been rushed into the city to reinforce the local personnel after the strike had begun. So sensational were these materials that they bowled me over. Convinced that I had stumbled upon a treasure trove, I resolved then and there to explore the events further, although other engagements prevented me from doing so in a sustained way until 1997.

In the intervening years, I did manage to locate and study much of the relevant published material, a matter that deserves a few words. I was in Petersburg again in 1995, to review the Russian translation of my biography of Plekhanov. Incidentally, during my month in residence I had the unusual experience for a foreigner of being on the payroll of the Russian National Library. My stipend as a senior research-scholar, no doubt the going rate at the time, was a munificent $125. Not far into my stay, I looked in on the library's *uchennyi sekretar'* (research consultant), a historian of early modern Russia with whom I had previously become acquainted. I presented to the library, in his person, copies of the two volumes of my collected articles on Muscovite Russia, and I also mentioned in passing that I was interested in the Novocherkassk events.

Imagine my surprise and delight when he immediately rang up the relevant library department and requested the compilation of a bibliography on the subject for me. This stroke of luck brought forth a list of eighteen newspaper articles produced in the years from 1989 forward. These articles by zealous investigative reporters traced the episodic disclosure of information about the strike, the massacre, the trials that followed, and the cover-up. When I had completed my work on the Plekhanov translation, I devoured these exciting materials. Beside providing a great deal of valuable information, they referred in passing to the existence of sources which, I felt certain, it would be necessary to track down and consult: a mass of letters sent by readers to the authors of the first article on Novocherkassk to appear in the national press (1989); a documentary film on the strike; an eight-volume record of the most important of the trials; and thirty-one volumes of testimony collected by the Chief Military Procuracy in the course of an investigation mandated by the government in the early 1990s.

I noticed that the individual most relentless in the pursuit of information on the Novocherkassk story was Iurii Bespalov, a correspondent for *Komsomol'skaia pravda*, and decided to try to contact him. It required a number of phone calls to learn that he was based in Rostov-on-Don and to obtain his number. My spoken Russian is imperfect, and I had almost never had a conversation in that language on the phone, so I had to muster a good deal of pluck to initiate these calls, especially the one to Bespalov. However, while no doubt perpetrating mistakes, I made myself understood and Bespalov was clearly interested to learn that a foreigner was seriously concerned with an affair in which he had invested a good deal of himself. Should

I come to Russia in the future, he promised, he would readily give me access to materials in his possession, and he assured me that a Novocherkassk organization that had been created to perpetuate the memory of the 1962 events would surely assist me as well.

Some other positive developments should be noted. While in Moscow, toward the end of my month-long stay, through the good offices of an American friend employed by USAID, I became acquainted with the head of a committee of jurists whom Yeltsin had appointed to design legal reform for the new regime. He, too, expressed interest in my project and promised to do what he could to help me gain access to the eight-volume trial record. That same year, one of our graduate students, Jeff Jones, had worked in the archives at Rostov. Although his focus lay elsewhere, he was interested in labor history and had come upon and copied several important publications on the Novocherkassk affair by local journalists Irina Mardar' and Olga Nikitina. He had also identified a number of relevant archival documents. When he learned of my interest in the subject, he generously put these materials and information at my disposal, enabling me to expand my stock of information and the roster of persons I would need to contact. Aware as I was that Bruce Menning had in recent years succeeded in doing research in sensitive military archives, I sought his aid in following suit with reference to the Military Procuracy's thirty-one volume collection alluded to above.

By then, fascinated with the subject and wishing to follow the many leads uncovered, I applied to IREX for a five-month research stay in Russia. My application featured a carefully drawn prospectus and was accompanied by strongly supportive letters from a group of scholars it would be impossible to improve upon—Robert Tucker, Alexander Dallin, and David Joravsky. I was so confident that the grant would be mine that I was inexpressibly shocked when word came that my proposal had aborted. The reality of age discrimination in the allotment of awards was brought home to me—I have since learned that it is pervasive, if understandable—as thirty-five or thirty-six of forty awards went to graduate students or junior professors. One of the few fortunate exceptions was our fellow-contributor to this volume, Richard Stites. Yet, too committed to abandon my project, I was ready to travel to Russia at my own expense.

A more attractive alternative option appeared. The University of North Carolina-Chapel Hill prides itself on being a "research university"; but, paradoxically, once a faculty member retires, he or she becomes ineligible for research support. Knowing this to be the norm, I decided to take a long shot and plead my case before our Provost, with whom I was only slightly acquainted. He listened attentively and indicated that he would examine the documents I had brought along. A few days later, he magnanimously consented to fund the six-week research expedition that I had proposed. My luck, no inconsequential factor in any endeavor, was buoying me up—but I suppose I can take some credit for resourcefulness too.

Late in May 1997 I flew to Russia, intending to carry out research in Rostov, Novocherkassk, and lastly Moscow. I timed the visit so that I could be in Novocherkassk on June 2, the anniversary of the 1962 massacre, which each year was memorialized in a public ceremony. In Rostov I hoped to work in the provincial library and in the former party archive where Jeff Jones had spotted relevant documents, but first of all I was keen to meet Olga Nikitina and Iu. Bespalov, journalists who had done the most to bring the long-suppressed Novocherkassk story to light. I had read and was impressed by a couple of Nikitina's articles and, upon learning that a television newsman from Rostov was attending a workshop at neighboring Duke University, had contrived to meet him and ask him to alert Nikitina to my planned visit. In Rostov she readily agreed to see me and, as we strolled toward an outdoor café, a lively conversation got under way.

I had had time immediately after arriving in Rostov to find and read her groundbreaking article on the Novocherkassk events, which had appeared in June 1988 in *Komsomolets*, the organ of the Rostov Province Komsomol. After expressing my admiration for what I truly regarded as her "historic" achievement, I began to speak of what I hoped to accomplish during my stay in Russia. Among other things, I mentioned that I had written to the Chief Military Procuracy, asking permission to examine the thirty-one volumes it had compiled, but had received no response. At that, she revealed that there existed a thirty-second volume, a 170-page summary of the preceding thirty-one volumes. I was simply stunned when she added: "I have a copy of the last volume, and here it is," whereupon she handed me an unpublished tome enclosed in wrapping paper. Almost speechless, I managed to ask haltingly whether I would be able to make a copy for my use. She retorted that she would contact Major General Iu.M. Bagraev, who had conducted the investigation, and presently give me an answer. Days later she phoned to say that the general had stipulated—unhelpfully, to my way of thinking—that I was free to use the facts laid out in the summary, but not the opinions. As for making a copy, what I was told seemed equivocal. However, Nikitina set no deadline for returning the tome, which remained in my possession for three weeks, and I took this to mean that I was free to do as I pleased.

Of course, I was pleased to reproduce the summary, but it seemed hazardous to ask one of the many copying establishments in the city to copy what had the earmarks of an official document. Accordingly, it behooved me to proceed clandestinely. It so happened that the American Bar Association had a small office in the same building that housed the local IREX staff, and I had become acquainted with the young attorney in charge. His office equipment included a copying machine, and he had two Russian assistants. By this time, the Soviet regime was long gone, but there was no way of knowing whether the Russian employees might be informants of the FSB, the successor of the KGB. So after the attorney had agreed to my proposal to use the copying machine, I suggested that it might be well to do the work after office hours, and I did so.

Obtaining this material was a coup of the first order: the volume contained the testimony of a hundred and twenty individuals, not only government officials—military, KGB and police personnel, both high level and rank and file—but many workers and bystanders as well. The compilation included ample testimony by individuals who, thirty years after the events, felt free to provide evidence decidedly at odds with the official version. Indeed, after having studied it very closely back in the United States, I concluded that it is, unquestionably, the single most important source I have found on the strike and the massacre. Fearful that I might run into trouble getting this treasure out of the country, I again felt obliged to resort to clandestine measures.

Nikitina generously assisted me in other important ways. For one thing, she told me the fascinating tale of how it came about that she was able to publish her article, the very first to appear on the Novocherkassk events in an official publication. With glasnost in full cry and revelations of past CPSU misconduct breaking into the news daily, a leader of the Rostov Province Party organization became convinced that the flow of information was unstoppable and decided on a counter-move. If the Novercherkassk events would inevitably leak out, he reasoned, the local party organization should publish the first report on the matter, a version that would take the steam out of those who were bent on sensationalizing the story and blackening those in power. He assigned Nikitina the task, but what she, a conscientious reporter, wrote could not have entirely pleased him. Nevertheless he favored publication, a step that local KGB officials refused to allow until the eleventh hour. With the weighty title "Days of Darkening, Days of Illumination" and the subtitle "History with No Torn-out Pages," it is understandable why they objected.

Nikitina also introduced me to the daughter of the deceased General M.K. Shaposhnikov, who was second in command of the North Caucasus Military Organization in 1962, and who, with the advent of glasnost, was lionized in the progressive media for having supposedly refused to order his men to fire on the strikers. Nina Shaposhnikova willingly looked through her father's papers for relevant material, but found none. (Her father, she told me, had kept a diary for years, but had destroyed all his material on the Novocherkassk events.) I resolved to examine everything on this subject I could get my hands on—Nina helped me, calling my attention to articles in obscure publications—and I have devoted half a chapter to this intriguing figure. The other half portrays someone who was on the other side of the barricades—P.P. Siuda, one of the strikers, who was arrested, tried, and sentenced to a long term of imprisonment. He was released after four or five years and, in the late 1980s, emboldened by the perestroika atmosphere, launched a zealous campaign—with leaflets, speeches, and articles in nonofficial publications—to have the shootings and the trials reviewed. More than any other individual, it was he who instigated the reexamination of what had occurred in 1962. I was able to treat this dimension of the story in some detail thanks to Bespalov, who possessed Siuda's papers and graciously put them at my disposal. He also imparted his thinking on how it came about that Siuda was found dead on a Novocherkassk street in 1991. While many concluded that he was a victim of foul play—Siuda's wife, whom I met, insists on this—both Bespalov and Nikitina advanced a less sensational but more believable explanation.

Rostov was my base in southern Russia, but of course I made a number of visits to Novocherkassk, some twenty-three miles away. I went the first time with the television reporter I had met at Duke, who was driving there to cover the ceremony marking the thirty-fifth anniversary of the massacre. It was moving to be present at the solemn public meeting, held on the very square where the massacre had occurred. There were speeches by the town's officials and others, notably Valentina Vodianitskaia, a very articulate woman who had participated in the strike and been imprisoned. I was introduced to Vodianitskaia and other one-time strikers; to Siuda's widow; to Irina Mardar', who had produced the fullest and best account to date of the 1962 events; and to the archaeologist who had facilitated the finding of the secretly buried corpses, and their exhumation and transfer to a specially designated space in a Novocherkassk cemetery.

When I revisited Novocherkassk repeatedly, both in 1997 and when I returned for a month the following year, these persons were of inestimable importance, consenting to interviews and subsequent questionings, putting me in touch with other individuals I wished to meet, allowing me to copy documents, and providing me with copies of relevant videos they had produced or collected. The archaeologist, who had a rattletrap car, kindly acted as my chauffeur, enabling me to familiarize myself with the terrain on which the key events had occurred. For one who had been occupied chiefly with Muscovite Russia for the preceding quarter of a century, having contacts with living witnesses, sallying forth with voice recorder and camera, and being involved in clandestine activities was a heady experience. The exhilaration I felt was priceless, but it certainly impaired my ability to rest easily through the nights.

In 1997 I was granted admission to the former Party archive in Rostov and was provided with the *opis'* (inventory) of holdings; the young woman who oversaw the reading room sequentially brought all but one of the files I requested. These were detailed accounts of the meetings of the Novocherkassk and Rostov party leaderships in the months preceding and following the strike—and they were most revealing. My dealings with the archive's administration, which had begun auspiciously, were soon beset with difficulties. In order to use my time efficiently I had brought a laptop computer but was advised that it was impermissible to use it. I was also notified that materials in which I was interested could not be copied. Another episode was more startling. On the day that I began studying the documents, I jotted down many notes. When closing time arrived and I set about packing up, the reading-room attendant advised that I would have to leave my notes behind so that they could be examined. I was astonished and objected vociferously. Far from mollifying me, after the attendant glanced at the notes, she quietly continued: "No one here reads English, so you'll have to write your notes in Russian." Furious, I complained to a couple of well-placed Rostovians who, shocked to learn that Soviet-style restraints were still in play, offered to intervene, but then decided it would be futile. The atmosphere having become unpleasant, I decided to complete my work in the archive as quickly as possible—but I complied only outwardly with the designated procedure. I purchased a second notebook, in which I inscribed English notes amply but in less detail than I would have liked, while setting down extremely cursory jottings in Russian in the other.

A year and a half later, when I returned to Rostov, my agenda did not include a return to the archive. However, after having completed the work I had planned, there was time to spare, and I thought it would be useful to peruse again, in a less hurried fashion, the documents I had examined before. The head of the History Faculty at Rostov State University with whom I discussed the matter thought it would be fruitless to try to seek admission. His counterpart in the Pedagogical Institute believed it was worth a try. He phoned the previous head of the archive, with whom he was friendly, and subsequently made an appointment for the two of us to call on the present head. When we entered the administrator's office, her demeanor left no room for doubt concerning her implacably negative attitude. I went through the motions of making my request and, as I had anticipated, she spewed out a litany of reasons why I could not be accommodated. At that, my companion entered into what became a protracted and rather heated argument. Inclined to think it was a waste of time, I could not have been more surprised when the administrator eventually gave way. I was then permitted to work in the archive, everything I wanted was promptly furnished, there was no talk of leaving notes for examination, and the woman in the reading room generously offered to bring me other materials that might prove useful. Fulfilling my objectives, I was forcefully reminded of how important connections can be in doing historical research.

Before concluding, I must relate the story of one more encounter. Before I left Rostov in the spring of 1997, Nikitina suggested that I meet Bagraev in Moscow and promised to advise him by phone that I would be contacting him. He agreed to my proposal and asked me to meet him outside of the compound wherein the Chief Military Procuracy was located. He escorted me past a guard-post to his office, where we conversed for about an hour. He was impressed, I believe, by how much I knew about the Novocherkassk story, but parried the brief I made for gaining access to the thirty-one volumes. There was no need for that, he argued, since I had examined the summary volume and everything of importance was contained therein. For my part, I laid out reasons why a historian could not be satisfied with a summary. Bagraev turned out to be an urbane and intelligent man, willing to listen and discuss rather than simply stonewall—by the way, he raised no objection to the taping of our interchange. Finally, he said that he could see no reason why I should not be allowed to view the volumes, but he would have to check with a superior and would phone me in a few days.

I took this to be a brush-off, but he did in fact call me and indicated that I would be given access. When I returned, he gave me an oral overview of the collection and some advice as to how I might most fruitfully proceed. He brought me the three volumes I requested and later provided tea and a snack while I worked away at the documents in a fever pitch of excitement. He was out of town for the next several days, and I could not gain admission to the compound without him. The next time I contacted Bagraev—he had advised me that I would need my passport to gain admission to the compound—the private soldier on duty at the guard station indicated that his instructions forbade him to allow someone with an American document to enter. Rather than pull rank on the soldier, Bagraev asked me to wait outside while he consulted the commandant. He returned about fifteen minutes later and ruefully told me that I would need special permission to continue work on the Novocherkassk volumes, that I should write to an officer whom he named, but ought not to be very hopeful about receiving a positive response. He had obviously cooperated with me on his own, had been called to order, and now he spoke sorrowfully about the persistence among many individuals of the old mentality of suspicion and secrecy. Needless to say, I was terribly disappointed, but also grateful to him for having stuck his neck out. The deputy director of the State Archive of the Russian Federation (GARF), whom I had told that I was to be admitted to the Military Procuracy headquarters, had exclaimed that this was a "miracle," but it turned out to be a short-lived miracle. This turn of events magnified my satisfaction at having the 170-page summary that Nikitina had handed me.

To tie up one other end, unreconstructed bureaucrats also frustrated the effort of the jurist who had endeavored to help me secure access to the eight-volume record of the most important of the trials. Fortunately, as the saying goes, there is more than one way to skin a cat. At GARF, the Moscow archive that is admirably open to researchers, I found the invaluable record of the detailed preliminary investigation that preceded the trial and undoubtedly foreshadowed closely the proceedings that followed.

The culmination of these adventures came in November 1999 when I received word that the Stanford University Press had agreed with alacrity to publish my *Bloody Saturday in the Soviet Union: Novocherkassk, 1962.*

Notes

1. I have expanded this point in "Recollections of a Life in Russian History," *Russian History* 17, no. 1: 35–36.

2. It is printed in Samuel H. Baron and Carl Pletsch, *Introspection in Biography: The Biographer's Quest for Self-Awareness.* Hillsdale: Lawrence Erlbaum, 1985.

3. I had coedited this volume (Columbus: American Association for the Advancement of Slavic Studies, 1977) with Nancy W. Heer.

4. S.V. Tiutiukin, *G.V. Plekhanov. Sud'ba russkogo marksizma* (Moscow, 1997), pp. 13–14; Samuel H. Baron, "Plekhanov, utopizm i russkaia revoliutsiia," *Otechestvennaia istoriia*, 1995, no. 5.

3

Discovering Rural Russia
A Forty-Year Odyssey

Priscilla Roosevelt

As I think back on my adventures and encounters from 1962, when I first went to the USSR, to the present, I envision them as a crazy quilt constructed of patches acquired over four decades, each of which has contributed something different to my current view of Russians and of their historical experience. I was trained at Harvard and Columbia during a period when the success of the Soviet experiment was by and large taken for granted. Post-1917 Russia was assumed to have little continuity with the old regime or, indeed, with any other society past or present. By extension, *homo Sovieticus* was virtually an alien life form. These assumptions, which took me years to set aside, impeded both my historical research on the old regime and my understanding of Russians I met both here and in Russia.

Until the early 1990s, the trips I took to Russia seemed like visits to a prison; I felt intense relief at their conclusion. As my own life experience broadened, I became more adept at sifting out the truly unique or abnormal in the Soviet experience and understanding that most Soviet citizens were just normal people trying to deal with an abnormal situation. Soviet Russia came to seem less a prison than an occupied country. I concluded that the Russia of great culture, passionate debate, and honest feeling I so admired still existed, but was in hiding; I viewed myself as a courier, bringing news and supplies to my dissident Russian friends, members of an underground resistance.

In such a risky business, I assumed—as did we all—that mail was censored, hotel rooms bugged, and all foreigners objects of intense interest to the dread KGB. The system certainly was very effective at isolating and dividing its citizens, and keeping contacts with foreigners to a minimum. On a long train ride from Leningrad through the Baltic states to Berlin in the late 1970s, I shared a compartment with a Lithuanian doctor and son, and a Russian woman living in Lithuania. For the first few hours we exchanged meaningless pleasantries. Then the Russian woman, who in the corridor had privately complained to me about the system that forced her to go all the way to Leningrad to buy food exported from Lithuania, left the train. The Lithuanian doctor immediately began to tell me volubly why he resented the Soviet regime, and to describe the system of underground churches in Vilnius. When I asked why we hadn't been talking openly some hours earlier, he said he could never speak of such things in front of "that Russian." It was obvious that she is a real Soviet. I could not convince him that she was just as much a Lithuanian patriot as he, and that she shared his resentment.

Two incidents at last convinced me that the occupation forces were actually pretty inefficient. In 1981 I was briefly detained in the police station of the Novgorod Kremlin. A young mechanic whom I had met in the park had urged me to climb up some scaffolding on a wall to get a better view of the city and, predictably, the local police swooped down on us. The police chief seemed mainly amused, and I am fairly certain that he did not even report the incident to the authorities at the Intourist hotel where I was staying. A few years later I landed at Sheremetevo with a small shoe box of writing materials I had been asked to bring for Andrei Sakharov, just banished to Gorki, along with a letter and some photos of his grandchildren. I was strip-searched, everything confiscated and, no doubt, painstakingly copied. After four hours everything was returned, but needless to say I decided not to deliver the shoe box in person. Though I feared future visa problems, in fact there were absolutely no repercussions; the record of my incriminating documents probably never left the airport.

Though the system turned out to have few dangers for me, it had painful effects on the lives of Russian friends. A curator in the Hermitage with children the ages of my own told me that her thirteen-year-old daughter had larded an essay on medieval Europe with irrelevant quotes from Marx and Lenin, telling her mother that the quotes would mean a better grade. "What do I, as a parent, do? Say, 'That's great,' and help her to succeed in this system, or tell her the truth? This will condemn her to failure, and possibly put us in prison if she gets angry with us one day." The memory of such painful conversations has erased whatever nostalgia I might have for the intense discussions of taboo subjects around the kitchen table, or for the special type of bonding and trust they engendered.

My intellectual odyssey has had just as many fortuitous moments of illumination and redirection. For two decades after writing my senior honors thesis on the provincial agronomist, designer of estate parks, and prolific author Andrei T. Bolotov (1738–1833)[1], I thought of myself as an intellectual historian. My doctoral dissertation was an intellectual biography of the historian Timofei N. Granovskii,[2] whose written oeuvre was small yet whose personal legacy was immense. In the course of reworking the dissertation into a book, I began a slow migration toward what is now called "material culture," and then, via social history, back to the world of provincial estates, the milieu to which Bolotov had devoted his labors and writings, and in which Granovskii had grown up. This *ricorso* began with curiosity about the sources of Granovskii's famous charisma. Many of his contemporaries dwelt on physical factors unrelated to the lectures and articles on which I had focused. Herzen, for instance, after talking about Granovskii's long, dark, wavy hair and luminous eyes, commented, "When Granovskii came back from Berlin, he had a blue velvet frock coat of a very particular cut." Though I never did identify this cut, I became fascinated by costume, recalling that Granovskii actually sent fashion plates from the thick journals, along with bolts of cloth, to his sisters on the family estate, Pogorelets, near Orel. My attempts to find out something about this estate became an obsession and were fruitless. When I asked a few colleagues about estates of the time belonging to other members of Granovskii's circle, I discovered that life in the provinces was more or less a blank page for all of us.

The final impetus to work on estate life was a friend's offhand comment as we were looking at an illustration of a marvelous ruined Gothic tower that Thomas Jefferson designed for Monticello. "The Russians *must* have had follies," she said. And so they did, I learned, as I perused the pages of *Starye gody* (Bygone Years) and *Stolitsa i usad'ba* (The Capital and The Estate) in the University of Illinois library. It suddenly occurred to me that I needed to reread Bolotov's memoirs. Then I learned of a special program offering a short course in estate culture. This intensive three-week program in England, "The Attingham Summer School on the British Country House," run by the British National Trust, features visits to many houses in different parts of the country and daily lectures on numerous discrete subjects. By the end, one has a very good picture of the constituent parts of the field and of the terminology for the subject. Attingham is usually fully subscribed by active practitioners: house museum curators, antique dealers, and academic specialists in all conceivable areas of the decorative arts. I filled one of the slots for people who, though not technically in the field, can make a good case for needing the schooling. Another was occupied by a practicing architect from Houston.

I had read numerous memoirs by eighteenth-century Russians who had toured the great English houses, and I determined to put myself in what I fancied would have been their mindset. This left me feeling overawed, during the first week, by the wealth of antiquities and the meticulously maintained archives. But midway in the course as I sat in a deep alcove at Petworth, catching my breath, I asked the practicing architect why he was doing the course. "Why, Priscilla," he answered, "my clients like their houses *big*. I'm getting ideas!" Suddenly I realized that my eighteenth-century Russian aristocrats hadn't toured these houses feeling like cowed provincials; on the contrary, they were wealthy and confident, the Texans of eighteenth-century Europe. They knew that if they wanted to re-create a Blenheim or Chatsworth in the wilds of Tambov or Saratov provinces, they had the resources to do so.

The Autumn of 1992 and Beyond

Few things have so changed my understanding of the Russian experience as an extended trip sponsored by the International Research and Exchanges Board (IREX) in the fall of 1992. For over a decade I had been working on the provinces, and had just completed the basic draft of *Life on the Russian Country Estate*.[3] During this time a great revolution had occurred in Russian attitudes both toward their past and toward foreigners, and for the first time I could move freely around the countryside, visiting and photographing the estates I had chosen to write about. One Russian friend had lined up a car and a driver, and Dmitrii Shvidkovskii, a superb architectural historian, planned the itinerary. Looking at the map, I had assumed that we would have some bases other than Moscow: Tula, for instance, or Kaluga, to explore the estate region south of Moscow. However, Dmitrii thought otherwise. In fact, save for a few nights in Yaroslavl and a few in Viazma, we left Moscow early each morning, armed with provisions for the day, and returned late each evening. Where we were going, there simply were no decent hotels, cafeterias, food stores, or toilets.

There were also virtually no road signs for estates that had been converted into tuberculosis sanatoria, mental hospitals, or homes for mentally defective children. Often there were no paved roads. On many a rainy autumn day, the brave driver of our little Moskvich followed muddy tracks that no American driver would have attempted. One of these took us through the village of the "A.T. Bolotov" state farm. We ended up at the newly reconstructed little manor house of Dvorianinovo, still flanked by the cascading ponds Bolotov had so proudly constructed, a place I had never expected to see.

The truths of the Soviet period came tumbling out in conversations with the locals we ran into. As we were walking around the remnants of Mar'inka, the former Buturlin estate, admiring the well preserved neo-Gothic stable and searching for the remains of other buildings, an aged babushka—the only person in sight—approached us. She announced that she was the caretaker of the stables, now a Pioneer camp, and that she had been a young child at the time of the revolution. What had happened? I asked. She launched into praise of their "golden *barin* (master)," who had paid the estate children for berries they collected in the woods. One day, she said, there was a huge noise and an airplane landed in a neighboring field. "None of us had ever seen an airplane, of course." The *barin* went into the house, collected a few things, and then got into the airplane. "He went up into the sky and hasn't been seen again!" she said, her eyes rolling upward.

We then talked about her life since then and at present. What had happened to the once expansive neo-Gothic manor house I knew from pictures? Well, she said, after the revolution some of the local families moved into it and were quite content until the early 1930s. Then some young activists arrived, told the peasants such a luxurious house was unnecessary, and burned it down. The families were resettled in a miserable replacement. Her father, a *kulak* (prosperous peasant), was deported, but she was allowed to stay on and when the Pioneer camp opened, she was put in charge. Recently, she said, her life had gotten worse. The nearest store was about five kilometers away, there was no bus service, and since she could no longer walk that far or carry anything back, she was dependent on handouts from the few people who dropped by.

Another historical vignette came from a peasant woman who lived next door to the church at the Chernyshev estate, Iaropolets, west of Moscow. I had been eager to see this estate, and particularly the unusual double church, designed with altars at both ends. We arrived to find the house a crumbling ruin, though its two flanking dependencies, in use by local farmers, were in good shape. Across the road, we crept through the churchyard fence and inside the building to find a vandalized, graffiti-covered shell. When we emerged, the aged neighbor hailed us from her apple orchard. While we sampled some of her apples, she told us that the house had been used as a hospital through the war period and her mother had worked as a nurse there. Then there was a fire (a very common occurrence) and the hospital closed, but the church continued to operate into the 1950s. It was one of the 50,000 casualties of Khrushchev's onslaught against religion. As she described the church being shut down, she began to cry. "I sang in the choir, and this was the only beautiful thing in my life," she said. "Now there is nothing."

Some of my most enlightening moments that fall came during my days as the guest of Viktor E. Kulakov, restorer and director of Khmelita, the Griboedov estate near Viazma in Smolensk Province. He drove me out from Moscow during the first real snowstorm of the season, worrying about the fate of the potatoes in his basement and talking volubly about all the former estates we were passing on the 200-kilometer trip. After ascertaining that the potatoes were not frozen, he took me for a closer exploration of the ruins in a twenty-mile-square area around Khmelita. He also took me to Aleksino, the Baryshnikov estate near Dorogobuzh, which I knew well from memoirs. This is a remarkable eighteenth-century ensemble, now a stud farm, whose director is both knowledgeable and concerned about its fate. In the manor house there were still some original ceiling paintings, and he showed me old photos of the elegant Etruscan-style frescoes that were concealed by Soviet whitewash in the former reception rooms.

On another morning Viktor took me to the remains of the Khomiakov estate, Lipitsy, near Khmelita, and then to Vysokoe, a wonderful estate ensemble designed by the well-known artist Alexandre Benois for Aleksandr D. Sheremetev at the turn of the last century. Almost all of the estate buildings have survived, including a log estate house of the 1840s, the far grander 1890s estate house in *style moderne*, a huge neo-Gothic stable and riding ring, the steward's house, and even the laundry building. Looking at the graffiti-covered church, which seemed familiar, I learned that Sheremetev had been the last owner of Ostankino, the famous Moscow showplace created by his grandfather, Nikolai Petrovich Sheremetev. For Vysokoe, Aleksandr Sheremetev had commissioned a smaller replica of Ostankino's seventeenth-century church. When I asked how this ensemble had survived Hitler's invasion (which went right through the region), Viktor said that a Sheremetev descendant had returned as an interpreter with the German troops. They occupied the house and spared it out of respect for him.

At one point during this touring, Viktor turned to me and said, "Priscilla, I bet you're glad you've finished your book." This was certainly true. Had I known in advance how very many estates there used to be, how many personal stories were connected with them, and in what a sorry state they now were, I might never have had the courage or the heart to write the book I did. For three days I stayed in the restored wing of Khmelita, borrowing *valenki* (felt boots) to trudge through the crisp snow on starry evenings, visiting various dilapidated huts in the village. In one, the owner, who seemed to be about eighty years old, offered us inedible *sala* (salt pork) and *samogon* (home brew) that was true firewater. As we were leaving, he gave me a huge primitive painting he had done of St. George slaying the dragon, copied from a magazine. On the way home Viktor explained that *Ded* (Grandfather), as this elderly man was called, was a veteran of World War II and a revered figure in the village, even though his primary occupation after the war had been informing for the KGB.

Offering a short course in the current socioeconomics of rural Russia, Viktor pointed out the "estate" of the director of the local collective farm—a handsome house, with several good-looking horses out to pasture. Viktor also proudly showed me around his nearly finished, smaller house on a hill overlooking a pond, with a view of Khmelita, surrounded by twenty hectares of land that he insisted belonged to him. In the mornings, listening to Viktor cajole his workers at Khmelita, I couldn't help thinking of Bolotov, steward of the imperial estate Bogoroditsk and owner of Dvorianinovo.

Dmitrii and I had a terrible shock the week after my stay at Khmelita. We were full of anticipation as we approached Ol'govo, the Apraksin estate north of Moscow. In the 1920s it had been one of many local estate museums, crowded with memorabilia collected by four generations of Apraksins. Then it had been given to the local administration. As we drove up, we saw the entrance obelisks, stable and cattle courtyards, and then the freshly painted wings, all in good shape. Then we rounded the corner, to find that the main house had fallen down completely. Dmitrii, who had visited the house five years previously, was speechless. Like the Chernyshev manor house, obviously the Ol'govo mansion was of no use to the local population and had proven too difficult to maintain; it was being gradually dismantled and the building materials put to other purposes. We found the great neo-Gothic mansion at Marfino still standing, but a wreck. We pushed our way in through a back door to find the flooring ripped up and twenty-foot, solid oak French doors lying on the rafters. There was abundant evidence that the roof had sprung leaks. As I was videoing the house, a young man passing by paused and said, "Good for you for photographing it—in ten years it will be gone."

My tours with Viktor have continued. In 1997 we spent a rainy autumn week on the road, our main goals Talashkino outside Smolensk, Pushkin's Mikhailovskoe in Pskov Province, and Mussorgsky's estate in Tver Province. All three are museum estates and in quite good condition. But on the way to Mikhailovskoe, we stopped at Glubokoe (Pskov Province), once owned by Count Heiden, marshal of the nobility, who had bought Khmelita for the dowry of his daughter, Varvara Volkov-Muromtsov. Here again I confronted devastating loss. The "Holy Gates" to the church and the main house, which I knew well from pre-revolutionary photos, had disappeared completely. The once prosperous factory on Lake Glubokoe that had produced wooden lanterns for export down to the revolution had crumbled to its foundations. Yet we ran into a local schoolteacher who had a collection of pre-revolutionary photographs and newspaper clippings, and knew the history of the estate well. She was excited by our visit and delighted to learn about the family link between Glubokoe and Khmelita.

The following year Viktor humored my desire to try to find what was left of the former Grabbe estate, Mikhailovskoe, on the border of Smolensk and Moscow provinces. Again it was raining, but he took a side road off the highway (so good that Viktor speculated it was military) and we traveled about forty kilometers before finally seeing the small sign for Mikhailovskoe. My expectations were low, as Count Paul Grabbe, who remembered the place from his childhood, had told me that the house had burned down in 1913. But down the road through the drizzle the outlines of a substantial house gradually and unmistakably appeared. We ran around it in the dusk snapping pictures, noting the apparently solid tin roof, the evidence that the *bel étage* had at some time been split into two floors, and the presence of an electric light inside. But we found no signs or people to enlighten us as to its current use—if any—by the sparse local population.

Experiences like this, reinforcing my sense that some houses I had written about were vanishing, and with them an important part of local history, and that others were alive but invisible, played a large part in the creation in 1997 of our foundation, American Friends of the Russian Country Estate (A-FORCE). Perestroika had a terrible impact on estate research and on the old support system for Russia's great houses, as both were dependent on government money. As the government budget shrank and inflation destroyed the value of the ruble, institutes, publications, and museums became equally underfunded; numerous sanatoria and resorts were shut down and the houses left to rot. The goal of A-FORCE is to help Russians salvage some of their cultural heritage in the countryside, represented by these houses; I am convinced that its very existence has given hope and moral support to those Russians who understand the significance of these old buildings and care about estate culture.

Since 1992 I have acquired a raft of new Russian friends who, like me, are trying to ensure the survival of what remains of the former grandeur of the countryside. Some are museum directors or curators. Most are members of the Society for the Study of the Russian Estate (OIRU), a small group founded in the 1920s, repressed by Stalin at the end of that decade, and reborn in Moscow in 1993. In 1996, shortly after my book came out, I was invited to a meeting of the board of directors of OIRU. (I was fairly nervous about this, imagining what a Russian who had written the first big book on the culture of the antebellum South might encounter were he or she to be summoned to the Center for Southern Culture at Ole Miss.) Various members had been assigned a chapter of my book to critique. To my surprise, they had nothing but praise for it. This was the ultimate reward for my long odyssey.

For the last five years I have been working on a second volume that takes the story of Russia's estates from the emancipation through the Revolution of 1917, the Civil War, and the Soviet period. The many scholars and museum personnel who have befriended me in the last decade are an invaluable resource in this endeavor. OIRU is actively researching estates throughout the country, discovering a great deal of illuminating material suppressed during the Soviet era. In Iaroslavl, a chance encounter with a young curator in the local history museum produced an unexpected reward when she loaned me an unpublished article by one of the original members of the Society. Gradually such "lost" manuscripts are coming to light. It is emblematic of the new mentality in Russia that "A Wreath for the Estate," written in Solovki prison in 1931 by A.N. Grech, a founding member of OIRU, surfaced after spending sixty-four years hidden in the bowels of the Historical Museum and was published in 1995.[4]

OIRU also has a few members actively involved in the practical problems of estate restoration. Through them I have had some extraordinary visits: to Pokrovskoe-Rubtsovo near Istra, built for the tycoon Savva Morozov in the early twentieth century, accompanied by Savva's granddaughter Tatiana; and to Znamenskoe-Raek near Torzhok, a masterpiece of Russian Palladianism designed by Nikolai Lvov at the end of the eighteenth century, in the company of the former mayor of Tver. Both these houses are now abandoned sanatoria that will perish from neglect unless someone comes up with a creative idea for their re-use and a source of funding for the plan.

Other members represent one of several recently created Russian foundations which, like A-FORCE, are trying to grapple with the enormous difficulties of implementing creative solutions to halt the decay of estates like these. The Pushkin Foundation, inaugurated by Academician Dmitrii Likhachev, is attempting to resurrect the estates connected with Pushkin and his friends in Tver Province. One of the foundation's board members was formerly head of the Iakovlev Aviation Institute; our first meeting took place at this top security institute, another place I had never imagined I would visit. As I looked at the earliest prototypes of Russian airplanes from 1913 in their museum of Russian aviation and then at the spy drones active during the Cold War, I could not help thinking of Count Buturlin vanishing into the ether and of the cosmic changes that Russia has witnessed in the twentieth century.

As elsewhere in the world, so too in Russia preservation efforts have engendered turf battles and considerable conflict, both theoretical and practical. During a preservation seminar A-FORCE sponsored at the Open Society Institute in 1999, my colleague Rodney Cook presented a development plan for Grand Duke Konstantin's palace, Strelna, near Peterhof (a joint venture abandoned after the financial crisis of August 1998). With one exception, the Russian academics in the room voiced a strong preference for allowing Strelna to fall down completely rather than letting it become a partially commercial venture. (Since then, Vladimir Putin has decided to renovate Strelna as a summer residence.) Recently, a barrage of publicity about such endangered sites has done much to soften this attitude.

Another challenge is convincing rural villagers clinging to unprofitable collective farm life (whose despair at their situation is, in most instances, palpable) that the restoration and re-use of a moldering house will benefit the community by creating jobs and income. In the poverty-stricken countryside, any display of wealth is deeply resented. This was brought home to me in January 1995, when an impressive group of international visitors gathered for the opening of the Khmelita museum. The festivities were widely covered in the press and on TV. But as a few of us walked around the village, we met a disgruntled old woman lugging a water jug to a nearby well. Her own, closer well was out of commission, she said. "That's how it is nowadays! They can show Khmelita on national television, but they can't fix my pump."

This resentment is susceptible to change. Twice I have brought Western preservation specialists to Vysokoe. The entire village has turned out for us; they seem to be proud of its history and anxious to find a good use for the manor house that will bring them income. The same is true at Lipitsy, the former Khomiakov estate, where they hope to restore the remaining wing as a museum, and at Aleksino. But as the director of Aleksino's state farm recently said to me, any plan to save the historic eighteenth-century core of the estate through privatization (one of the options he foresees) must deal equitably with the 400 people who now live on the property; they cannot simply be dispossessed.

* * *

Though the last forty years have seen numerous changes, many of them overwhelmingly positive, for me the eternal question "Whither Russia?" remains unanswered. A British colleague, John C.Q. Roberts, in his recent memoirs of his decades of work in Russia, likens the tortuous process of decoding Russia to exploring a mountain landscape. He writes, "Its lower slopes are covered by mysterious forests, punctuated by occasional clearings, in which one might perceive some feature or movement. Higher up, as the cover becomes thinner, one begins to appreciate the shape of things more certainly. Then, finally, there are the brighter uplands of freedom, hope, and understanding. But the top of the mountain, as with most real ones, is periodically shrouded in mist."[5] My entire generation of Russianists undoubtedly empathizes with that sense of having tried to discern the familiar in an unfamiliar landscape, of having felt on firm ground only to have the comforting landmarks again shrouded from view. This has been my experience. I too am grateful for the clearings, which have made me happy that I chose, so unwittingly and so many years ago, the "Russian enigma" as my field. And I remain hopeful—though not certain—that the mist may ultimately disappear.

Notes

1. "Bolotov and his Role in the Russian Enlightenment." (Radcliffe College, March 1963).

2. "Timofei Nikolaevich Granovskii: Universal Historian and Russian *Intelligent.*" Columbia University, 1977. Published as *Apostle of Russian Liberalism: Timofei Granovsky* (Newtonville: Oriental Research Partners, 1986).

3. *Life on the Russian Country Estate: A Social and Cultural History.* New Haven: Yale University Press, 1995.

4. "Venok usad'bam," *Pamiatniki otechestva*, no. 34 (January 1995).

5. *Speak Loudly into the Chandelier.* London: Curzon Press, 2000, p. 6.

4

Catherine the Great and the Rats

John T. Alexander

Sisters can bruise the ego. When Johns Hopkins University Press sought a title for my study of bubonic plague under Catherine the Great, my younger sister facetiously championed "Katya and the Rats." Maybe that would have boosted sales beyond its stodgy academic title.[1] Fortunately for my pride, in view of the decade-plus efforts invested, the book gained marvelous evaluations by reviewers more expert than Susan Stamberg on National Public Radio and William McNeill in *Slavic Review.*[2] In retrospect I am amazed at how blithely I tackled the topic, which I thought might merit an article. Instead it plunged me into diverse fields of epidemiology and medical history, historical climatology and ecology, urban affairs and Moscow's social structure, demography and topography, Cliometrics, and Russian religious and church history. Abundant assistance accrued from many individuals and institutions in several countries. All of which underscores that multidisciplinary, international scholarship entails group enterprise.

A crucial stimulus appeared by chance. In early 1965, while a doctoral candidate exchange scholar working in the Central State Historical Archive of the USSR in Leningrad, I stumbled onto a handwritten order by Empress Catherine II. Labeled "secret" and dated September 24, 1771, her single convoluted sentence urged the Governing Senate to undertake removal of all large manufactories from Moscow. No reason was given for such an extraordinary measure although the note was filed among correspondence relating to the epidemic then raging in the old capital. What the relationship might be between pestilence and industry was not obvious.

I had come to Leningrad the previous autumn to work with Professor Vladimir Vasilevich Mavrodin (1908–1987) and his team of historians producing a multivolume study of the Pugachev Revolt of 1773–75.[3] It was my first visit to Russia and my first archival work there. My Slovak-born and Russian-speaking bride Maria and I were the single American couple assigned to the "hardship" post of Leningrad. The first few months we spent getting acclimated, exploring the beautiful city and environs, sampling the

49

lively cultural life, and pressing for archival access despite repeated assurances that all Pugachev-related materials had been transferred to Moscow. When I was finally admitted to the Leningrad archive, it proved to hold just the documents needed and more. Catherine's order seemed to be just an unrelated curiosity.

Still learning eighteenth-century Russian script, I made my own handwritten copy and then forgot about it. Amid research for my dissertation and first book on the imperial Russian government's policy-making during the Pugachev Revolt,[4] I discovered references to the "plague riot" of September 15–17, 1771, and assumed that the empress's order had been provoked by the Moscow violence. That assumption was buttressed by readings about various anti-government manifestations during the first decade of Catherine II's reign (1762–96). Although no Marxist in my approach to history, I was much influenced by "crisis" notions from undergraduate mentor Sigmund Neumann (1904–1962) at Wesleyan University and also stunned by the turbulent late sixties worldwide and locally at the University of Kansas in Lawrence, where I began teaching in 1966. Upon completing two books and several articles concerning the Pugachev Revolt and translating S.F. Platonov (1860–1933) on the Time of Troubles in Muscovy, I sought a new topic in social history that would facilitate intellectual growth and further professional advancement.

Such pragmatic considerations led back to the Moscow plague. Preliminary research at the Library of Congress in August 1969 confirmed the existence of a wealth of sources and a dearth of scholarship. I returned to Lawrence certain there was a book in the subject and applied to the academic exchange, the International Research and Exchanges Board (IREX), for seven months in Moscow in 1971. Maria and I thought it would be educational to take our son and daughter, ages four and two. Since a cholera epidemic had struck Ukraine in 1970, we all got cholera shots in preparation for Moscow, where we arrived on January 8, 1971, and were housed at the Hotel Pekin in central Moscow. Within days our daughter, Darya, came down with diarrhea and fever and was taken by ambulance to the hospital. Maria and I alternated staying with her overnight for fear that she would be frightened alone in a strange place. She stayed for a week and the women doctors urged leaving her longer, reminding us that the care was free. Our dear little Darya, or Dashenka as the Russians called her, left the Soviet hospital happy as a lark and never saw the inside of another. Some weeks later we got a bill for 72 rubles, a whopping sum the hotel personnel advised us to ignore. When it came again through the mail, we turned to the U.S. embassy and it was quietly dropped.

This initial experience unnerved our first few weeks. Eventually we arranged for both kids to attend a preschool five days a week, including break-fast and lunch. This school was run entirely by women, and despite elaborate rules covering one wall, it proved to be delightfully anarchic. Our kids picked up handy Russian phrases such as "I'll give it to you!" and "Hands up!" (many of the boy-toddlers came in toting plastic burp guns). Just starting to talk, Darya babbled ungrammatically with an excellent accent that charmed all and sundry. In a nearby park we met Andrei Stroev, his wife Svetlana, and son Maksim with whom we became friendly. The Stroevs were the only Soviet family we knew with a car, and we went out riding with them several times. Fortunately, too, Maria arranged via the maids on our floor to move us into a three-room suite with a refrigerator and TV, and an embassy friend supplied a crib and a stroller. Everyday life became more bearable.

Within days of our arrival I met consultant Professor Mikhail Timofeevich Beliavskii (1913–1989) of Moscow State University (MGU) at his apartment, where he was recovering from flu, to go over my research proposal. An extrovert impaired by war wounds, with a shock of dark hair and a Bolshevik-style mustache, he smoked incessantly. He opened our first meeting by asserting that the plague riot wasn't worth further investigation. But his attitude softened when I reiterated that my primary focus would be the epidemic in a socioeconomic context. He agreed that the public health and environmental setting might be worthwhile.

Soon I started working in the Central State Archive of Ancient Documents (TsGADA), the main repository of manuscript materials predating 1800. In 1965 I had toiled there for almost six months, so presumably my Pugachev research helped gain immediate access to the voluminous plague materials. Besides, the topic raised no Soviet objections, perhaps because the eighteenth century seemed ancient history, and there was no established field of medical history or much active research therein. Based on Catherine's order of September 1771, I pursued the question of industry in Moscow and pored over huge files relating to the outbreak at the Big Woolen Court (*bol'shoi sukonnyi dvor*), the empire's largest textile manufactory. I knew that it had been an early locus of the outbreak and that its central location just across the Moskva River from the Kremlin had galvanized officialdom to action. At Beliavskii's suggestion I visited the Museum of the History and Reconstruction of the City of Moscow, where I purchased a mammoth compendium of materials detailing the evolution of Moscow by the great local expert P.V. Sytin (1885–1968). Later in the spring, when I had to stay indoors because of bronchial woes, I learned much from Sytin's scholarship.

With a grant from the American Philosophical Society I purchased books and ordered Xerox and microfilm copies of relevant materials from the Lenin Library. An incident with a Xerox machine sticks in the memory. Going upstairs to order copies (self-service was not available), I watched a young man with a fire extinguisher tending to a smoking copier. When switched on, the machine spewed flames while he continually squirted it with foam. No wonder the copies were barely legible. Fellow exchangee Bruce Lincoln (1938–2000) of Northern Illinois University believed that the machines must have been totally worn out before being sold to the USSR, even then infamous for abysmal maintenance. It all recalled humorist Mikhail Zoshchenko's tale from the 1920s, "The Dictaphone," recounting how Soviet office workers get hold of an American Dictaphone that they finally break by foolhardy abuses—a delicious satire on "technology transfer."

Through a Soviet historian of the United States whom I had met in Lawrence and accompanied to lunch with former governor and presidential candidate Alf Landon in Topeka, I met two senior scholars at the Institute of History of the Academy of Sciences of the USSR, Lev Vladimirovich Cherepnin and Nikolai Ivanovich Pavlenko. The former, a corpulent medievalist (1905–1977) who had survived the Stalin era to become an eminent member of the Academy, I found rather curt although he did praise the work of Yale's George Vernadsky. With Pavlenko, however, an ebullient Ukrainian of about fifty who specialized in the history of eighteenth-century Russian industry, I discovered much common ground. He thought the plague an excellent research topic and mentioned several relevant archives. We talked about his current work on Peter the Great's personality, and he disdained Beliavskii's crude attack on Catherine II "as if with an axe" and thought the significance of the Pugachev Revolt much exaggerated—sentiments I shared. He also explained that the Ukrainian term *chumak* (from *chuma*, plague) was derived from salt-haulers who visited the Crimea in the eighteenth century and smeared their clothes with pitch as protection against disease. Though unsure about the medical history angle, he cautioned against amateurs dabbling in history. Later he supplied me with offprints of his latest work, and he has sent me books and articles over the years. A chance meeting with the charming elderly Petrine specialist Elena Petrovna Pod"iapol'skaia also elicited praise for the topic and archives to consult. Such positive reinforcement energized my infatuation with the topic.

After three abortive attempts we finally managed to spend ten days in Leningrad amid the white nights. We were warmly received by several friends. Mavrodin, my former mentor, greeted me affably, as did his genial assistant, Valeriia Al'bertovna Petrova, my paleography tutor. The Leningrad archive provided some interesting tidbits. We spent a pleasant day at suburban Pushkin/Tsarskoe Selo, where I photographed the Orlov Gates, a monument to Grigorii Orlov's heroism in captaining the antiplague campaign. Our last few weeks in Moscow were quite frenzied. After repeated requests I finally gained access to one hefty file on the plague riot that had been unbound to permit microfilming. It proved quite valuable, so I am glad I persisted. I also perused many files transferred to TsGADA from the Moscow city archive concerning the Plague Commission set up in October 1771 to oversee antiplague policies. We left Moscow at the end of July 1971 after dinner with Father Louis Dion, the Catholic chaplain who kindly conveyed us to the Kiev railway station. Returning home via Slovakia, Norway, London, and Wales, our kids quickly forgot Russian, Darya puzzling over how we got to "Londongrad."

The first year back I began processing the sources and reading Russian works on medical history, for I had decided to do more with that neglected dimension. In line for a sabbatical, I arranged a year and two summers off with supplementary funding from the National Library of Medicine. The witty, iconoclastic history of plague in the British Isles by J.F.D. Shrewsbury also encouraged me to challenge much received wisdom. I continued investigating the question of industry in Moscow for a presentation at the Southern Conference on Slavic Studies in Coral Gables, Florida, in October 1972. That report was read in my absence at a memorable session that included two other much cited papers, by David Griffiths and Brenda Meehan-Waters. All three subsequently appeared in major journals.[5] By then my understanding of Catherine's order of September 1771 had changed radically as a result of a broader context and greater theoretical grasp of bubonic plague. The plague riot receded in significance to rank as only one of several police, public health, and environmental concerns that gave birth to the proposal to remove large manufactories.

By coincidence I missed the Florida session in order to attend the first colloquium of U.S. and USSR historians in Moscow. This elite conference was planned in the aftermath of rancorous disputes at the World Congress of Historical Sciences in Moscow in August 1971. The topics were ostensibly non-controversial: "Town Development and the Enlightenment in the Eighteenth Century." With Marc Raeff of Columbia University, I was flattered to be one of two commentators in the delegation of five U.S. scholars charged to comment on the two Soviet papers. The American headliners were Henry May of UC-Berkeley, Bernard Bailyn of Harvard, and Jacob Price of Michigan. Meeting at the Moscow House of Scholars, Pavel Grigorevich Ryndziunskii (d. 1993) spoke knowledgeably about town development, whereas my former consultant Beliavskii delivered an inept report on "Franklin and Lomonosov." Inadvertently I enraged Beliavskii both by questioning his contention that the two men came from lower class backgrounds, and by labeling Lomonosov (a Soviet icon) the son of a wealthy "businessman," unaware that in Russian the term implied "dirty business." At lunch after this contretemps the charming wife of academician N.M. Druzhinin, Elena Ioasafovna Druzhinina (1916–2000), assured me that despite mistaken terminology I had been right about the principal issue.

More importantly, I met several Russian specialists in American history: Nikolai Nikolaevich Bolkhovitinov and Gennadii Petrovich Kuropiatnik of the Institute of General History of the Academy of Sciences, Svetlana Grigorevna Fedorova from the Institute of Ethnography, and graduate student Iurii Rogulev of MGU. All were eager to meet Americans in anticipation of visits to the United States. (All three men did in fact visit the University of Kansas in the next few years, and Svetlana Fedorova attended an international conference in Chicago, where she was overwhelmed by a visit to Marshall Field's.) The American conferees also visited Leningrad, where we stayed in the venerable Astoria Hotel. Providentially we escaped a near vehicular crash at Tsarskoe Selo and later visited Novgorod for a day. A long conversation with Bud Bailyn about my paper on industry in Moscow, which I had thoughts of submitting to the *American Historical Review*, sharpened its focus and steeled my resolve.

Shortly after the Moscow colloquium I attended a tercentenary conference on Peter the Great organized in Chicago by Richard Hellie. My paper on medical developments in Petrine Russia introduced me to a wide array of Russian and Soviet scholarship on medical history, with emphasis on the numbers, types, origins, and academic training of the various medical practitioners. Arcadius Kahan of the University of Chicago graciously provided a copy of an unpublished listing of epidemics in Russia, just one of several topics in which we shared an interest. Stimulated by the Chicago discussions, I later pursued additional lines of inquiry at the National Library of Medicine in Bethesda, where I was assisted by a longtime family friend and librarian, Mrs. Dorothy Hanks, and by James Cassedy and John Blake in medical history. In June 1973, at the New York Public Library's fine Slavonic Collection, I utilized N.N. Novombergskii's compilation of sources to reassess some obscure Petrine plague outbreaks.

The Moscow colloquium of 1972 yielded ancillary benefits in raising my status in Soviet eyes. When I returned to Moscow three years later to complete archival research, I was viewed as more than just another promising young scholar. Indeed, when my industry paper came out as the lead article in the *American Historical Review* in June 1974, it won widespread recognition. Nikolai Bolkhovitinov commented that Catherine II had been right about the need to remove big factories from overcrowded and polluted Moscow: just look at it now! An inquiry that had begun with the assumption that Catherine's order would show what a panicky female she was ended by concluding the opposite. Although her order had arisen from varied motivations dating well before the plague, it was not implemented fully because the epidemic killed so many bondaged workers at large manufactories that none was large thereafter.

Amid the Watergate hearings in the spring and summer of 1973 I revised the industry and Petrine papers and drafted several chapters of the book. For several months I feared that Nixon might suspend the Constitution. The next spring Iurii Rogulev visited Overland Park with a Soviet exhibition, and I arranged for him to meet colleagues in twentieth-century U.S. history. The artist-journalist Oleg Visniakov sketched five-year-old Darya in a "granny" dress, a portrait printed a year later in the mass-circulation *Soviet Woman*. After Nixon's resignation Iurii later recalled that when the Soviet exhibition had moved on to Denver, the American visitors unanimously condemned Nixon, whose visit to Moscow in the summer of 1974 was described by embassy friends as like that of an automaton.

Teaching full time again in the fall of 1973, I reapplied to IREX to spend four months alone in Moscow. The aim was to wrap up research on the expanding study, of which I had already drafted eleven chapters, the core of the book. This final, longish sojourn in Moscow began in early February 1975. Luckily, customs did not detect a picture book on horror films for Andrei Stroev, which might have been confiscated as pornography. My reception committee of two graduate students told me that a review article had just come out criticizing my Pugachev publications.[6] My main consultant was again Beliavskii who, after a few minutes' amiable conversation, suddenly asked: "Aren't you Dzhons?" Robert Jones (UMass-Amherst) was scheduled to arrive a few weeks later, Beliavskii mistaking me for him. This ambiguous start looked even worse when I was met frigidly at TsGADA by a "Gogolian creature" bureaucrat who insisted they had nothing more for me. In fact, the huge repository housed more than I could have digested in many months.

My lone protracted struggle for archival access—amid these relaxed months of détente—involved materials from the medical administration (*Meditsinskaia Kollegiia*). After weeks of protesting TsGADA's refusal as unfounded and enlisting the assistance of Beliavskii and the U.S. embassy, something worked. The "Gogolian" politely conceded the materials in question and said that I might see inventories to speed my selection of documents. This was a satisfying minor triumph although, ironically, the medical administration materials proved disappointingly thin. One file of plague treatises could not be found anywhere. Some files were so hefty as to be extremely awkward to read because you had to stand to view the script. My Pugachev research had prepared me well for the script; nevertheless, one letter took half an hour to decipher because of two simple words. Most documents were clearly written, many pierced with holes from hot needles or singed by flames to disinfect reports from suspect localities. Some archivists expressed alarm about handling such papers, but I assured them that plague bacteria could not survive so long.

At TsGADA I met the authors of the critique of my Pugachev publications, Sergei Martinovich Troitskii (1930–1976) and Redzhinal'd Vasilevich Ovchinnikov (elderly though still active at present). Both greeted me cordially and accepted offprints of the AHR article and my small Pugachev book.[7] Some days later Troitskii and I had a heated discussion in the hallway; he dismissed the plague as an inconsequential topic, easily forgotten like the weather. The AHR article he criticized for skimpy use of primary sources. Stung by such one-sided criticism, I pointed out that 100,000 deaths did not seem inconsequential, and I stalked away seething. The next day we reconciled, acknowledging lost tempers on both sides. He remarked that my criticism of Soviet Pugachev scholarship showed that I, too, could dish out criticism.[8] Later he gave me some more offprints, and Bob Jones told me that Troitskii had also castigated him for his recent book on Catherine II's Provincial Reform. Both critiques were later reprinted with Troitskii's posthumously published essays.[9] By contrast, Ovchinnikov seemed delighted at my use of his publications, and he gently hoped their critique had not offended. Nikolai Bolkhovitinov sagely advised that I should not assume that the sentiments voiced in the published critique were their own. Unlike Troitskii, moreover, Ovchinnikov praised my current topic and suggested several archival files to check.

I also met with Pavel Ryndziunskii, who had given one of the papers at the 1972 colloquium. He received me and the AHR offprint affably, and recommended looking into the role of the Old Believers during the plague—a fruitful idea. The demographic historian Vladimir Maksimovich Kabuzan proved quite helpful in my efforts to estimate Moscow's pre-plague population. Additional archival guidance came from Svetlana Romanovna Dolgova, librarian at the Main Archives Administration, whom I had met in 1965 and who had a serious research interest in Archbishop Amvrosii (d. 1771), a major victim of the plague riot. During this sojourn I enjoyed more hospitality from Soviet colleagues than during all previous visits combined.

For public presentation I prepared a shortened version of my AHR article in Russian with the assistance of Andrei Stroev. I gave this first at a festive meeting of the Moscow University Russian History Department on April 9, on the occasion of the retirement of G.A. Novitskii as its head. It took about thirty-five minutes and the audience of thirty-five was not very attentive, Beliavskii accusing me of neglect of the political aspect. My reception in Leningrad for the same report in mid-April could not have been more different, with Mavrodin genially presiding over a much smaller and more receptive group.

Mavrodin praised my scholarly success and treated me like a favorite son. For the first and only time he invited me to a family evening at which I also met the eminent art historian Aleksandr L'vovich Kaganovich, a strikingly handsome scholar who later gave me a tour of the Academy of Fine Arts. The Leningrad historians who attended my talk included Lidiia Nikolaevna Semenova (1937–1993), an eighteenth-century specialist in social history and wife of Ruslan Grigorevich Skrynnikov, eminent authority on the Muscovite era. They invited me to dinner with their two cute kids, the first family I had met with more than one child. I also went out with several old friends who were delighted to see photos of our family and the portrait and story about Darya in *Soviet Woman*.

My most exciting research adventure was finding manuscript weather data at the Chief Geophysical Observatory outside Leningrad. From reading some theoretical and current discussions of bubonic plague as a disease, I had become aware of the importance of temperature and humidity in governing its behavior. Somewhere I had found a reference to weather data collected by Dr. Lerche in the 1770s. Since Mavrodin knew almost everybody of significance in local scholarly circles, he directed me to a friend who provided guidance. Three successive buses took me to the suburban village of Voiekovo, northeast of the city, where I spent the afternoon at the Metereological Museum housed in a quonset hut. At the director's desk I leafed through Dr. Lerche's temperature logs for the early 1770s in St. Petersburg, Kiev, and Moscow. So far as I know, I may be the only person ever to examine this data, which confirmed the crucial role of temperature and rainfall in the Moscow plague.

Back in Moscow I immersed myself in TsGADA materials with renewed fervor. Unfortunately, Beliavskii's wife died in early May and I never saw him again. Because of the May holidays the archives and libraries closed and shortened their hours, hence I had to rush to accomplish the maximum work before leaving at the end of the month. Providentially, I finished working at the Manuscript Section of the State Historical Museum (GIM) on Red Square, the tiny reading room that could accommodate only ten readers. There I happened upon a fascinating petition by prominent Muscovites in November 1770 voicing fears of disease because of offal from slaughterhouses and unusually warm temperatures for early winter. This information came from police materials that historian I.E. Zabelin (1820–1908) had collected and which remained among his papers. Other lucky finds were materials on the plague in Yaroslavl that Dan Morrison, a doctoral student from Columbia, had discovered and which I supplemented by data from the Moscow City

Archive. Furthermore, Bob Jones shared population statistics from the Novgorod region that showed the plague's inroads there. Another tantalizing tidbit, a published Senate report to Catherine in October 1762 supporting her ban on new manufactories in Moscow, turned up out of sequence in *Senatskii arkhiv* in 1904, a publication difficult to find in the United States. It supported my contention in the AHR article that Catherine's ban was based on economic, police, and sanitary considerations.

On May 3, I spent the day at Bolkhovitinov's going over his paper for a conference at the Library of Congress celebrating the American Revolution in international perspective. It was sad to see that he did not yet know whether he would be permitted to attend (in fact he did go). He was more confident about traveling to San Francisco for the International Conference of Historical Sciences, because he would be part of a large delegation at an official forum useful for broadcasting Soviet views. Though invited to stay on as a fellow after the LC conference, Bolkhovitinov was told it couldn't be arranged so soon. Likewise, Svetlana Fedorova could not accept an invitation to lecture in Alaska that summer. "What an inhuman system," I wrote Maria on May 2; and again on May 13: "Right now I feel as if I never want to come on the exchange again." I revisited Russia only in 1993, after the demise of the USSR.

The last month I was in Moscow my psychological state became quite fragile, a consequence of missing my family, the end-of-sojourn syndrome, and mounting frustration over petty inconveniences such as abortive telephone calls to and from home. Maria was told by people at the hotel that I no longer lived there. She could not reach me because I had been put in a different room after returning from Leningrad with my surname listed as Dzhon (Alexander is always a forename in Russian). We finally made contact when I sent a telegram with my new room and telephone number.

Even so, I nearly got into trouble trying to mail phonograph records home. A woman postal worker refused my package, claiming such boxes had to be of wood, and though I pointed out that I had sent such packages before, she wouldn't budge. Enraged, I shook my fist at her, to which she reacted by screaming "Unconscionable!" and "Insolent!" After telling her off, I stamped out, so furious I couldn't think of any swear words in Russian. Andrei Stroev calmed me down, thankfully, and made fun of the whole thing imagining *Pravda's* headlines: "American professor shows true face—assaults helpless old woman!" Later he drove me to the main post office where we mailed the package promptly without incident.

Bob Jones and Rex Wade were also frustrated by hassles about a trip to Leningrad, which spawned their fable explaining the lack of Russians in hell: 1) it will be closed for repair; 2) the Devil will be on break; 3) the line will be too long. When I stopped by the Graphics Section of GIM to pick up some prints, the kindly old lady I had talked to by phone was astounded that I was an American: "You've slain me," she expostulated in mock horror. I doubt my spoken Russian has ever been so good as it was at the end of this sojourn. Somewhat earlier I had sat at supper with some unknown Soviet men and was cheered when told they had thought I was Bulgarian.

Upon arriving home I found myself utterly exhausted, so plans for a summer of writing faltered. Still I started sorting out the materials stock-piled, drafted several chapters, and redid my paper for an American Historical Association session in Atlanta in December 1975 with Arcadius Kahan and William McNeill. The listing of my paper in the AHA program put me in touch with John D. Post of Northeastern University, an economic historian with a major interest in weather cycles and their effect on subsistence crises in modern Europe. Offprints of his work began in 1976 a regular correspondence about mutual research interests. This affirmed my thinking about the importance of historical climatology and its crucial significance for plague epidemics, an angle of the Moscow epidemic totally ignored by previous scholarship. Yet there was strong evidence for weather's pivotal role in the events.

It took several years to draft the book entirely because of teaching duties and additional research. Several chapters were presented as talks to different groups on campus and elsewhere. Maybe the most unusual was in costume at the annual Halloween festival at Fort Hays State University. Numerous articles resulted: about ten up to the mid 1980s and another dozen encyclopedia entries on individual physicians and diseases.

The book finally came out in the spring of 1980. Regrettably, it is little known in Russia although Mavrodin privately declared it a "book for the ages." Still, it did bring a trip to London in 1985 for a small conference on the history of plague at the Wellcome Institute for the History of Medicine.[10] In 1996, on the occasion of an international conference on the bicentenary of the death of Catherine the Great, I donated a copy to the Russian Academy of Sciences in Saint Petersburg. A recent article translated from German, which capitalized on my plague scholarship, has appeared in a conference volume in Russian.[11] One final irony befits "Katya and the Rats." As grand duchess in 1754, she turned out to be unique in having actually recorded the presence of rats in Moscow.

What did these adventures produce? An unconventional topic stirred me deeply for many years during which I received a great deal of encouragement and many specific leads from Soviet and other scholars. I had the rare pleasure of discovering massive amounts of fresh documentation, beginning with Catherine's enigmatic note. My findings surprised me by contradicting many initial assumptions. Rummaging through hundreds of documents bearing direct traces of the horrific pestilence certainly brought home to me the mysterious power of a catastrophic epidemic. My radical revisionism was emboldened by concepts arising from current understanding of the disease that aided my effort to imagine how eighteenth-century physicians and lay persons encountered the plague. The whole experience made me more deeply interested in Catherine as a ruler and a person subject to an array of unusual pressures.

Notes

1. *Bubonic Plague in Early Modern Russia: Public Health and Urban Disaster.* Baltimore and London: Oxford University Press, 1980.

2. *Slavic Review*, vol. 40 (1981): 106–7.

3. V.V. Mavrodin et al., *Krest'ianskaia voina v Rossii v 1773–1775 godakh: Vosstanie Pugacheva*, 3 vols. (Leningrad, 1961–70).

4. *Autocratic Politics in a National Crisis: The Imperial Russian Government and Pugachev's Revolt, 1773–1775.* Bloomington: Indiana University Press, 1969.

5. David M. Griffiths, "Catherine the Great: The Republican Empress," *Jahrbücher für Geschichte Osteuropas* 21 (1973), 323–44; Brenda Meehan-Waters, "Catherine the Great and the Problem of Female Rule," *Russian Review* 14 (1975): 293–307; John T. Alexander, "Catherine II, Bubonic Plague, and the Problem of Industry in Moscow," *American Historical Review* 79 (1974): 637–71.

6. S.M. Troitskii and R.V. Ovchinnikov, "Noveishaia Amerikanskaia istoriografiia Krest'ianskoi voiny pod predvoditel'stvom E.I. Pugacheva," *Istoriia SSSR*, no. 5 (1974), pp. 173–90.

7. *Emperor of the Cossacks: Pugachev and the Frontier Jacquerie of 1773–1775.* Lawrence: Coronado Press, 1973.

8. "Recent Soviet Historiography on the Pugachev Revolt: A Review Article," *Canadian Slavic Studies* 6 (Fall 1970): 602–17.

9. S.M. Troitskii, *Rossiia v XVIII veke: Sbornik statei i publikatsii* (Moscow, 1982), pp. 115–39.

10. John T. Alexander, "Reconsiderations on Plague in Early Modern Russia," *Jahrbücher für Geschichte Osteuropas* 34 (1986): 244–54.

11. Martin Dinges, "Nemetskie vrachi v Rossii vtoroi poloviny XVIII v.: konflikt kul'tur," *Russkie i nemtsy v XVIII veke: vstrecha kul'tur* (Moscow, 2000), pp. 160–88.

5

Exploration and Adventure in the Two Capitals

Richard Stites

A Master of Wrongheaded Topics

The big picture. . . . Let me begin by charting the chronology, topicality, and geography of my research career in Russian history. Phase one encased the years 1967 to 1976—the long, long road of turning my Harvard dissertation into a book on Russian women's history. Then came a decade of work that produced a study of utopianism at work in the Russian Revolution, followed rather quickly by a contracted survey of popular culture.[1] The first was researched at the Widener and New York public libraries, Leningrad, Helsinki, and a few other places; the second, mostly in Helsinki and Leningrad; the third, almost wholly in Moscow and Leningrad.

Wrongheaded topics? Let me explain. In 1958, I walked into the office of the Chair of the History Department at George Washington University (GWU) where I was beginning my M.A. in European history. This extremely friendly and helpful man—an elegant historian of United States diplomacy—asked what branch of history interested me. I pulled from my jacket a paperback copy of Jacques Barzun's, *Berlioz and His Century* which I was devouring with great relish. He smiled somewhat pityingly and turned my attention to the "real history" offerings at GWU. I proceeded to get a very good foundation in the diplomatic and political history of Europe and the Middle East, but learned little about their cultures. Decades later I gave a lecture on Russian popular culture at Helsinki University. At the end, the eminent scholar Walter Kirchner (whose books I had read ages before) came up to me and said tactfully: "Mr. Stites, that was very interesting, but it is not history."

On the dissertation topic—women in the reign of Tsar Alexander II—I had good luck with my advisor, Richard Pipes, who actually selected it from a small list I had drawn up to show him. He thought it a good one and long overdue; he even told me he had been suggesting it to his female Ph.D. candidates. But when I got to Leningrad on the exchange in 1967 for the next phase of the book and told my Russian advisor, Naum Grigorevich Sladkevich, about my topic of research, "the woman question," he was really puzzled. Other Soviet historians told me that it was a subject suitable only for females. When I started to work on the next book, *Revolutionary Dreams*, Soviet colleagues again wondered at my academic judgment. Finally, for book number three on popular culture—begun in Moscow—I got one of two kinds of reaction: "We have no popular culture here in Russia." or "Why study trash?" Conversely, at home in American academic circles—especially among the younger generation—I received generous moral and intellectual support for all three enterprises, which I needed and appreciated immensely.

In the 1990s, just when I thought I had found a pretty conventional subject of investigation—art, music, and theater in early nineteenth century Russia—I bumped into bafflement again. Well over a decade after the onslaught of glasnost and other reforms, the mentalities about work and information in Russia had not changed very much. The cause for this runs deeper than xenophobia or political suspicions. It is rooted in an intellectual structure. Among the most friendly and helpful of my librarians and archivists—and these were many—lurked a deep skepticism about the ways of Western scholarship and their habits of the *problématique*. Librarians in my own country are not only trained superbly in technical skills, but have been raised in more or less the same intellectual environment as their historian clients, who are generally accustomed to oblique formulations, a broad scope of inquiry, and interdisciplinary approaches. To American reference librarians, "Russian history" does not simply mean the "DK-designated shelves" (in the Library of Congress cataloguing system) where everything one needs can be found. They are well aware that most cataloguing systems were founded in a long gone age when the definition of history was narrow—amounting as it did largely to "topography" and the political chronicles of the nation in question. Thus many of the books that modern historians must use are shelved in social sciences, economics, religion, art, music, literature, military science, philosophy—indeed in all the categories of library catalogue systems.

The old Soviet and the new Russian librarians are also very well trained in information retrieval (though rarely equipped with the updated technical means that we now have at our disposal—computers, on-line resources, the Net, etc.). They know at least where to get what they have. In some ways they were advanced, due to the herculean labors of those who built the famous *kartoteka* system. These card catalogues of periodical articles by subject and author are a truly awesome instrument, far superior to our older methods of "guides to periodical literature." But when it comes to imaginative searches or even physical placement in reading rooms, rigidity sets in.

A case in point: The last time I received a reading card at the Publichka in St. Petersburg (in 1997), the desk manager wanted to put me in the social sciences reading room because I had identified myself as an historian. When I asked for the literature and arts reading room instead, she replied in genuine puzzlement: "But you are an historian, not an art historian or literary scholar [*iskusstvoved ili literaturoved*]." Once installed in the room of my choice, the librarian there, after I had ordered and received books not only on early nineteenth-century Russian culture but also about cities, social classes, railroads, history of manners, serfdom and other things, suggested in friendly tones that I relocate to the social sciences reading room. When I explained that my study of the arts was related to the social system surrounding them, she smiled and said: "Why don't you make up your mind?"

I invoke these moments not because they generated any real problems, but to illustrate the kinds of mentalities that scholars have to confront at present when old disciplines are blurring rapidly. Great programs have been launched by various American and other countries' institutions to assist Russian libraries with the most novel technical means of storage and delivery of information. I think it might be time to arrange courses for Russian professional archivists and librarians about modern ways of "thinking" about information and sources; and particularly the way people of different cultures—not only Western ones—think about those things.

Going to the People

In all my enterprises, I have tapped living sources. Some of this was oral history. For the book on women, I did manage to talk to a few female veterans of World War II, but the source base was mostly printed. For the popular culture book, things came more alive especially as I reached the final chapters. I could draw on acquaintances among musicians, comedians, film directors, ice skaters, managers, entertainment journalists, and so on. But more important than direct testimony about events and processes have been the indirect clues that living Russians unwittingly offer about larger matters. I speak not about any dubious kind of native "essentialism" or racial characteristics, but of real inherited habits and attitudes toward life. One can read a good deal about the "double lives" that Soviet citizens led, the dual behavior exhibited in the private and public spheres. But there is no substitute for seeing it at work in all walks of everyday life. Like most foreign scholars, I gained much in the way of historiographical assistance and intellectual stimulation from conversations in the kitchen with academic colleagues, but I tended to favor association with the less exalted, particularly young people.

I found that I could apply what I learned from the immense divergence between the public and private faces of contemporary Russians to the processing of printed sources from the historical past. This experience sharpened the skeptical approach to received data that we all learn as a matter of course when we become practicing historians. The intuitive instruments so developed in the hundreds of encounters with Soviet people of all classes heightened the natural urge to supplement every public statement—to the extent possible—with private thoughts embedded in letters or the occasional private revelations contained in memoirs and autobiographies.

The Amateur Archaeologist

A sense of place, distance, and materiality has always played an essential role in my attempts to recreate mentally what the historical characters— whether individuals or crowds—might have thought and felt. In my book on women's history, I traced on foot the route of Tsar Alexander II on his last journey from the Winter Palace to the Manège to the site of his assassination; followed in the steps of Sofiia Perovskaia as she took up her post as signaller to the assassins; stood inside the tiny cell at the Schlüsselburg Fortress where Vera Figner spent about twenty years in solitary confinement; and strolled along the Griboedov Canal to find the home of Aleksandra Kollontai. As the sense of place fleshed out and illuminated for me the written word, I began to think about the condescending ways in which professional historians (including myself) sometimes look upon—for example—the American Civil War buff who haunts the battlefields of that tragic struggle. If their venture is antiquarian, then so was mine—in fact it was a kind of romantic antiquarianism that played more to emotions than to intellectual analysis. And yet it was essential for my motivation and helped to turn an academic enterprise into adventure.

I have described in the prefaces of *Revolutionary Dreams* and *Russian Popular Culture* the venues, media, and technologies that I pursued in coming to grips in an intimate way with the culture of revolutionary utopianism in the 1920s and the popular and mass culture of the twentieth century. Here the sense of place, people, and things was integral to the study: People's Houses (*Narodnye doma*), sites of Bolshevik festivals, old cinema palaces, circus, jazz and rock clubs, TV and radio stations, and a dozen other kinds of venues offered not only written records and oral testimony but also the physical environment of production and consumption.

In my present work, *Serfdom, Society, and the Arts, 1790–1860*, the search for the sites and artifacts of expression is once again a part of the research adventure. Printed materials on these huge subjects abound, both published and archival. Although there are no living sources to tap, persisting attitudes to the arts—many dating back two centuries or more—survive in full force. Briefly, my book is the story of how the arts intersected with tsarist society and vice-versa; in other words, a social history of cultural experience under serfdom, experience that includes creativity, management, intertextuality, and audience reception. The treatment of the arts of this period in standard textbooks and—I would guess—in most of our lecturing tends to offer a skimming of high culture: a few examples of academic painting and architecture followed by an early "realist" canvas or two of the 1840s–50s; the emergence of Glinka and *A Life for the Tsar* (1836); and a nod to the dramas of Griboedov, Pushkin, and Gogol. This pretty much follows the canonical model we get in the history textbook discussions of early Russian literature. In trying to break out of this narrow and impoverishing channel in my present book, I am hoping to encourage a richer integration of the arts into the mainstream of Russian history. Both inside and outside the archives and libraries, I set out to find ways of tying the technical aspects of art and cultural history to the throbbing life around it during those bygone decades ruled over by Alexander I and Nicholas I.

Make Mine Music

Until the founding of the conservatories in the 1860s, symphonic music in Russia had no central training center or permanent concert hall. The Petersburg Philharmonia Society, founded in 1803, had no orchestra of its own. Its concerts migrated for a half-century from site to site, mostly to private homes or clubs. The principal venue was the second floor of the Engelgardt House near the corner of Nevsky Prospect and the Catherine (Griboedov) Canal—a building that most of us have probably walked past a hundred times. In 1997, sitting in the Public Library, I read how in the 1840s the budding composer Aleksandr Serov was brought to rapture when he attended a solo performance by Franz Liszt there during one of the numerous virtuoso appearances in Russia. That evening I attended a recital at the Engelgardt (now Glinka) Hall. As I listened, I inspected the architecture of this rather small recital space, counted the seats, looked over the decor, and wondered how Hector Berlioz—also in the 1840s—could have squeezed a chorus and orchestra of well over 300 people onto the stage and pit. My reveries conjured up Berlioz's public, the elegant Petersburg *beau monde*, in period costumes, chattering in French before being mesmerized by the performance of his *Requiem*. When I script the Engelgardt episodes in my mind for the historical recreation, contemporary prints provide the decor; memoir literature provides cast and plot. But it is the visual and physical remembrance of those evenings that frames the narrative.

Of course, it was the hall of the St. Petersburg Assembly of the Nobility, whose building we all once knew as the Leningrad Philharmonia, that eventually became the regular home of orchestral concerts. Here I shift to another aspect of the cultural–social life of old Russia, the gentry ball. Readers of Pushkin, Iurii Lotman, or Priscilla Roosevelt's magnificent volume on country estates are aware of the crucial roles these occasions played in the life of the upper classes.[2] Aside from court balls at the Winter Palace, those held in the stately hall on a corner of what is now Square of the Arts loomed high above all others. While listening to a classical concert in the superb acoustical environment of the Philharmonia, one can mentally remove the seats, add liveried footmen and potted plants, install a serf orchestra in the balcony, and picture the gaiety and sociability tempered by hierarchical formality that in a sense reified the social and psychological structure of a class long vanished from the scene. And from a quite different historical source base, one can also tap into the complex and often agonizing experience of serf musicians who provided the music for such entertainments.

Theaters of Life

Leonid Grossman many decades ago and Julie Buckler very recently described in minute archeological detail the innards of St. Petersburg theater buildings during this era as well as the social structure of the audiences.[3] The Public Library and the Theater Library are adjacent to the Aleksandrinskii Theater and to the old imperial theater and ballet school on Carlo Rossi's celebrated Theater Street. As I made my way from a day at the library table to the ticket office of the Aleksandrinskii, I could ponder about theater-going audiences then and now, and summon up visions of coachmen warming themselves and drinking tea on winter evenings at the specially maintained fire in the drivers' pavilion, while their masters and mistresses attended Racine's *Phèdre* at the Aleksandrinskii. *Phèdre* still plays there regularly as it did all through the Soviet period. The interior architecture and decor of this classical edifice are still in place; and the European-style hierarchal seating system still speaks eloquently of the way in which class was concretely translated into space.

Theater in early nineteenth-century St. Petersburg—as we approach it from a sociological viewpoint—provided almost nightly four different performances, casts, and dramas. These were staged on the square, in the house, backstage, and on the proscenium stage itself. Coachmen, footmen, lackeys, and valets—most of them serfs—acted out their script around the stove in the shelter on the square. In my mental reconstruction, I tried to evoke the moment by standing on winter nights outside the Aleksandrinskii and on the huge Theater Square between the Marinskii and the Conservatory (edifices not yet built in the era I was reliving) where once stood the imposing St. Petersburg Bolshoi Stone Theater, the main site of opera and ballet. How marvelous if we could have a record of their conversations! We can do no more than extrapolate what we know about the life and work of serfs and servants in the entourages of Russia's aristocratic families. Around the stove, the minute social gradations would be on display in diction, apparel, and occupation; and one might well hear, amid the general grousing and camaraderie, the one-upmanship rooted in status, gossip about the masters, and perhaps a bit of bragging about them as well. This is a lost and secret drama, a hidden transcript. Whatever elements we fantasize into it are fictional, and the historian will not commit them to paper as real history. And yet without trying to envision such a scene with its props—the icy wind, the frosty breath of the horses, the roar of the fire—any recreated picture of Russian theatrical life is relatively sterile and superficial.

Inside the house the second drama unfolds with the audience as cast playing very stylized social roles. There are many ways to get at this in conventional sources: secondary works, contemporary memoirs and journals, and literary treatments. The front of the house was a living seminar room on class, gender, sexuality, and the body. The nearly ascriptive character of the seating culture, only faintly affected by the market, speaks for itself. And if one's place in the geography of the audience were not enough, costume, mannerisms, and language would do the rest in plotting one's status graphically long before the show began. By sitting at different times in the stalls, a box, or a cheap seat, I felt an aura of immediacy that no written source could provide as I connected my angle of vision and distance from the play to the social roles and identities of those who sat there two hundred years ago: satin-gowned misses with décolleté and lorgnettes; dandies and officers glancing into the female sector of the second tier, signalling to their mistresses on stage, or hissing the "unfavorite" of the moment; rich merchants from Gostinnyi Dvor basking in the elevated milieu of the imperial theater; destitute students and government clerks straining to see both the audience and the stage from their lofty places in the gallery.

Drama number three is the most animated of all: the backstage scenario, starring actors of every level, management, artisans—even policemen sometimes called to restore order in the wings. Unable to get backstage at any of the Petersburg theaters, I did manage to wangle a private tour of the Malyi Theater in Moscow, the celebrated house "built by" the serf actor Shchepkin and the playwright Ostrovskii. In this huge complex, standing beside (and predating) the Moscow Bolshoi Theater, the backstage space is three times larger than the house itself. Green rooms, dressing rooms, makeup and prop departments, opulent mini-lobbies ringed by offices, and the immense machinery chamber below the stage, resembling the engine room of a huge ocean liner—all these together represent the inner heart of this theater. In the early nineteenth century, the backstage world of the imperial theaters presented their own plays-within-plays: realistic dramas of competition, jealousy, and rage among the actors; farces and burlesques featuring mischievous and drunken cast members; melodramas of villainous managers and vulnerable players; tragedies of seduction and the ruin of actresses by their lordly patrons. These were real life dramas, not dramaturgical works of the imagination. We know about them from the sources. Standing and strolling amidst the huge interior where the cast once lived added for me a level of empathy not available by any other means.

Now we come to the final drama: those works of art and artistry actually performed on the stage by actors for the audience. Access to this is easiest of all: we have most of the texts. I have never acted in a Russian theater and surely never will. Instead I walked the length of the Malyi stage, stood near the footlights, peered out into the dark and empty house, and tried to imagine what it might have been like for the actors on the opening night of Ostrovskii's *The Storm*. Like a cinematographer who splices scenes from various locales into one sequence, pretending it is shot in the same locale, I made my imaginative historical montage out of the squares and interiors of St. Petersburg theaters and the backstage empire of a Moscow theater in an effort to reimagine theatrical life in the round, in its social and cultural setting. All this is not so much in the spirit of scholarly research as a way of furnishing my mind as a writer of history with the pictures and scenarios of real people who dwelt in a real world long ago.

Up in the Attic

Writing about Russian painting without being an art historian is an adventure in itself, as is writing about music and theater. My primary purpose was to see how and where artists worked, what they saw, what they painted, and who saw what they painted. In pursuit of some of these answers I worked in the Tretiakov Gallery in Moscow and in the Russian Museum and Academy of Arts in St. Petersburg—all of them housing libraries as well as pictures. Although training centers in Moscow and the provinces existed in the early nineteenth century, the main schooling took place at the Academy and its branch in Rome.

The character of an edifice—the distribution of space, shape of its rooms, walkways and fenestration, and its entire visual system—can have a profound effect on the lives of its denizens and on what they create, or fail to.

The Academy remains to this day an astonishing piece of architecture and one of the glories of the vaunted Neva Embankment. One does not take a casual stroll through this building. A careful studious circling of the perimeter and its facades takes a good hour; exploring its three stories of corridors, circular galleries, multitudinous rooms, and out-of-the-way attics and storage space is the labor of a week. The Academy building is a massive rectangle with four courtyards at the corners and a huge circular yard in the center along which run three floors of galleries, offices, sketch rooms, and classrooms. Facing the river is the Conference Hall, the administrative and ceremonial heart, where careers were made and broken. On the opposite side of the building is the interior Orthodox Church, now reopened after the long decades of closure under the Soviets. The attics still contain a Gallery of Antique Art. Faculty apartments are no more, but the present administrators can still look out on the river Neva.

What happened inside this huge complex? Nothing less than the formation of Russian neoclassical art, a school now more or less despised by world opinion and largely devalued in the world marketplace. But during the period in question, it was *the* art of the Western world, though soon to be overshadowed by romanticism and realism. Like the backstage theater world, the Academy building houses many old narratives: inspiring tales of creativity, sordid ones of ego and dissoluteness, sinister ones of thwarted talent. Once again, I plugged in the connectors. Sitting in my heavy coat in the library on the first day, I perused student memoirs about how cold and drafty the building was in the 1820s and 1830s. I peeked into the chamber where Alexei Venetsianov and his students would pose a model dressed as a peasant woman around whom they would later paint in a landscape. Only a short walk across the nearby bridge stood Theater Square and up river a few blocks was the university. Yet the students at the Art Academy had virtually no contact with these institutions. In this hothouse of art training, serfs mingled with other classes until a new director expelled them in 1817 as bad moral examples for the other students. And yet enrollment of a serf in the program could and did lead to emancipation. Here around me rose yet another shrine where the highest of high culture was being created or performed by those from the lowest ranks of society.

The Russian Museum in St. Petersburg served a double purpose in my visual and aural research. Those of you who know the fine works of the late W. Bruce Lincoln will recall that this building, once the Mikhailovskii Palace, was an incubator of reformist ideas.[4] In the 1850s, Grand Duchess Elena Pavlovna held a kind of exalted political circle—she called it her morganatic salon—where a mixed company gathered to talk of coming reform and of the emancipation of the serfs. Less well known perhaps is that in these same rooms Elena Pavlovna hosted musical evenings and that her musician-in-chief was the soon to be celebrated founder of the St. Petersburg Conservatory, Anton Rubinstein. How this son of a Jewish merchant from the Pale came to move in such lofty circles is itself one of the remarkable stories of pre-emancipation Russian history. During his sojourn at the palace, Rubinstein not only composed what was once one of the most popular recital piano pieces in the world—the Melody in F—but also floated the idea for a conservatory of music to the Grand Duchess.

Getting to work on art at the Russian Museum was a minor misadventure, but one so familiar to those who have faced Russian bureaucratic hassles that I will not bore them with it. Viewing the works shown in the public museum was no problem. But I wanted access to the unhung collection in the attics, thousands of pictures that are displayed only periodically or never at all. Having done the work on neoclassical art at the Academy and elsewhere, I now wanted to explore the mountain of "realistic" genre canvases stored in the upper reaches of the museum. One of the problems was that the museum was under major renovation in readiness for the one hundredth anniversary of its founding as a public museum in 1898. Large sections and the main entrance were closed off, virtually excluding access to the storage rooms. I finally muscled my way in.

As expected, the staff was as pleasant and helpful as could be once the ice was broken. Each day I would appear in the office at one of the outer wings for a document check; a librarian would be called to come and escort me on a labyrinthine route through several buildings, up and down several staircases, to the dark recesses near the roof. There awaited a treasure house of numbered paintings stored on racks. By means of an elaborate index file, paintings could be found on all the themes I wished to examine: daily life in town and country, peasants at work, blacksmiths, industrial forges, drunken tavern scenes, bourgeois interiors—the whole gamut of urban and provincial life in pictures (good and bad) that caused much consternation among the authorities and critics when they were first done, and still do among modern Russian curators. There I found both "minor" works of famous painters and the works of unknowns—all dealing with subject matter so unpalatable to art museum officials, who always want to show the best to the art-viewing public—Russian and foreign. Without seeing these, a scholar would come away with a prettified and distorted tableau of what life was like and how art portrayed that life in the early nineteenth century. This was the relatively neglected early "realism" that predated the vaunted social realism of the Wanderers School of the later nineteenth century. It was exactly what I sought: the point where art came closest to intersecting with life as actually lived.

Looking Back

In my four major (and many more minor) research sojourns in the USSR and Russia, I have always worked in libraries and archives. This constituted the solid bedrock and the intellectual frame of my books. Nothing I could say about the nature of these institutions and their peculiar cultures would be new to readers of this book. Instead I have focused on what used to be called "non-conventional sources": buildings, pictures, musical scores, recordings, films, and so on. This is the part that feeds my historical imagination and provides quasi-cinematic material for my narratives. It was a major part of the adventure—a corollary to the required poring over of documents, the acquisition of languages, the torturing of sources, the building of arguments. I tell my doctoral candidates that a historian must be an archaeologist, a rabbi, a lawyer, and a poet. The true scholar must dig up the sources, read with deep commitment, marshal evidence, and write it all up in style. To reach that much longed-for poetic moment when we write our histories, I believe that adventure is a required ingredient.

Notes

1. *The Women's Liberation Movement in Russia: Feminism, Nihilism, and Bolshevism, 1860–1930*. Princeton: Princeton University Press, 1978; *Revolutionary Dreams: Utopian Vision and Experimental Life in the Russian Revolution*. Oxford: Oxford University Press, 1989; *Russian Popular Culture: Entertainment and Society Since 1900*. Cambridge: Cambridge University Press, 1992.

2. Iurii Lotman, *Besedy o russkoi kultury: byt i traditsii russkogo dvorianstva (XVIII-nachalo XIX veka)* St. Petersburg: Iskusstvo, 1994; Priscilla Roosevelt, *Life on the Russian Country Estate: A Social and Cultural History*. New Haven: Yale University Press, 1995.

3. Leonid Grossman, *Pushkin v teatralnykh kreslakh: kartiny russkoi stseny, 1817–1820* (Leningrad, 1926); Julie Buckler, *The Literary Lorgnette: Attending Opera in Imperial Russia*. Stanford: Stanford University Press, 2000.

4. W. Bruce Lincoln, *In the Vanguard of Reform: Russian Enlightened Bureaucrats, 1825–1861*. DeKalb: Northern Illinois University Press, 1982.

6

Leningrad, 1966–1967
Irrelevant Insights in an Era of Relevance

S. Frederick Starr

American society is always shifting between self-indulgent contentment and self-critical activism. Anyone graphing the interplay of these polar forces would surely place the years 1966 and 1967 as a time when unease was on the rise. The sixties had made their belated debut and earnest people, among whom graduate students always stand at the forefront, were beginning to sense that the era called for them to be engaged and, as they said, "relevant." Relevant to what? The word no longer required a prepositional phrase following. Everyone knew that relevance meant contemporary politics, Vietnam, social and generational issues, and changing values. Deeds would soon count more than words. But for now, ideas were still held to be important, at least in the most junior ranks of the academic world. Among these, ideas arising from the social sciences, especially sociology and political science, exercised the greatest influence.

As the graph of unease began to rise, the annual band of American graduate student exchangees set out for the Soviet Union. Most went to Moscow. I was among six who chose Leningrad instead. As usual, the group had spent a couple of summer months at Indiana University, where everyone received training in the Russian language and in Soviet living, a regimen that was relieved only by illicit swims in the glorious abandoned limestone quarries that surround the college town of Bloomington.

To spend a year in the USSR was not, to paraphrase Tolstoy, "like crossing a field." We were not Fulbrighters of the 1950s, heading to Paris to sip aperitifs in Left Bank dives frequented by Jean-Paul Sartre or Henry Miller. Ours was an entirely more serious enterprise, one that was somehow connected to "the national interest." Many of us had received National Defense Education Act fellowships or "funding" (the older term, "money," was becoming obsolete) from the Ford Foundation. All benefited from the Inter-University Committee on Travel Grants (IUCTG), which justified itself in terms of the country's need to understand the Soviets. Whether or not we acknowledged it, our group of exchangees had been coopted into the Cold War, and by some of the very people and institutions that within three years would be vehemently attacked on campuses across America.

The growing disquiet in the broader American society did not seem to touch us. With only a few exceptions, we were still politically inert, certainly by comparison with our successors only a few years later. More precisely, we were thoroughly, self-consciously, and even proudly "irrelevant." None of us aspired to provide sound bytes on Kremlin politics for the news networks. When Bobby Kennedy, Senator Tydings, and then a parade of other Washington dignitaries came to Russia and held carefully staged "informal meetings" with Russian students, we contemptuously dismissed them as trivializers.

The reason for the profound "irrelevance" of the generation of young men and women who headed to Russia in 1967 is that we were all, to a degree that now seems amazing, already thoroughly acculturated as scholars and academics. True, many of us eventually pursued careers outside the classroom. But for now, scholarship—not just the writing of dissertations, but the vocation of scholar—struck us all as a noble calling in itself and not just a step to something else. Vladimir Nabokov, David Lodge, and Joyce Carol Oates were all writing, or preparing to write, their droll novels of academic cupidity in these very years. But we were still true believers in the enterprise.

In my own case, undergraduate studies in Classics and Classical Archaeology at Yale and two years spent studying Slavonic languages at King's College, Cambridge, had accustomed me to seeing the entire world through footnotes and citations, "Leben im Zitat," in the words of the Austrian novelist Peter Handke. As a graduate student at Princeton I had listened with abject humility as Father Georges Florovsky, his thin white beard stained with nicotine and his cassock dusted with dandruff, advised us, as we left the library each night when it closed, to check out a year of any one of the nineteenth-century Russian historical journals and pore through its contents as we fell asleep. No wonder that our heroes were scholars and our talk and gossip were of scholars. The entire ethos of the IUCTG and then of IREX supported the view that real scholarship counted, and that even the most seemingly irrelevant topics—a failed reformer of the early nineteenth century or a forgotten poet of the 1920s—would somehow enrich our understanding of the Russians.

A second characteristic of much of the research that young Americans conducted in Russia in my time as an exchangee was its strong focus on the past rather than the present. American taxpayers would surely have been surprised to learn that most of the money they were spending to develop experts on the USSR was actually going for the support of research on the seventeenth-century Russian Orthodox Church, the Muscovite capture of Kazan in the sixteenth century, or the novels of Turgenev. But this was precisely the case.

There was a very practical reason for this. With few exceptions, Soviet authorities were unwilling to open their borders and their archives to young Americans writing on anything pertaining to the Soviet era, let alone on the present. Occasionally a brave graduate student would propose some innocently antique topic in the hope of gathering information *sub rosa* on some hot contemporary issue. But these occasions were few and far between, and only partly because Soviet vigilance extended to virtually anything having to do with the social sciences. The deeper reason for the emphasis on historical studies and literary history is that a deep-dyed historicism prevailed among us. Like Victorian biologists or nineteenth-century German historians, we assumed that to really understand something meant appreciating its development through time.

In my own case this philosophical view, or prejudice, had been developing since childhood. Having spent seven years doing archaeological work in the Midwest and in Turkey, I was used to the notion that all social arrangements are impermanent. To behold a huge and ruined Roman aqueduct in the bleak and remote upper reaches of the Euphrates is to ask the question, "What happened to cause this to be constructed, and what caused it then to be abandoned?" All societies rise and fall over time, and the challenge is to ferret out the causes of each phase of this organic development.

My training at Princeton reinforced this orientation. Historical studies at the time I was a graduate student there were rapidly falling under the influence of the French Annales School. But Russian studies (and also art history) continued under the old banner of historicism, thanks to James Billington and Father Florovsky. Even the head of Russian studies, Cyril E. Black, based his theories of modernization as much on historicism as on the function-structure analysis he derived from the social sciences.

The intellectual fountainhead of this current was the Oxford philosopher Isaiah Berlin, whose links with Russian culture were forged during his brief, platonic, but intense encounter with the Leningrad poet Anna Akhmatova in 1945. Billington had studied under Berlin and was responsible for bringing him to Princeton to teach a memorable seminar on German romanticism. Berlin's great essays on Giambattista Vico and Johann-Friedrich Herder, the twin fathers of historicism, exerted a profound influence on me, not least because they seemed to validate views of life and history that I had developed on my own since childhood. There was absolutely no doubt in my mind that history, properly understood, is the queen of the social sciences and certainly the key to any real understanding of Russia. That this happened to coincide with the practical constraints under which the exchange program operated was convenient but irrelevant.

It was no wonder, then, that once in Russia I did what half the other graduate historians there did and purchased a copy of the massive 1898 edition of the Brockhaus Effron encyclopedia, which served as the Internet for Russian historical bibliography back then. My copy came from the second-hand bookshop on Herzen Street in Leningrad, a hallowed shrine of Russian letters where one was likely to meet the distinguished historian Dmitrii Likhachev or the pianist Sviatoslav Richter prowling among the stacks. The task of spiriting these eighty volumes to Moscow and then persuading someone in the U.S. embassy to send them all home by pouch was only one of many logistical challenges to be faced that year.

A third general attitude that prevailed among my cohort of exchangees was the conviction that culture was more important than politics. Again, one might argue that this was the only reasonable response to Soviet policies that threatened with expulsion any visiting scholar who stuck his or her nose too deeply into the political affairs of the USSR. At the very least, this made me cautious, for example, in a late-night conversation with a Russian student who was only then, in his late twenties, becoming aware of the political realities behind the Communist slogans that had heretofore defined his world. This same student, incidentally, later emerged as a prominent figure in Gorbachev's entourage. Similar caution arose when the driver of the No. 7 bus one day announced the stop for the university by shouting out sarcastically "Leningrad State University, named in memory of Mr. Zhdanov." The passengers all froze, for they knew full well that this was the same Zhdanov who, as Stalin's henchman, had led the post-war purges. I avoided my fellow passengers' glances.

Political control over our actions was entrusted to the Communist Party folks in the Foreign Section (*Inotdel*) of Leningrad State University. These were people to be avoided. At one point, however, they convinced themselves that I was not only the spokesman (*starost'*, literally "elder") of our small American group but also an American spy. Earlier, KGB people, presumably working with the *Inotdel*, had tried to recruit one of our number to report on the others. When that failed, the KGB turned to me. Arriving at the historical archives in the old building of the Holy Synod one day, an elderly female assistant told me with quavering voice and trembling hands that I was wanted "downstairs." The stark basement room to which I was shown was furnished with two chairs and a desk pitted with cigarette bums. Two gentlemen proceeded to inform me in menacing tones that they "knew all about my activities" but that I would be allowed to stay if I would agree to meet with them from time to time to discuss foreign students in Leningrad. It was a classic scene from a bad spy movie, missing only the grainy black-and-white format. I politely declined, explaining that unfortunately "my activities" consisted mainly of long days spent in the archives. When I told them that I was therefore the last person who could be of any use to them, they were clearly crestfallen and at a loss over what to do next. I tried to help by suggesting they contact instead a Swede who spent all his days drinking in the dormitory and who I knew had departed for Stockholm the day before. I never heard from them again.

Even if the Soviet authorities had not prevented foreign students from taking too keen an interest in political issues, I would still have favored culture, broadly defined, over politics. Besides the interest in archaeology, my formative years had left me with a passion for music of all sorts and a boundless curiosity about the history of architecture, which I saw as the crystallization of a people's ideals on the good life and how to live it. Thanks to the institution of a city-manager system of government back in the 1920s, my home town of Cincinnati had seemingly solved the problem of politics for all time. This, at least, is what I had grown up believing. Politics was important, but only as a means, not as an end. The end was a good life, which had to do with reading interesting books, passing pleasant hours with friends, and music-making in congenial settings. Yale had reinforced this view, as had my years at King's College, where E.M. Forster was a living presence and the aura of Bloomsbury still hung in the air.

At Princeton I had been fortunate to fall into the circle of the Russian émigré novelist Nina Berberova, who had earlier taught me Russian at Yale. Nina Nikolaevna held court each Sunday at her small faculty apartment for a small group that included future fellow-exchangee John Malmstad and Ellen Chances, who later took over Berberova's professorial post. At her table one might meet and talk with George Balanchine or hear the composer Nicholas Nabokov read from his memoirs. The particular passages with which he regaled us, as I recall, featured a detailed account of his childhood experience of watching elephants mating in the Odessa zoo.

All this biased me in favor of culture as opposed to politics, which seemed pallid and dull by comparison. We were well aware of the armed clashes on the Chinese-Soviet border that were taking place during my time in Leningrad, and I had friends with brothers who perished in the fighting. We also followed Soviet press accounts of the dreary last days of the Khrushchev era, and helped celebrate the fiftieth anniversary of the October Revolution by marching in the great parade with workers from a factory on Vasilevskii Island. But I took no interest in the Kremlin dignitaries assembled like puppets on the reviewing stand that had been erected in front of the Winter Palace in honor of the great day. Rather, my attention was riveted by the lugubrious Sicilian marches being played by the inebriated members of the factory's twelve-piece brass band. Dressed like derelicts but wearing impressive 1910–style military hats issued by the company, the musicians gave the event the anarchic mood of a Fellini film, effectively canceling out the intended political message.

The topic of my research embodied awe for professional scholarship, belief in the importance of history, and prejudice against politics that many participants in the 1966 exchange shared in common and which all my limited experience to date seemed to affirm. However, the moment I announced my topic to my two academic advisors, Professor N.G. Sladkevich and Professor S.S. Okun, I knew something was terribly wrong. Sladkevich, who daily wore the same green suit over the six years I knew him, was a sad, gentle man who was watching his wife die and his own life's work as a loyal Communist scholar begin to fade before his eyes. Okun, by contrast, was a Petersburg *intelligent*, wry and avuncular, with a solid record of research on the Pushkin era. When I declared my intention of writing a book on the topic "Decentralization and Self-Government in Russia," both of them, for all their differences, burst into uproarious laughter, which kept erupting anew during the waning minutes of the interview. Finally Okun, wiping his eyes, wished me well and asked me to inform him "of any sightings." I agreed to do so.

Today, when the Soviet Union has collapsed into fifteen separate countries and centrifugal forces have reduced Moscow's centralized control to a hollow shell, Russians have good reason to ponder the question of decentralization and self-government throughout their history. They also have good reason to ask to what extent their entire experience prepares them to function as a self-governing and civil society, in which citizens manage their own affairs under law rather than submit to control exercised from above. I could not foresee any of this in 1967, of course. But my reading had convinced me that the relentless centralization and state control that both Russian and Western historians had projected onto the entire Russian past left too much out of the picture.

What about the self-governing village communities that the German traveler Baron August von Haxthausen had described in such detail and offered as the very essence of Russian life? Or the elected provincial and local assemblies (*zemstvos*) that Tolstoy wrote about in *Anna Karenina*? Or the many manifestations of local feeling that kept popping up in the Soviet era? I noticed that whenever the central state weakened, local forces turned out to be alive and well and ready to assume responsibility for the well-being of citizens. I decided to concentrate my analysis on one such period in which this occurred, the era of the "Great Reforms" that came on the heels of Russia's defeat in the Crimean War in 1855.[1]

This idiosyncratic topic arose at least as much from my personal experience as from any understanding I had of Russian history. My upbringing in Cincinnati and northern Kentucky had been intensely local in character. Over four summers I worked on archaeological projects that put me in daily contact with hundreds of farms and farmers in several counties on both sides of the Ohio River. As a jazz musician I had grown up playing music that was deeply rooted in the culture of Ohio and Mississippi River towns, but which scarcely penetrated fifty miles inland. My entire experience focused on the specificity and authenticity of local and regional life, rather than the generality of national and international experience. In exploring the theme of decentralization and local self-government in Russia, I was simply calling on what I knew best to help me understand what I knew least.

The externals of our lives as exchangees in Leningrad during 1966 and 1967 were uneventful. In retrospect, it is clear that the city was still recovering from the war, with poverty an accepted way of life. Graduate students were housed at the back end of Vasilevskii Island in the notorious dormitory at No. 2 Shevchenko Street. Constructed by Soviet graduate student "volunteers" only a few years earlier, the building was already crumbling. I later met one of these indentured builders, who told me that he and the others had all been so angry at having been dragooned to work that they missed no opportunity to wreck the structure as it was being built.

Responsibility for the building, and for us, rested with the *vakhtior* (janitor), a Ukrainian peasant and World War II veteran named Nikolai Nikolaevich. Most of the time Nikolai Nikolaevich was peevish and taciturn. But at the monthly dorm meetings he came alive, for this was his time to lecture the assembled intellectuals on uplifting subjects relevant to our life together. As a rhetorician Nikolai Nikolaevich stood squarely in the baroque tradition, and Gogol himself might have envied even his less ornate orations. His invariable subject was *cleanliness*, which was in noticeably short supply at No. 2 Shevchenko Street. Typically, he would begin by paying elaborate homage to "you visionary scientists, far-seeing scholars, and, yes, our own dear learned ladies who, together, will build the future and enable the radiant sun of socialism to warm our mortal lives." Then, like a high diver who does multiple flips only to end up in the mud at the bottom of the pond, he would ask, in a voice oozing bathos, "How could such people as you, in whom the mothers of Russia and the Communist Party itself have placed such unquenchable hopes, throw shirts in the toilet?" At this point Nikolai Nikolaevich would brandish the offending garment, his face distorted with genuine anguish.

Each morning I would head for the archives on the Semyorka (No. 7) bus. As winter set in I would sometimes stop for a second breakfast at a grubby eatery near the Naval Academy. The food was excellent, even without the tumblers of cognac that were standard for most denizens of the place, and the conversations with officers and midshipmen were always interesting. The archives were a brightly lit and well-heated haven within the cold and murky gloom of Leningrad, and work there proceeded smoothly. For lunch I would occasionally invade the Union of Architects' private restaurant, which was situated·in the colorfully ornamented leather-walled dining room of the old Panin mansion nearby. There was something appealing about lunching at the table of one of the men whose papers I was poring through.

On the few evenings when there wasn't a concert to attend, I would pick up bread, cabbage, and carrots and drop by the neighborhood butcher, whose shop was near the end of the Semyorka line. The poor man had lost three fingers in combat with carcasses on his butcher's block. To my astonishment, I discovered that he cut the meat in such a way as to leave as much bone and fat as possible on each hunk, tossing the pure steak into a corner of his vitrine reserved for the cheapest cuts. The reason for this was that most of Leningrad's population was made up of peasants who had been recruited to fill the jobs of people who had perished in the war or in the 900-day Nazi blockade of the city. As their forebears had done, these migrants continued to consume most of their meat in soups, and took little interest in the finer cuts.

If food seems to figure prominently in this account of daily life in Leningrad in 1966, it is because everything beyond the most basic rudiments was still so scarce. Fresh vegetables were a great rarity and citrus fruits nonexistent. Any person on the street could tell you there was plenty of food in the countryside but that the government was unable to get it to urban consumers before it spoiled. Thanks to the occasional sale of eggs miraculously stamped "Made in Finland," Leningraders were also aware that people abroad were eating better than they were. The only people I knew who always ate well were two scientists from Tashkent who roomed across the hall. Both knew Turkish and liked to speak it with me, and both took pleasure in teaching me some basic Uzbek. Royally provisioned by means of regular shipments from home, they ate like kings and skillfully used their Central Asian feasts to attract Russian women. Thirty years later I was to meet one of them again in his home town, which was by then the capital of an independent Uzbekistan. He was now a wealthy businessmen in partnership with Turks, happily married to a Russian, and an ardent Uzbek nationalist.

The same elements of my personal background that fueled an interest in the fate of decentralization and self-government in Russian all but guaranteed that I would immerse myself in the city of Leningrad. The old imperial capital that had once inflicted centralized rule on all Russia was now itself a provincial outpost, thanks to the policies of Lenin and Stalin. Editorial offices, publishing houses, and such leading local artists as Shostakovich had followed the shift of political and economic power to Moscow. What remained, aside from a few giant industries like the Elektrosila plant, was the decaying husk of the former capital and the greatly reduced but still proud residue of its cultural life. I embraced both with a passion.

Every free moment was consumed in exploring the city. With the help of rare monographs acquired at the antiquarian book store on Herzen Street and a well-thumbed 1909 Baedeker, I soon knew every old street name and the street address of practically every figure in nineteenth-century Russia in whom I had any interest. Not content with perusing the outsides of buildings, I became adept at talking my way past guards and watchmen in order to examine the interiors as well.

It was intriguing to ferret out the rooms where Russia's post-Napoleonic reformers, the Decembrists, met in their Masonic lodges; where Gogol penned some of his greatest early works; where Beethoven's patron Prince Razumovskii assembled friends to hear the renowned quartets (Opus 59) that he had commissioned; or where turn-of-the-century liberals gathered to hear lectures on democratic socialism at the Free Economic Society. Even more startling was to discover how Dostoevsky took pains to set his *Crime and Punishment* or *The Idiot* in real locales that he depicted in utmost detail. And how Andrei Belyi used similarly concrete settings as points of departure for his utterly fantastic novel *Petersburg*. Far from leading me to concur with Soviet critics who insisted that virtually every Russian who wrote anything worth reading was a realist, this immersion in the authors' physical world gave me a deep appreciation for the way in which art transforms reality.

As my appreciation for the specificity of Petersburg deepened, my sense of connectedness with the city and its culture grew apace. It did not hurt to know that my great-great-grandfather, William Edmondson, had spent the years 1818–25 in the Russian capital as part of a small group of Quakers invited there by Tsar Alexander I. It took no time at all to locate the outbuilding of the grand Bezborodko estate where Edmondson had lived, the same house, it turned out, in which the World of Art painter Alexandre Benois later spent much of his childhood. This, along with the fact that these Quakers made a cameo appearance on the pages of Tolstoy's *War and Peace*, aroused in me an almost tactile identification with the subject of my study.

Anyone with the slightest knowledge of social science methodology knows how subtly and thoroughly such an identification can distort one's perspective as a dispassionate observer. Did the Petersburg world that Vladimir Nabokov so lovingly described in his memoir, *Speak Memory*, ever really exist? Surely it did not in any objective sense. But the fact that it existed only in Nabokov's memory does not in any way diminish its compelling reality as art. It simply means that art and science, beauty and truth, are different. The problem for me was that I was in danger of creating a mythic Petersburg, an aesthetic Petersburg that fitted my own emotions more closely than it accorded with the gritty truth of history. Much later my friend Andrei Voznesensky presented me with a collection of poems with the disturbing title *Nostalgia for the Present*. He understood that I was in danger of succumbing to the tendency to personalize and romanticize what should instead be viewed with the cold gaze of a clinician.

The person who prevented this happening, while at the same time preserving the sense of connectedness that gave Petersburg meaning for me, was the historian Iurii Mikhailovich Denisov. A great specialist on the architecture and art of Russia, Denisov knew every nook of the city and was generous enough to share his vast store of insights with an American who possessed far more enthusiasm than knowledge. This soft-spoken embodiment of the old Petersburg intelligentsia had a warm and truly proprietary relationship to the historic city, yet at the same time he had just the right degree of analytic distance. It is more than a pity that the circumstances of Soviet academic life did not enable this formidable authority to set down his remarkable understanding in a great monograph on Russian culture. Nor has post-Soviet life treated him any better. I have recently been shocked to learn from a mutual friend that he is nearly destitute.

Thanks to Denisov, I gained a solid appreciation of how nineteenth-century ideas and ideals lived on in the USSR. In America, the condition of unceasing ferment creates something akin to the "permanent revolution" of which Leon Trotsky dreamed. As John F. Kennedy observed, the only thing that is permanent is change. Not so in the USSR. Whatever the Bolshevik Revolution touched was changed fundamentally, if not destroyed. But whatever escaped its force continued unchanged. Indeed, by some dialectical process the revolution created a powerful drive for continuity among broad sectors of society and particularly among the intelligentsia. Over the years this drive proved to be immensely fertile in terms of cultural creativity in many spheres. Nothing quite like it exists in America with the exception of the South, which underwent its own revolution during the Civil War and Reconstruction, and which, as a consequence, has generated more than its share of great literature.

Gradually I came to understand that this drive for continuity amidst discontinuity accounted for many of the things I most admired in Russia. In 1966–67 Dmitrii Mravinskii still conducted the Leningrad Philharmonic. When this great orchestra performed in the stately hall of the Noblemen's

Assembly one could still hear the specific musical timbres of the age of Tchaikovsky, Borodin, and Rimsky-Korsakov. The dark, muffled horns playing with broad *vibrato*, the commanding sound of the Russian bassoons, and the incredible string section all represented a direct laying on of hands from the nineteenth century. Above all, Mravinskii's deliberate tempos and the orchestra's ability to play with collective *rubato* gave it a totally distinctive voice with no parallel in Moscow or, for that matter, in western Europe. It may have been a throwback, but this was the orchestral sound through which Dmitrii Shostakovich spoke in the greatest symphonies of the twentieth century. Much the same can be said of the Vaganova style at the Kirov Ballet, which was linked with the premier of Prokofiev's immortal *Romeo and Juliet* back in 1937, and which was still alive and well in the 1960s.

Particularly confusing for me as an American was my discovery of how continuity and innovation, far from being opposites, are actually related to each other. Few thoughtful Europeans would consider this insight particularly startling, but it hit me like a bolt of lightning. The person who set me on the path to this understanding was once more Iurii Mikhailovich Denisov. Late one spring day I announced to him that I was heading for Moscow for a few weeks and wondered if he could suggest any particularly notable buildings for me to see. He immediately produced a check-list of the best avant-garde structures from the 1920s. And he suggested that I would find the architecture of the great "rationalist" innovator Konstantin Melnikov especially challenging. A pious Orthodox Christian from a peasant family, Melnikov had managed to gain admission to the prestigious Moscow School of Painting, Sculpture and Architecture and to study with Russia's greatest neoclassical painters and architects on the eve of the revolution. A born innovator, Melnikov produced new building forms that were so unprecedented and stunning that he became a kind of cult figure in Paris in the 1920s and was featured in the first exhibition held at the new Museum of Modern Art in New York. And yet Melnikov drew inspiration not from Lenin's militant ideology but from his faith and from the rich vein of mysticism and neo-Platonism that had long been a part of Russia's intellectual culture. Indeed, his thinking had far more in common with the worldview of traditional Russia than with what was espoused by the Communist Revolution that eventually crushed him.

I eventually learned that Konstantin Stepanich had survived three decades of forced inactivity and could be found at Moscow's Central Hospital, situated on the outskirts of town. We met, and in the course of conversations extending over many days an unlikely bond grew between us. When later he died it was clear to me that no one else was going to write his biography. Since all the materials were in my hands and since I also had my notes on those hours of reminiscences, I undertook to do so, even though I had never studied architecture or architectural history.[2]

Besides his radically utopian vision of architecture and life, the most startling thing about this great Russian artist was his utter and complete independence of spirit. The Soviet move to crush him came when he was at the height of his powers. Had he been willing to compromise, the state would surely have lionized him as it did the writer Maxim Gorky and many other artists who caved in. Melnikov refused. And, as I gradually came to appreciate, so did an impressive number of others. Some asserted their independence overtly. Others simply withdrew into private realms.

Returning to Leningrad from Moscow, I was fascinated by the intricate maneuvers which individuals, groups, and whole communities undertook to construct their separate realms of autonomy within the massive structures of Soviet life. Avoiding confrontation, they simply went about their affairs. For most, this was not so simple as a binary choice between being part of the system or living outside it. Men and women who in their workaday lives were pillars of the Soviet establishment were often those most persistent in asserting their autonomy once they left the office. Sometimes this took uproariously funny forms.

For example, when the pipes at No. 2 Shevchenko Street froze (doubtless another case of deliberate subversion by the unwilling builders), all of us turned to the city's public baths. After much research, I began frequenting an establishment situated a few blocks behind the Naval Academy. After several visits at the same day of the week and hour, I formed a nodding acquaintance with about a dozen of the regular denizens. Soon we were sharing jokes. After some weeks we were sharing beer, soon supplemented with ample supplies of more potent fluids, as well as sausages, pickled garlics, and so on. The stories grew increasingly bold and irreverent. Gradually I sensed that every member of this informal men's club was living at least a dual life, with one set of activities and attitudes for the workplace and another, often far more developed and active, for the majority of the time that he spent on his own.

I assumed that I had fallen in with a bunch of rowdy malcontents whose greatest pleasure in life derived not from participation in the Soviet system but from the micro-worlds they and their friends had laboriously constructed in the invisible crannies of that system. Eventually the pipes thawed and most of us went back to bathing in our apartments or dormitories. Before doing so, however, we decided to hold a banquet at the shabby but still elegant Evropeiskaia Hotel. Imagine my surprise when, at the appointed hour, an extraordinarily diverse group assembled for the champagne feast, among them several senior naval officers who arrived in dress uniforms, two truck drivers, three minor public officials, a night watchman, an appliance repairman, and a forty-year-old deckhand! Never having seen one another clothed, everyone there was as surprised as I.

Being a lifelong musician, I regretted being unable to play my clarinet in Leningrad. The university's orchestra was pathetic and I was not in good enough practice to try out for one of the Conservatory's ensembles. And so things stood until I heard that factory band wheezing away at the fiftieth anniversary celebration. I managed to chase them down at one of their "rehearsals," and they invited me to join their ensemble. As a result, I spent a number of evenings adding to the general cacophony. They issued me a collection of dog-eared music, none of which had been published since 1917. In addition to those morose and comical Sicilian marches, our repertoire consisted of waltzes dating from the 1880s and, because officials at the factory seemed to be dropping off daily, a grandiosely morbid rendition of Chopin's *Funeral March*. We played *fortissimo*, with palsied *vibrato* that was positively creepy, and with a bone-chilling disregard for pitch.

What struck me, besides the way fourteen players could equal the volume of the entire Red Army Band, was the sheer conviction with which everyone played. Much later 1 learned that the great American composer and innovator Charles Ives had made the same observation concerning small-town bandsmen in his native Danbury, Connecticut. The reason soon became clear. These amateur musicians found in their self-organized brass band a realm of independence and autonomy that was lacking in other parts of their lives. The music was less important than the sense of association that this modest enterprise infused into their lives. Was this not an example of that independent communal spirit that Haxthausen had celebrated a century and a half ago?

Similarly trivial incidents convinced me also that Russians no longer buckled under submissively to official intimidation, if, indeed, they had ever done so to the extent some foreign observers claimed. When the Neva ice finally broke up and the first signs of spring began to appear, Iurii Denisov organized an expedition by water to the old Finnish town of Vyborg, with its splendid art nouveau and modernist buildings. Returning in the motor launch that he had commandeered for the trip, we passed among the serenely beautiful islands that sprinkle the northern shore of the Gulf of Finland. It was a warm day and I had helped finish several bottles of Georgian wine. Lying in the bow, I fell asleep. Suddenly Iurii shook my foot. As I opened my eyes, he quietly suggested that I look around but stay absolutely still. Looming up on every side were submarines: big and small, new and old, electric-powered and, yes, atomic submarines. Considering it a fine joke to take an American through the Soviet navy's biggest submarine base at the height of the Cold War, Denisov had calmly sailed us right through the midst of it all.

As such impressions piled up in my mind, it was increasingly difficult for me to take seriously most of the pompous generalizations about the nature of the Soviet Union that had been concocted by political scientists in the West. Most of these savants, I realized, based their theories on Soviet publications, which were by definition official and filled with the Soviet government's preferred image of itself rather than objective information. Some had benefited from occasional visits by Soviet officials and scholars who were deemed to be sufficiently reliable to send to Harvard or Columbia. If the older American "Sovietologists" had visited the USSR at all it was to attend conferences, travel along the few approved routes that the government had opened to foreigners, and stay at Intourist's carefully monitored hotels. Unless they were the sons or daughters of émigrés, they generally spoke atrocious Russian. Is it any wonder that they missed most of what was going on?

Nearly everything I experienced as a humble graduate student caused me to question their generalizations about a totalitarian government ruling over a passive society. True, the government did aspire to a totalitarian control that began with the state's ownership of all property and ended with the state seeking to mold the population's values, both public and private. But, as they say, there was a huge distance between the cup and the lip. The "irrelevant" reality of my daily life proved that these aspirations were not being achieved, and disproved Western theories that were based on the assumption that they had been.

With what should I replace these discredited assertions and theories? My research in the archives was helpful, at least on one level. The months wore on and the piles of neatly labeled folders of papers from the 1850s and 1860s grew to near-Himalayan altitudes on my desk. As I pored through them, it became increasingly clear that I was not the first to wonder whether Russian society would function better if it could manage its own affairs rather than have the state control everything for it. Throughout the nineteenth century there had been a strong undercurrent of Russian thought that held that the society would flower if only it were less fettered by the ponderous apparatus of state. Such thinkers denied that Russians were innately servile. They pointed to a variety of institutions, from peasant village communities to the urban merchant guilds and the assemblies of gentry, to defend the notion that Russians, too, were capable of responsible self-government. The fact that these thinkers ranged from high officials, jurists, and noblemen to Slavophiles, middle-class socialists, and radical anarchists gave weight to their argument.

But what had happened to this impulse during the Soviet era? Most of those who acknowledged its existence earlier argued that Lenin, with his boundless hatred for the world from which he himself sprang, effectively destroyed the "bourgeois" institutions of voluntarism, self-management, and pluralism. Whatever he had failed to accomplish, Stalin had finished. As a generalization on the era of Lenin and Stalin, this is more or less correct. Yet my own explorations into the arts and architecture under Stalin convinced me that, to paraphrase Mark Twain, news of the death of independent and pluralistic impulses under Soviet rule were premature. Why had a group of leading cultural figures banded together to protect Melnikov during the Zhdanov purges? What about all those artists and writers who continued to produce independent work that was widely exchanged in private, even during the worst years? And the underground churches, or the jazz fans who surreptitiously reproduced and disseminated recordings of the banned music on X-ray plates?

I saw one of these X-ray plate records during a visit to the Leningrad Conservatory. The person who showed it to me was the cellist and composer Iurii Aleksandrovich Fallik, who hailed it as proof of the resourcefulness of ordinary Russians. Much later I was to write an entire book, *Red and Hot*, to demonstrate that even when it was willing to exert any amount of brutal force in order to form tastes and values "from above," the Soviet state failed at its self-assigned mission.[3] Russians always managed to come together and do what they wanted to do, in this case to enjoy American jazz.

Beyond the insights that came from my research, I had only to observe the world around me to find more fitting generalizations about the nature of Soviet society in the 1960s. For example, on a visit to Estonia I met with a Lutheran pastor who, at the time Iurii Gagarin announced from space that he couldn't see God, placed a metallic orbit around the spire of one of the main churches of Tallinn. Or another example: for several weeks I went daily to the great Leningrad Public Library to work. En route I would drop by a commission store to admire the antique rugs from Central Asia and the Caucasus that were on sale there. Soon I discovered that most of these came not from impoverished Leningraders but from Turkmen, Azeri, and Dagestani entrepreneurs who brought them in on flights from the south. The "suitcase traders" of a later era were already plying their trade in 1966! I enjoyed speaking Turkish with some of these rough-looking characters, and learned that several of them had grown rich from the trade and were building comfortable private homes for themselves in Makhachkali, Alyat, and Krasnovodsk.

Such examples led me to the conclusion that the Soviet system was like a broken and uneven old sidewalk, with no few hard spots but with fresh green grass sprouting up everywhere between the constantly expanding and multiplying cracks. The new sprouts were healthy and strong. They could be trimmed or cut away but were bound to grow back, further cracking the sidewalk and creating still more room for more new sprouts.

Did the many signs of social vitality that I discerned in those years add up to anything beyond their numerical sum? For the time being I did not even pose this question to myself. In fact, it took more than a decade—actually, until the early 1980s—before I was able to entertain the notion that something akin to a civil society was emerging "from under the rubble," in Solzhenitsyn's phrase. For now I was content to look into smaller networks in the hope of finding evidence that some new (or very old) form of political culture was taking root within them. During my last months on the exchange I examined several professional organizations, including the Union of Architects, to see if they were capable of independent collective action. Most were not. I also attended meetings of a number of so-called societal organizations in an attempt to learn whether these governmentally sanctioned groups behaved anything like the "voluntary associations" depicted so vividly in the second part of Alexis de Tocqueville's *Democracy in America.* To my great disappointment, they did not either. By 1980 this, too, had changed, so that clubs and amateur groups of all kinds were becoming the seeds of a new civil society. To this day I ask myself whether I might have found more evidence of autonomy had I looked more closely at a few more groups back in 1966–67.

During my time as an exchangee in Leningrad I failed to arrive at any clear generalizations about the way Russians actually organized themselves in the 1960s to pursue common ends. I succeeded in tearing down one set of theories without developing better ones to put in their place. I could at least console myself that I was now raising the right questions, thanks to the insights that I had gained in Leningrad.

The same questions continued to bother me many years thereafter. I confess that I find them no less compelling today. Within a few years of my first Leningrad experience I was to be on the exchange again, now in the more exalted status of a young faculty member. This time, during the early 1970s, I plunged headlong into the world of voluntary associations and self-organized groups. I explored such entities in every conceivable sphere, including neighborhood improvement, medicine, religion, petty trade, and both the visual arts and music. These explorations were eventually to result in a series of essays on civil society in Russia, as well as the book *Red and Hot,* which used the fate of jazz in the USSR to address the same issues. To this day I bridle when an adherent of the old view of Russian society praises my "book on jazz," implying that it deals with a curious and amusing topic that in no way affects their cherished dogmas. For better or worse, all these projects bear the stamp of my time as a graduate exchangee in Leningrad.

A dubious habit that I inherited from my mother's Quaker forebears is to keep a diary. Over the course of my stay in Leningrad I filled several volumes with observations and thoughts. Glancing through them now, I am struck by three things. First, the diary entries are for the most part quite superficial. I was fascinated by the gentle but firm manner with which a group of young people handled an old drunk who wandered onto the bus one day, but failed to explore whether this was the result of village ways transported whole into the city, or if it was in fact some new and Soviet habit. I cursed under my breath at the old women on the street who would chastise me for going without a hat in November, but failed to ask myself whether Russia's communal heritage had turned everyone into irksome busybodies and would be rejected the first time Russians had a chance to do so.

Second, I am struck by how remote most of the concerns reflected in my diary were from the great political and international issues of the day. By the activist and politically engaged definition prevalent in 1966, I was thoroughly irrelevant. The exchange experience validated that irrelevance and made me less apologetic about it. The time spent in Leningrad helped me to focus on and prefer the irrelevant but real as against the relevant but unreal. Over time this inclination was to benefit me, both as a social scientist and in the personal realm.

Third, I returned from Leningrad with far more questions than were in my head when I arrived on the banks of the Neva. Some of these questions, like issues of voluntarism and self-rule as opposed to totalitarianism, pertained to Russia and its evolution through the centuries. Others had to do more directly with my own experience as an American and as a Midwesterner. Because they arose from living experiences rather than my readings in scholarly monographs, the questions with which I returned to Princeton pertained equally to my professional activities and to my private intellectual life. Finally, because they were posed under such strenuous and exciting circumstances, all these new areas of puzzlement and curiosity commanded my attention for many years to come. Answers to some of them came during further trips to the USSR throughout the 1970s when I headed the Kennan Institute of Advanced Russian Studies. Others gained clarity as the perestroika years began to unfold. Still others I am pondering even today.

Notes

1. *Decentralization and Self-Government in Russia, 1820–1870.* Princeton: Princeton University Press, 1972.

2. *Melnikov: Solo Architect in a Mass Society.* Princeton: Princeton University Press, 1978.

3. *Red and Hot: The Fate of Jazz in the Soviet Union, 1917–1980.* Oxford: Oxford University Press, 1983.

7

Adventures and Misadventures
Russian Foreign Policy in European and Russian Archives

Hugh Ragsdale

Though I am interested in the Russian tradition in the broadest sense, distinctly including cultural history, most of my published research falls into the presently awkward field of foreign affairs. I stumbled into the subject in a seminar of George V. Taylor on the French Revolution offered at Duke University in the summer of 1962. Just beginning graduate school (apart from summer school, at the University of Virginia), little did I imagine at the time the peculiar nature of that field of research in our generation. It was in two senses a manifestly inauspicious choice of field. On the one hand, it confronts the notorious traditionally Russian cultural phenomenon of secretiveness, which is even more obsessive in foreign affairs than in other subjects. On the other hand, our generation of historians has emphasized social and cultural history at the cost of other kinds, and the field of foreign affairs has been virtually dropped from the agenda of respectable subject matter.

There are compensations, however. Russian foreign policy is one field of research in which abundant documentation is, by its very nature, widely available beyond the reach of Russian agencies of control, beyond the borders of Russia; and the European diplomatic archives—located in some of the continent's most attractive cities—are readily accessible. Moreover, the exploitation of them makes the work of the Western historian of unusual interest to his Russian colleagues in the field,[1] as Soviet considerations of thought control and present Russian considerations of expense have practically excluded Russia's own historians from doing such work.

In addition, as I remind myself from time to time, while fashions come and go, genuine historical work is not a house of fashion and its values persist through generational fads. Meanwhile, as the new Russian Republic wrestles with the question of what its national interests and its foreign objectives both are and, more important, *ought to be*, the historians of the Russian Academy of Sciences have just given us the most authoritative work ever published on Russian foreign policy, and it clearly recognizes its debt to the few historians of the West who have joined in their endeavor.[2] There is hope, then, for an appropriate reorientation of attention and interest in the field, and when it occurs, the relatively small volume of work done by us in the West during the past generation or so will be all the more seminal for a new generation.[3]

My first effort at archival work in Moscow began as inauspiciously as possible. I arrived at Moscow State University (MGU) in mid-August 1968. On the morning of August 21, I awoke to the news of the invasion of Prague by the Warsaw Pact forces. An already poor atmosphere for cultural exchange turned to pure chill. I was soon refused all archival access whatever, although my subject, Franco-Russian relations during the years of Bonaparte's Consulate, scarcely threatened Soviet national security interests. I remained in Moscow until January 1969, working in the Lenin Library, which was useful but only marginally better than the New York Public or the Library of Congress and several American university libraries even in quite specialized and relatively rare historical literature—in other words, not a major asset. In short, it was a frustrating and painful semester but an unforgettably graphic introduction to Russian society and especially to the culture of Russian administrative and political control.

The following spring I spent on the same subject in the archives of the Quai d'Orsay, the London Public Record Office, and the Danish Rigsarkiv and Swedish Riksarkiv. The Quai d'Orsay and the Public Record Office are pretty conventional fare for us scholarly types, and there is no need to dwell on them here. What is worth emphasizing from my research of that period is the experience in the archives of Copenhagen and Stockholm. At the time of my first visit there, 1969, I scarcely read Danish or Swedish, though I later learned to do so (and later yet forgot). In any event I was working there entirely in diplomatic history, and the local languages were scarcely necessary, as all important documentation was in good, clear French. Several elements of my experience there are worth recalling.

First is the fact that the organization, cataloguing, and indexing in the two archives was more detailed and meticulous than any similar work that I have seen in other European archives. Second, in the period of my research, the late eighteenth century, considerations of national security made both Denmark and Sweden exceptionally vulnerable and sensitive to Russian policy, and they invariably kept in St. Petersburg experienced senior diplomats. In this case, Danish ambassador Nils Rosenkrantz (married to a Viazemskaia princess) and Swedish ambassador Count Curt von Stedingk consistently made an especially full and reliable record of Russian foreign policy. I emerged from the Danish archive in particular with the impression that I had probably seen there the single most authoritative record of Russian foreign policy for the period available anywhere in the world, including in the Russian archives themselves. I emphasize the word *probably* because, although, as previously related, I was unable to work in the comparable Russian archives, I read the unpublished correspondence with St. Petersburg from five European capitals as well as extensive published Russian documentation in the volumes of the Russian Historical Society's *Sbornik.*[4]

One unique feature of the Danish archive that I especially remember was the definitive authority in commercial and maritime questions of the Sound Dues Toll Book, the ancient Danish record of ships and cargoes passing the Sound, the narrow channel between Denmark and Sweden (Danish Øresund). In the winter of 1800, the second Armed Neutrality functioned as a kind of auxiliary instrument of Bonaparte's ban on English trade in northern Europe, the forerunner of his later Continental System, and I was curious to see how effectively it excluded English trade from the Baltic in particular. The answer was dramatically simple and clear: for a time no English ships whatever passed the Sound.

In the Stockholm Riksarkiv, I was given the only tour of the stacks that I have ever had in an archive. The building itself was a quite remarkable structure, designed as I was told to withstand all but a direct hit of a nuclear weapon, the stacks being situated deep inside a huge boulder that itself lay in Lake Mälären, and as I was guided from sector to sector large metal doors opened and closed in the fashion of the watertight compartments of warships.

I have referred to working in the unpublished Russian correspondence of five nations, and if you are counting, you have missed the fifth one. The fifth capital was Berlin, although in fact I did not work there. The Prussian archives of the period were housed in the Deutsches Zentralarchiv in Merseburg, German Democratic Republic. I asked for well-informed advice about dealing with it, and, acting on such advice, I simply wrote to the archival administration, outlining the papers that I wanted. I got a prompt response coupled with a gratifying proposal. If I would send several rolls of film from the papers of George Washington in the U.S. National Archives, Merseburg would supply film of the papers that I wanted. Although the process moved a bit slowly, it was eventually a fully satisfactory arrangement, and I obtained first-rate documentation.

Of course, the French and English newspapers of the period, *Le Moniteur universel* and the London *Times*, were readily available; the Moscow and St. Petersburg *Vedomosti* were available both in the Lenin Library and the Library of Congress; and, although I was skeptical, because of World War II strategic bombing, about the prospect of finding the crucial German papers of the period, in fact I found them well preserved, especially the important *Hamburgische Zeitung*, in the *Deutsche Presseforschung* at Bremen University. The Hamburg diplomatic documents of the period, which would have been valuable, were destroyed by a fire in the 1840s.

I went back to Moscow in the spring of 1981 with similar research in mind and had little more luck than in the first case. Ronald Reagan had just been elected, and he soon pronounced the words "evil empire." To make matters worse, his national security adviser, Richard Pipes, proclaimed that if the Soviets did not soon improve their behavior, World War III was a distinct possibility. In these circumstances, I got precisely the same archival access as previously.

It was during this visit, however, that I had one of my more engaging Russian educational experiences of another kind. My *rukovoditel'* (advisor) was the former chief of the hierarchy of Soviet historians, director of the Institut istorii Academic A.L. Narochnitskii. He had matured in Soviet life during some of the toughest times. He was an able and widely read person, an elder statesman of the academic *nomenklatura* (establishment selected by the Party), rather formal, a good linguist, who did not stray far from acceptable conventions. Still, he liked my work and took it seriously, and he told me that he had done his best to get archival access for me—without success. More surprisingly, he invited me to lecture to the Foreign Policy Division of the Institute of History. I was flattered, initially euphoric. Then it occurred to me that I would be speaking on Russian foreign policy to the most venerable and senior native specialists, a thought more than a little intimidating.

I drafted the lecture in Russian, and a colleague assisted me in correcting it before we gave it to a typist for a legible format. In the meantime, it had occurred to me that I had real advantages to exploit in the circumstances. I was to speak on Russian relations with France during and after the Second Coalition. Though I had never had access to unpublished Russian materials on the subject, I had worked extensively in Paris, and none of my auditors had. Before I began to speak, I realized that I could treat them to a version of their history fresher than they could imagine, based on materials that no one else present had consulted and no one among them could dispute. An essential part of my subject was a document of sensational disrepute, the Testament of Peter I, a notoriously controversial piece of apocrypha in which Peter allegedly prescribed for his successors the means of conquering all of Europe.[5] It is not hard to imagine the attention with which they followed my suggestion that the Russian policy of Napoleonic France was based flatly on the understanding of Peter's Testament as an authentic document. They were fascinated. I did not neglect to insist that our Western understanding of their foreign policy, sympathy for it, and confidence in their representation of it would be vastly improved by open access to the arcana of the archives. They did not demur, but, as I soon had reason to believe, they exercised nearly as little influence with their archivists as we ourselves did.

I spoke and/or read from my text for about forty minutes, and the discussion that ensued lasted for a couple of hours. In the course of it, there was a lively conflict of opinion between Narochnitskii and the distinguished historian A.M. Stanislavskaia, and I began to realize that I had unwittingly served as something of a stick with which to beat the rebel faction that, as was explained to me on another occasion, had recently attacked the director of the whole Institut istorii and *"svergnuli ego"* (overturned him), reducing him to chief of the Foreign Policy Division.

It was at the Quai d'Orsay that I had stumbled inadvertently across what is probably the basic text of the Testament of Peter I, and it quickly became clear that the French foreign office from the 1770s through the Napoleonic era believed that the document was genuine (notes of Alexander d'Hauterive) and conducted its Russian policy accordingly. (Incidentally, Harry Truman believed the same thing until he got a note about it from George Kennan; and the *Christian Science Monitor* perversely used the Testament on page one to explain the Soviet invasion of Afghanistan on December 31, 1979. In response to my letter, the *Monitor* subsequently printed a correction.) In any event, the treaty of Tilsit of 1807 was in part the product of that French misunderstanding. Napoleon intended to seduce the Russians to a French alliance by offering the bait of the Balkans and the Turkish Straits, while of course he never intended to deliver on his promises.

The Testament aroused my interest in a similar Russian project of conquest, the equally notorious Greek Project, in which Catherine II allegedly presumed to drive the Turks out of Europe and to divide the spoils with the Habsburg Empire. The authenticity of the project had been denied by two prominent historians, one Soviet, O.P. Markova, and the other, the German Balkanist Edgar Hösch (Munich). So I decided to try Moscow again. This was 1986, and, fortunately, glasnost was afloat, and Reagan and Gorbachev had just had a cozy little meeting in Reykjavik. On this occasion I was met at the airport by a colleague who informed me that I had already been approved to begin work on the following day in the *Arkhiv vneshnei politiki Rossii* (Archive of the Foreign Policy of Russia). My experience there was ambivalent, ironic, initially discouraging, and eventually fortunate.

I wanted the diplomatic correspondence with three foreign capitals, Paris, Vienna, and Constantinople. I was given no inventories or finding aids; I simply described what I wanted, and the materials were brought. When I was given the French and Austrian files, I found that huge sections, up to thirty pages running, had been removed. I inquired about it and was given a brush-off. In fact, the withholding of these materials did my research little damage, as I had already read the Russian correspondence in both Paris and Vienna, but it led me to expect the worst when I requested what I knew would be the most valuable material, the Turkish correspondence. Much to my surprise, however, I was inexplicably given all of it without any omissions. It was incredibly rich. According to the register, it had been read by six or eight persons whose names I did not recognize and who had never published from it. I was evidently the first Westerner ever to have seen it. I realized that I had unusually good material. I was able to demonstrate, in my opinion, not without considerable help from the materials in the Vienna Haus-, Hof-, und Staatsarchiv, that the Greek Project was quite real. Because of the strength of expertise on Catherine II on the editorial board, I sent the article to the *Slavonic and East European Review* (University of London), where it was published in 1988.

The Soviet historian Markova had made the apparently telling point, in denying the significance of the Greek Project, that it was nowhere mentioned in the published record of discussions in what was in effect Catherine's cabinet, the *Gosudarstvennyi sovet* (State Council). I checked the text and found that Markova was right.

It was here, however, that the materials in the Vienna Staatsarchiv were so important. My first experience there was discouraging, because Emperor Joseph II had decreed that all official papers during his reign were to be done not in the usual diplomatic French but in German. That in itself was not the big problem; rather it was the style of German handwriting of the time, *Kurrentschrift*. When I first saw it, I recognized none of the letters of the alphabet. It was a shock. I went across the street and had a couple of drinks, which unfortunately did not advance the cause. Persistence, on the other hand, did, and in about ten days I was reading it well enough, and the information in it was dramatically informative.

Although Markova denied that the Greek Project had ever been discussed in Catherine's State Council, in fact the president of the College of Commerce, A.R. Vorontsov, had given the Austrian ambassador, Louis de Cobenzl, a full account of the extensive discussions of it there. Cobenzl reported that Catherine herself had introduced the subject, and her correspondence with Potemkin on the warfront in the south confirmed the evidence of his reports. If, therefore, you are using the published stenographic record of the State Council, beware of its relative reliability and by all means check it against the Austrian diplomatic reports. Don't forget, however, your *Kurrentschrift* alphabet.

More recently, I have succumbed to the appeal of an old fascination far from my traditional field of research, the question of Moscow's potential military intervention in support of its Czechoslovak ally in the Munich crisis. I realized that we knew from published diplomatic papers and memoirs all there was to know about the policy of three powers that were a party to it, Britain, France, and Germany. After glasnost and the Soviet collapse, however, I thought that we had a new opportunity to examine in East European manuscripts the disputed question of potential Soviet intervention. In reading the literature, I found a clear discrepancy between the confidence of Western historians that Moscow would not have intervened, of East bloc historians that it would have, and the conspicuous dearth of East European, especially Russian, sources in the arguments of Western historians. I also thought that I would learn more from military than from diplomatic documents, that they were intrinsically more likely to yield the secrets of Soviet intentions. As I pored over the pious, monotonous, and often antiseptic collections of Soviet diplomatic documents, I was unable to forget Stalin's observation that honest diplomacy is like iron wood or dry water. So in 1996 I went back to Moscow.

My initial experience there was literally fantastic, the stuff of an historian's fantasies. I worked entirely legitimately in an archive that, because of political pressure subsequently brought on it, I cannot afford to name. I found in it the richest collection of largely unexploited materials that I had ever imagined to see in a Russian archive. In the period that interested me, two subjects in addition to Munich were especially fully represented. On the Soviet purges, there was a considerable variety of material, including accusations, confessions, suicide notes of the accused, and quarterly inventories of the purge process. I thought at the time of the series of running debates between Robert Conquest and his critics, Arch Getty and others (on how big a toll of life the purges took), and reflected that we were obviously still far from having the whole story. The other conspicuous subject was Soviet involvement in the Sino-Japanese War and Soviet relations with the Kuomintang, including the transcripts of long interviews of Soviet agents with Chiang Kai-shek. I was unable to resist the temptation to sample some of these materials before turning to my own proper subject.

I ordered documents on Soviet activity in and around the Munich crisis from detailed *opisi* (inventories), and I was given everything that I ordered on the following day. The content of the documents was mind-boggling. I saw a good deal of correspondence directed to Stalin, though no replies to it, as well as correspondence of Litvinov, Voroshilov, Tukhachevskii, and Beria, the responsible chiefs of foreign policy, defense, and the police. Litvinov would write to Stalin with an important question. On the following day, as we can now see from the published log of visitors to Stalin's office in the

Kremlin,[6] he would be received for an answer to his question, and the next day he would execute an official document directed to one diplomatic legation or another reflecting the decision taken.

I soon found unpublished documentary evidence to support at least the purely factual version of the Soviet historiography of Munich. I saw the manuscripts of documents both published and unpublished, and no evidence of any distortion of the factual record. I discovered that a week before the Munich conference the Soviets mobilized and posted to the border areas about half a million men. More surprisingly, I found that the army organized agitprop meetings in which the clear message was that the Soviet Union intended to honor its treaty with Czechoslovakia if the Wehrmacht attacked it. There was no reference to the contingency of a prior French military intervention, as the treaty stipulated. The documentation here was from the very grass roots, i.e., NKVD (security police) reports of the reaction of enlisted personnel coming from those meetings. I saw everything that appeared to be of interest on military developments in the Kievan Special Military District. This was the good news.

Of course, in Russian affairs there is always bad news. At the end of ten days, as I was turning my attention to the papers of the Belorussian Military District, I was informed that the archive was closing at once for lack of funds to keep it open. More specifically, the closing was attributed to both budgetary and technical problems—at different times, *"lift ne rabotaet"* (the elevator doesn't work), *"po biudzhetnym prichinam"* (for budgetary reasons), and *"po tekhnicheskim prichinam"* (for technical, i.e., mechanical, reasons). I was disappointed, but, I thought, I already had the heart of the matter in hand. I had at least advanced the cause of throwing light on the subject.

My disappointment was soon aggravated. Some months later I was asked not to make reference to any document that I had seen there. I telephoned and protested but to no avail. I have published a couple of articles from this research without citing these unpublished sources, and I am working on a book on the subject without having decided yet what to do about that problem.

Meantime I searched in the old Party Archive, *Rossiiskii tsentr khraneniia i izucheniia dokumentov noveishei istorii* (RTsKhIDNI: Russian Center for the Preservation and Study of Documents of Recent History), now *Rossiiskii gosudarstvennyi arkhiv sotsial'no-politicheskoi istorii* (RGASPI: Russian State Archive of Sociopolitical History), for whatever discussions/decisions of the Politiburo I could find. I found only *protokoly*, i.e., decisions, not records of discussions; and two categories of decisions, defense and police affairs, were still classified for the period after 1934. The archivists attempted to divert my attention to Comintern records, and I actually read the reports of Tito from Yugoslavia in the 1930s and a few materials from Czechoslovakia as well—all documents were there in English, French, German, and Russian—but these materials were not productive.

The logical next step was to turn to Prague. I consulted first the specialists at the Historical Institute of the Czech Army (*Historický ústav armády České Republiky*), who told me that most of the pertinent materials had been destroyed upon the entry of the Wehrmacht in March 1939. They were right. Although the staff at the Military History Archive (*Vojenský historický archív*) was very helpful, none of the reports of Colonel František Dastich, the Czech military attaché in Moscow, survived for the period around Munich. I found one long and useful diplomatic dispatch from the Czech ambassador in Moscow, Zdenek Fierlinger, but nothing more. On the other hand, I located a few incidental documents from Dastich among the copies of Russian archival documents in the papers of General Dmitrii Volkogonov at the Library of Congress Manuscript Division. They show that he was ostracized by his Soviet military counterparts and shadowed relentlessly by the NKVD, rendering his presence in Moscow largely useless. The Czechoslovak General Staff complained about this state of affairs, but to no avail.

In the meantime, a colleague furnished me with one sensational document from a Polish historical journal, the correspondence of the Polish consul in Kishinev, Bessarabia, or eastern Romania in 1938. Romania was in a crucial position during the Munich crisis, as it provided what appeared at the time to be the unique feasible route for a Soviet army to go to the support of the Czechs (the Poles would have resisted militarily). A week before the Munich conference, the Polish consul reported whole trainloads of Soviet military equipment passing through Romania on the way to Slovakia. Wonderfully intrigued, I decided to go to Bucharest to check the matter out for myself.

So I spent two periods of research in the archives of the Romanian army and the Romanian foreign office. I was received most cordially. At both places, I was invited to publish my research in Romanian historical journals, and I have obliged with two articles. I discovered a variety of facts pertinent to the story but unavailable from other sources: (1) the Romanian army was committed to facilitating the passage of the Red Army to Czechoslovakia; (2) the Romanian foreign office and King Carol II vetoed the plan; (3) the inadequacy of Romanian railroads made it impossible in any event, as the Germans were well aware, hence they were not concerned about it; (4) the report of the Polish consul was utterly false or deluded, or both. The intelligence reports of the Romanian army from the Soviet frontier on the river Dniestr contain no such dramatic material as the Polish consul reported. On the contrary, what they reported was comically trivial: stories of the poaching of fish, the stealing of firewood, and drownings in the river. The nature of the

dramatic developments alleged by the Polish consul there are fittingly sym-
bolized by a couple of stories.

On August 22, the mare of Volea Vişman went to the Dniestr to drink and
was swept by strong currents to the Soviet side of the river. Several weeks of
negotiations with the Soviet side established that the mare was not a bourgeois spy, and she was eventually returned to her owner, whereupon she was
submitted to the examination of a veterinarian and found to be free of Communist diseases. A month later, on September 28, the day before the gathering at Munich, the Romanian army was concerned with nothing more
momentous than the issuing of a new cut of uniforms to the border guards.
Their instructions stipulated white gloves and yellow cartridge belts to be
distributed preferably to soldiers tall and good-looking, who were then assigned to the more important border posts. The circumstances on the Roma-
nian-Soviet frontier make it abundantly clear that the Czechs were hopelessly
lost whatever the uncertain French did, and so we were not almost spared
World War II by Soviet intervention.

As must be apparent by now, I am one of those weird birds who find
archival research, apart from a few dull days, nearly endlessly fascinating,
but my experience in the Soviet and contemporary Russian aspect of it prompts
a lot of almost macabre reflections. Like most other foreign researchers in
Soviet and post-Soviet Russia, I have had a lot of wonderfully heartwarming
cross-cultural encounters with the Russian intelligentsia, and I remember
them very fondly. Still, in retrospect, I wonder why people like me invest
their careers in discovering the history of a country at times so capriciously,
so obsessively committed to condemning us all to utter ignorance of it. At
times it threatens to blight my whole conception of Russia and to overwhelm
the memory of such things as Chekhov, *shchi* and *kasha* (characteristic Russian dishes, cabbage soup and porridge), and kitchen conversations.

Though I went to Russia annually for over thirty years and still have an
active correspondence with my Russian colleagues, especially those with
whom I have collaborated in publishing projects, I have not been back since
the blight of my research in the military archive in 1996 and can foresee no
future for myself in my kind of subject matter inside the Russian frontier (I
am also not indifferent to stories of incurable tuberculosis). The experience
of Russian culture has been a stimulating element of my own education, and
I am grateful for much of it. On the other hand, the cost has been high. Some
of my American colleagues in the field can, and some cannot, easily imagine
the frustration of spending a career of research between the indigence of a
puny provincial American university library and the obscurantism of the
Neanderthal gatekeepers of Russian archival documents. The fact that I have

had ready access to the foreign-affairs archives of Russia's diplomatic partners in Western and Central Europe has always made my work of considerable interest to my Russian colleagues, much more so than to my American colleagues, whose interest in foreign affairs is mysteriously if fashionably negligible. My Russian colleagues have always appreciated what they regard as my impartial if not sympathetic approach to their history, but it has precisely no influence among their archivists. The Anglo-American students of Soviet social history have been ever so much more fortunate, at least in this generation. Of course, all of this problem is properly perceived as an essential feature of Russian tradition. I sometimes reflect with a kind of rueful consolation that when the nineteenth-century dean of Russian historians, Sergei Solov'ev, was invited to publish the jubilee biography of Alexander I on the centennial of the emperor's birth in 1877 (*Imperator Aleksandr Pervyi*), he was not able to cite a single archival reference. *Russkaia pravda!* Russian justice: Plus ça change . . .

Notes

1. See, e.g., Hugh Ragsdale, "Prosveshchennyi absoliutizm i vneshniaia politika Rossii v 1762–1815 godakh," *Otechestvennaia istoriia*, 2001, no. 3, pp. 3–25.

2. A.N. Sakharov et al., eds. *Istoriia vneshnei politiki Rossii (konets XV veka-1917 g.)*, 5 vols. Moscow: Mezhdunarodnye otnosheniia, 1995–1999. See review (forthcoming): Hugh Ragsdale et al., in *Slavonic and East European Review*.

3. See, e.g., Hugh Ragsdale and Valery N. Ponomarev, eds., *Imperial Russian Foreign Policy*. New York/Washington: Cambridge University Press/Wilson Center Press, 1993.

4. *Sbornik imperatorskago russkago istoricheskago obshchestva*, 148 vols. St. Petersburg: Stasiulevich, 1867–1916.

5. It is generally agreed among people who have examined the question carefully that in this case—as perhaps in most other such cases—the document mimicked demonstrable historical reality.

6. *Istoricheskii arkhiv*, 1998, passim.

8

Reclaiming Peter the Great

James Cracraft

For an American of deeply provincial antecedents, it could be said, the very idea of doing research in *Russian* history was an adventure in the standard dictionary sense of the term: "an exciting, very unusual experience," if not "a bold, even risky undertaking of uncertain outcome." Until college, I had never met a live Russian, and then they were of the émigré variety, wistful bearers of ineffable sufferings who had somehow landed on our shores. I can still remember being stunned, one very wintry day in March, a teenager delivering newspapers in south Minneapolis, by the biggest headline I'd ever seen: STALIN DEAD; and later, a comparison of the writings of Dostoevsky and Tolstoy, no less, was the theme of a senior high school English paper—largely cribbed, as I recall, from a book by a sometime professor with the thrilling name of Ivor Spector. "Russia" was the land of the firebird fairy tales we'd read as children, and the home of the huge threatening armies we saw pictured in *Time* magazine. It surely was "a riddle wrapped in a mystery inside an enigma," as the revered Winston Churchill had said.

College was Georgetown, and Frank Fadner's popular introductory course on Russian history began to open my eyes to a subject that was even more colorful and complex than I had imagined. Georgetown is in Washington, D.C., then (the early 1960s) The Capital of the Free World and undergoing a post-Sputnik boomlet of anxious interest in that emergent superpower, the Soviet Union. Anatolii Dobrynin, the Soviet Ambassador, was a major figure in town, especially during and after the Cuban missile crisis. I saw him at the theater one night, sitting in a mezzanine box across the hall from the box holding President and Mrs. Kennedy. The Bolshoi Ballet was on stage and the dancers, constantly glancing up at the President's box and then at the ambassador's, made several obvious slips. Nobody minded; most of the audience were similarly triangulated. For this Georgetown senior, working part time on Capitol Hill and thinking maybe about law school, it all seemed to come together right about then—the early impressions, the introduction to an exotic history, the sometimes sinister, but often glamorous, Cold War. I was hooked.

One quickly learned that the initial challenge, after tackling the language, was to study Russian rather than Soviet history, the former being the domain of the more learned, cosmopolitan, and charming members of the first (post-1917) emigration, the latter, that of the founding generation of Cold Warriors, all honorable men no doubt but grimly determined to get it right as a matter of national security. They tended to wear gray suits and military haircuts, and usually also came from deeply provincial backgrounds. But one also quickly learned to appreciate the monetary subsidies and political valence these mandarins could lend to careers in Russian history, a subject, as they saw it, that could unlock the deeper codes of the often baffling Soviet conduct of the day. In their view, Russian history was also the potential wellspring of a Russia freed someday from the awful blight of communism, a matter of documenting any parliamentary and capitalist initiatives, however feeble, taken under the Old Regime and of magnifying, however possible, the calamity of the Bolshevik Revolution. One was not really supposed to spend much time on the former pursuit, to be sure, lest one seem excessively academic, or worse, politically naive. The enemy was at the gates.

Scholarships in the field were forthcoming, and this student with a growing interest in earlier Russian history soon found himself at Oxford University, the home of a veritable pleiad of charming émigré scholars and their sometimes equally illustrious British colleagues. Situated well to the east of The Capital of the Free World, in the heart of old Europe itself, Oxford was also the destination of an astonishing number of real Russians, as it were, or Russians fresh from Soviet Russia itself: spouses of British exchange students who had been "let out," or exchange students themselves (junior KGB-types I'd discover pretending to study international law); senior Russian scholars ensconced in Oxford libraries for months at a time and quietly available for conversation; and, wonder of wonders, a string of visiting high-cultural stars. Just during my *stage* there the latter included dissident Andrei Voznesenkii for a poetry reading, with Professor Dmitrii Obolensky simultaneously interpreting (Voznesenskii was astonished to have a genuine Russian prince doing the job); Academician Dimitrii Likhachev for a big lecture (another chapter in the controversy over the origins of the famous *Igor Tale*, long thought to be the greatest monument of medieval Russian literature—the view that Likhachev defended—but considered by some scholars to be a much later fake); and, most memorably of all, Anna Akhmatova, the grandest of modern Russian poets, to receive an honorary degree. She was the guest of her friend, the distinguished Oxford philosopher, historian, and Russianist, Professor Sir Isaiah Berlin; at a reception in his fancy house she sat in a throne-like chair receiving the homage of the admiring throng. Nobel prize winner Boris Pasternak's sister, resident in Oxford, stood by Akhmatova's side while her host hovered solicitously (we learned later of their chilling, touching encounter in Leningrad just after World War II). It was all quite amazing—all the Russians, all the interest in Russia, the fine drama of it all, and not a Sovietologist in sight.

These were among the primal adventures of one budding student of Russian history, which increasingly seemed a way of having your cake (doing historical research) and eating it too (helping in some small way to overcome the potentially disastrous East–West divide). The riskier adventures naturally came with working and living in the Soviet Union, which entailed, in those old days, steering one's scholarly course between the usually discreet pressures of U.S. officialdom and the doggery of its Soviet counterparts. In my search for a safe but important dissertation topic—"safe" with respect to official Soviet sensitivities—I'd hit on certain "progressive" aspects of the reign of Peter I and particularly his church reform, a subject that had not been adequately investigated by Soviet or "bourgeois" historians, most of whom were indeed engrossed, one way or another, in the question of the Bolshevik Revolution ("the teleology of 1917," as an American colleague later put it). It was not a topic I embraced with any great enthusiasm; it needed doing, I'd shrug, I'd try to do it in a rigorously secular, empirical kind of way. It was also a project that could be completed in acceptable scholarly fashion without direct access to the Russian archives. In fact, at the crucial juncture in my work they did prove inaccessible: some *skandal* had temporarily shut down the Central State Historical Archive in Leningrad—perhaps the one, as we later heard, precipitated by the discovery in the Holy Synod's files of a petition from Lenin's maternal grandfather requesting acceptance into the Orthodox Church (aha, he was!—he was not!!—a Jew). At any rate, I had to content myself with the contemporary printed works of relevance and the scholarly monographs and articles to be found at the main research libraries in Moscow and Leningrad, which enabled me to finish the dissertation and then the book in a form that was subsequently well received by Soviet historians (in person, be it said, rather more than in print).[1]

Those were the 1960s, a time of formative experiences to be sure, halcyon years as they now seem. I went back to Russia in 1972, intending to research eighteenth-century Russian political and literary history with a focus on Feofan Prokopovich. Here again was a personage and a topic that resonated positively in Soviet scholarly circles, where Prokopovich was seen as an important literary exponent of political absolutism, a doctrine that they also regarded as "progressive" for the times. For these and other plausible reasons Soviet scholars saw Prokopovich as the Russian Hobbes or Grotius, no less, and as the first local champion of Copernican heliocentrism (no such interest was shown in Prokopovich the churchman and theologian, an important omission I again thought to repair in my moderately positivist fashion). So I was quietly welcomed by specialists in Leningrad and Moscow, younger scholars like myself who helped me circumvent the Stalinist "dragons," as they called them, guarding the archives and rare book and manuscript collections. In one quite exceptional case one of these conspirators, markedly braver than the rest, abetted my clandestine efforts to photograph rare materials—at night in my hotel—when official permission to arrange it was flatly denied, apparently because I was a foreigner, and worse, an American. In another instance this same fellow personally transcribed eighteenth-century manuscripts to which I'd been denied access and passed his transcriptions on to me wrapped in newspaper (his handwriting proved as hard to read as the originals would have been!). On yet another occasion he and some colleagues contacted me at my hotel and asked that I meet them in a nearby vacant lot, where they presented me with a rare and most valuable volume of expertly edited Petrine documents (it had been published in Russia during the brief thaw after World War II and proved to be a work of such fine, disinterested scholarship that a promised companion volume could not be published). I might emphasize that these young scholars and particularly the chief conspirator here acted without the overt demands for payment in cash or kind that in the 1980s became routine in dealings with Soviet archives and libraries. We exchanged cigarettes; I would try to obtain copies of Western scholarly works of interest to them, and they would secure other Russian items for me. But mostly it was unfettered conversation they wanted, and the opportunity to vent their frustrations at the official obstructions that hemmed in their work and drastically restricted their career prospects. When I went home at the end of 1972, much of my research accomplished,[2] it was with a strong sense of frustration, but more on their behalf than my own.

This was the world in which the first generation of American scholars to conduct research in Russia from their graduate-school days forward lived and worked; my arrival in 1972 on the U.S.-Soviet Young Scholars' Exchange, not so unusually, had been delayed for months in official Soviet retaliation for the United States' expulsion of some Soviet spies. This was the cat-and-mouse game we all played then, from application to expulsion (as we joked), applying and reapplying to go on the exchange and, once there, pleading and bargaining our way through the archives and libraries of Moscow and Leningrad. Rarely could we get permission to work in the provinces, where the reception anyway was likely to be ice-cold, as I would personally discover in both Kiev and Novgorod. The game continued in our dorms and hotels, ever bugged and reported on, and in the streets and public parks, where we were often tailed, the official bonhomie of the Nixon–Brezhnev détente notwithstanding. With the collapse of the latter and the Cold War revivalism of the early Reagan years (early 1980s), if anything things got worse. Yet there were often moments of high relief, sometimes hilarious in context, even surreal. My comparison in reflecting on such moments is with my more "normal" archival, museum, and library experiences in Britain, the United States, Sweden, Denmark, and France— a normality, it might be noted thankfully, that today largely obtains in the corresponding Russian institutions.

I remember in the mid-1970s trying to get photos of some Petrine portraits at the Hermitage and enlisting the help of a friendly curator, who duly filched them from the files and slipped them to me in the usual plain wrappers. The thief asked in return for as many books on the life and works of Pablo Picasso as I could send him; by his count, the Hermitage had thirty-nine paintings by Picasso, few of which were ever on public display (his communism was suspect, his art "decadent"), but Picasso was his obsession. I felt honor-bound to comply, and once home in the United States found four or five such books in print. It had been agreed that they would best be sent in the regular mail, from my university to the Hermitage, all open and proper; I can still feel the anxiety as I dispatched them, out of pocket more than a hundred dollars. But a few months later, to my amazement mixed with mounting joy, I received the first of what proved to be a series of five postcards from Leningrad, each conveying on its back some part of an overall message of intense gratitude for the books—gratitude also mixed with amazement that they had actually arrived, and with unalloyed joy. We had prevailed, my curator and I, and somehow advanced the cause of fine art in Russia against the rampant philistinism of the system.

On another occasion, in 1979, at the Central State Archive of Ancient Documents (TsGADA) in Moscow, I was repeatedly denied access to records of the Preobrazhenskii Prikaz, the office of political police founded in 1696 by Peter the Great, on the grounds that, contrary to my own assertions based on citations in a recent Soviet publication, these records were not relevant to my research. It was a standard Soviet dodge; whatever the real reason for denying access—in this case, perhaps the risk that I, a foreigner, would uncover something that was somehow embarrassing to Soviet pretensions or Russian national pride—the archival official took it upon herself to declare the requested files unrelated to my stated research topic, and that was that. In 1979, too, my arrival in the Soviet Union had been delayed for months, this time in U.S. retaliation for the Soviet denial of a visa to a senior American scholar, the late Alexander Dallin of Stanford University. This time I had played the waiting game in stages, advancing in April from New York to London to work for a while, then to Copenhagen to work some more, and then to Stockholm and Helsinki, ever closer to the rainbow's end; but all to no avail. After nearly two months of this delay my U.S. sponsors called me back to London to await resolution of the quarrel, which finally came in June. So I went home in the fall of 1979 determined to seek access to those archives again, now with the advance assistance of the American exchange authorities, who agreed that we would make such access a condition of my participation in the exchange and, implicitly, of that of a Soviet scholar hoping to come our way. Again to no avail; repeated applications at last elicited the telegraphed response from Moscow, in English, that the archives in question were "closed to all investigators for a long time." There it was, blatant in its unadorned obstinacy, however oddly funny. But such stories should not be allowed to eclipse the support and assistance regularly received on the ground in the Soviet Russia of the 1970s, often with a wink and a nod, let alone the little acts of collegial heroism.

The year 1972, to return to more substantive scholarly adventures, was the tercentenary of the birth of Peter the Great and the occasion, I was surprised to discover once in the Soviet Union, of a kind of official rehabilitation of the first emperor. Or rather, looking back, it marked stage two of his reclamation in Russia since the collapse in 1917 of the empire he had founded. I refer now to Peter's place mainly in the serious historical literature but also in the public arena, the latter divisible into official status and popular esteem. Peter never lost the guarded affection of his people, it seems, as witness the flowers put daily on his tomb in the Peter–Paul church in Leningrad, right through the siege of World War II; but his official status and place in the historical literature have been subject to major alterations. In the militant Bolshevik era and on through the 1920s he was consigned along with all of imperial Russia's leaders to the limbo of non-personage, if not worse, to outright obloquy as mere agents of the erstwhile feudal and bourgeois orders. But with the 1930s and the "counter-revolution" of Stalin came the first, partial rehabilitation of Peter as a great builder of the Russian state and armed forces; indeed, in his proclivity for mixing with common folk and working with his own hands, he was hailed as Russia's "first Bolshevik." The rehabilitation was reflected not only in historiography but also in literature, most notably Aleksei Tolstoy's novel *Peter the First*, which won a Stalin prize in 1941 and was repeatedly republished in the Soviet Union after its first part appeared in 1929. Indeed, Peter's status as a great historical figure was strongly affirmed in the revival of Russian nationalism occasioned by World War II and again in the tercentenary observances of 1972, which also had at least semi-official support. In both cases the authorities were manifestly following the popular lead. At public lectures and in letters to the newspapers in 1971 and early 1972 ordinary Russians repeatedly called for official recognition of the tercentenary—an example of how, contrary to the models of most Sovietologists then, public opinion did function in the Soviet Union. Hence also the plain middle-aged man encountered in Moscow who, on learning that I had just come down from Leningrad, suddenly exploded: "Why the devil did they have to change its name? They could have named some other place after *him*! I don't know any 'Leningrad.' To me it will always be Peter's city [*grad Petra*]."

In 1972 a movie called *Tabachnyi kapitan* (*The Tobacco Captain*) premiered in Moscow, its title a play on Peter's well-known fondness for his pipe and its protagonist a nobleman's servant who rises in the tsar's new navy to become captain of a ship, with a gigantic Peter appearing as the ultimate hero. A grandiose new opera, *Peter the First*, loosely based on Tolstoy's novel, was staged at the famous Kirov Theater in Leningrad. Public exhibitions of Petrine memorabilia were mounted at every major museum in both cities. The many buildings and parks in suburban Leningrad associated with Peter were spruced up or thoroughly restored (the meticulous restoration of Peterhof, "Peter's Versailles," from the destructions of World War II had been under way for several years). All of these sites were crowded with tourists, mostly Russian. For the visiting historian it was all quite exhilarating, an adventure in historical discovery on a wholly unanticipated scale and an opportunity to witness a still supposedly repressed people busily hailing one of its heroes. But more telling in terms of research, *things* were on display now that were rarely if ever seen, unearthed from basements and storerooms: uniforms and other clothing, glassware and tableware, furniture and sculptures, assorted gadgets and instruments, tools, toys, weapons, medals, coins, standards and flags, books, paintings, drawings, maps, and prints, all of which had belonged to Peter or his close relatives and associates, and almost all of which were made in western Europe or newly fashioned in Russia after European models. It was an astonishing array of the physical, tactile remains of the era of great reforms or "transformations [*preobrazovaniia*]," as it was now being called again in Russia. And then there were all the Petrine buildings and parks to which one's attention was insistently drawn, all built or laid out in contemporary European (classical) style and standing as such in marked contrast to the architectural monuments of the preceding Muscovite age, romanesque as it were in their simplicity when not "baroque" in their structural complexity and decorative profusion.

The last point was forcefully made by the exhibition of "Russian Architecture of the Early Eighteenth Century" hosted in the fall of 1972 at the Shchusev Museum of Russian Architecture in Moscow. The contemporary sketches, drawings, maps, plans, prints, and models on display in four large rooms demonstrated in a most arresting way the quality and range of the Petrine ambition to transform the Russian-built world along contemporary

European lines. More visually impressive still was the exhibition "Portraiture of the Petrine Period" mounted at the Russian Museum in Leningrad and seen on a return visit in 1973; it filled nine large rooms and drew on at least a dozen different collections housed in Leningrad, Moscow, and the provinces. The prints and oil paintings on display, many also taken out of deep storage, depicted Peter himself, his immediate family (the tsar as family man!), and various other relatives and associates. Almost all were executed in the European Renaissance tradition of naturalistic portraiture, and almost all of the sitters, women included, were clothed in contemporary European dress; the few exceptions in either case antedated Peter's active rule and only served to emphasize, in their static, iconic poses and/or traditional Muscovite garb, the cultural gulf that had been crossed within a generation.

This impression was enormously strengthened on seeing the smaller but equally telling exhibition of "Icon Painting in the Petrine Period" which the Russian Museum had simultaneously mounted in adjoining rooms. Traditional in subject and style, often provincial in origin, and only touched by a stray Western influence, the icons on display embodied continuities and other historical actualities that were largely obscured for viewers—it seemed the great majority—who concentrated on the portraiture of the elite. What was the message here? A representation of two Russias, one traditional (church and masses) and one modern (the Europeanized elite), forever distinct if not opposed? The triumph of "realism" as embodied in the new portraiture over the supposed "formalism" of the traditional icons? And how did either theme link with the Soviet Russia of the present? Shunting back and forth between the two exhibitions, immersing myself in these juxtaposed repositories of contemporaneous visual material, was a truly exhilarating experience for this still largely book-learned, logocentric, would-be historian of Russia.

In fact, the tercentennial exhibitions in Russia proved to be a turning point in my professional life—if you will, its single greatest adventure. Gradually the multifarious impact of those visual encounters in 1972–73, written up in an article published in 1974,[3] coalesced in a single hypothesis: what had happened of greatest historical significance under Peter was not the achievement for Russia of the Great-Power status celebrated by generations of Russian and now Soviet historians, but a kind of cultural revolution—a quite sudden and lasting turn among the dominant elite away from practices and values of the Muscovite past to others of contemporary Europe, and most readily traceable in the material rather than the written remains of the period. This was not a welcome hypothesis among historians of virtually any stripe, however, not then or for long afterwards. For Soviet Marxists it was all quite beside the point, as it was for the so-called new social and/or people's historians in the West, where historical biography and particularly the study of dead white males was concurrently slipping out of academic fashion. So, indeed, was large-scale historical interpretation as such, the victim of reductive "deconstruction" along modish lit-crit lines even as "micro-history," or the detailed study of small groups in small places, was rapidly on the rise. Meanwhile Russian nationalists were instantly offended by the seeming implication of my hypothesis that Russia was not always an integral part of Europe, that Russians had to be inducted into the modern arts and sciences by Western hirelings, and so forth. Moreover in the strict division of the sciences obtaining in the Soviet Union, if not elsewhere, study of material remains was the highly specialized domain of archaeologists, art scholars, museum curators, and—as I gradually broadened my inquiry to include linguistic change under Peter—historical linguists and particularly historical lexicographers. Such study was the work severally but never jointly of these finely tuned specialists and decidedly not the domain of bumptious historians, whose sources were and are of course overwhelmingly written documents, especially those generated by organs of state power, which are typically subjected by them to little or no linguistic scrutiny. One way or another I was off on a lonely quest. Further research in visual as well as verbal sources and more on-site inspection of material remains seemed to strengthen my hypothesis, however, to the point where I began giving papers to report my findings. A trilogy on the subject eventually was planned to contain the ongoing research, and the first of the volumes, on architecture broadly understood, appeared in 1988, with the others, on imagery and on verbal culture, to follow.[4] In the meantime, a little sad to say, Feofan Prokopovich had been all but abandoned.

All but: in the Public Records Office in London in 1979 I happened on a document which indicated that Prokopovich had not actually written the major work for which he had long been acclaimed as the Russian Hobbes or Grotius, namely, *Pravda voli monarshei* or *Right of the Monarch's Will* in choosing the heir to his throne, first published in 1722. This tract was "the great *pièce justificative* of Peter's reforms," as Marc Raeff once called it, the original Russian statement of monarchical absolutism (the copy at the Library of Congress comes from the library of Alexander II). It was thus a political work of immense historical significance and I had evidence that its real author or at least co-author was an obscure Greek scholar who had come to Russia as a refugee from the Ottoman Empire. Another adventure in Russian historical research had begun. Preliminary investigations at the British Library, including perusal of an original copy of the *Pravda* in company with a local expert on eighteenth-century Russian literature, Professor Charles Drage, seemed to confirm the archival finding. I went on to discover that the conventional attribution to Prokopovich of various other writings similarly rested on sand, and reported as much in an article published in 1981.[5] There was space in the article only to suggest how a "Prokopovich canon," or list of works definitely authored by him, could be established; meanwhile, I hastened to add, we could still cite with confidence the contemporaneously published orations of Feofan Prokopovich, since there he is invariably identified as the author and confirmative evidence, for example, from eyewitnesses of the occasion on which he gave the oration, invariably a major public holiday, is readily available. Even then, it might be added, the standardizing influence on the published text of printers and press "correctors" must be considered. The whole experience suggested to me that quite anachronistic notions of authorship had been applied in the study of seventeenth- and early eighteenth-century Russian writings—a suggestion, again, that did not prove welcome, this time to literary scholars as well as to those of a Russian (or Ukrainian—Prokopovich was born in Ukraine) nationalist bent.

Enough already of the specialist's adventures in Russian historical research. I alluded above to the Nixon–Brezhnev détente of the 1970s and to the revived Cold War of the early Reagan years. The second of these developments could not help but impact, negatively, the work of Russianists wanting or needing to pursue their investigations in the Soviet Union. Many of us were thus drawn into the public debate over the alleged need to resist and contain the "evil empire," ultimately with the vast, and vastly expensive, anti-missile defense system also aptly named, given the same Hollywood source, "Star Wars." A prominent Russian historian briefly served as President Reagan's in-White House Soviet expert, urging him on. Others of us took a more cautious stance in the radio and television talk shows that called upon our supposed expertise, in the op-ed pages of newspapers and other publications intended for general readers, and before concerned civic groups. All Russians, we in our turn urged, were not in fact—and never had been—Communists (many were indeed religious); all Soviet practices—like the aggressively confrontational foreign policies of leaders from Lenin to Brezhnev—were not necessarily rooted in Russian history; many healthy developments, amid all the troubles, were now under way in Soviet society (the environmental movement for one, a lively youth culture for another, widespread attention to urgent public issues for a third); and anyway, economically if not otherwise the Soviet Union was a giant with huge feet of clay, so why press so hard? Future historians will be able to put the debate in proper perspective, the perspective of ensuing events: record defense-driven deficits in the United States and corresponding economic recession, on the one side, and the sudden collapse of the Soviet Union followed by the economic, social, and moral degradation of Russia and its other national components, on the other. To me it seems likely that after all due deliberation these future historians will conclude, in terms of universal human values, that a more gradual dissolution of the Soviet Union would have been better for all concerned, one coupled with a broadly consensual transition to freer, more open and equitable economies and societies. Even so, for those of us who took part in the debate it was another exhilarating part of the job—another great adventure, in its way, in Russian historical research.

As for Peter the Great, his full reclamation in his homeland is obviously well under way. His image is harnessed to the sale of beer, vodka, and cigarettes and to the promotion of banks and real estate. Ships are named after him, along with schools, streets, and museums. His tricolor mercantile flag, patterned on contemporary British and Dutch models, is again the Russian national flag; his great "window on Europe," as it was first dubbed in 1739, is again called St. Petersburg; his figure, embodied in a colossal new statue standing some fifteen stories high, now graces Moscow. When asked in a published interview to select a hero from Russian history, President Boris Yeltsin named Peter—a choice which once again, polls now indicated, enjoyed broad popular support. Acclamation has succeeded reclamation, it seems, however misguided or excessive it may sometimes appear. Meanwhile the massive scholarly edition of Peter's letters and papers, inaugurated in 1887, continues publication in Russia and new scholarly editions of other primary sources and of pre-Soviet works have appeared; so have numerous new monographs and interpretive studies as well as a major new biography.[6] A biography of similar if not greater scope has also been published in the West, where dissertations on Petrine subjects and other specialized studies have also appeared or are in progress.[7] This efflorescence of scholarly interest suggests a renewed recognition of the fact that major historical events and figures, those which directly impacted the lives of millions, cannot permanently be ignored or downplayed in service to prevailing historiographical fashion without doing serious damage to historians' basic credibility. Figures and events like the reforms of Peter the Great, in other words, must be periodically reinterpreted in the light of current values and by whatever methods now seem appropriate; they cannot simply be wished away or left to the tomes of a bygone era if historiography itself is to remain alert, convincing, "relevant." In this respect, at any rate, this one student's investment in certain aspects of the Petrine era seems to have been time well spent. But I'm also pleased to think that all of the renewed interest in Petrine subjects, which will surely intensify in 2003 with the tercentenary celebrations of Peter's founding of St. Petersburg, constitutes a very salutary reminder of Russia's huge, indeed measureless, European heritage. It is a reminder which at this juncture in history many Russians, and a great many others, seem to need.

Notes

1. James Cracraft, *The Church Reform of Peter the Great.* Stanford: Stanford University Press, 1971.

2. As recorded in Cracraft, "Feofan Prokopovich: A Bibliography of his Works," *Oxford Slavonic Papers*, n.s. 8 (1975), pp. 1–36.

3. Cracraft, "The Tercentenary of Peter the Great in Russia," *Canadian–American Slavic Studies* 8, no. 2 (Summer 1974): 319–26.

4. Cracraft, *The Petrine Revolution in Russian Architecture.* Chicago: University of Chicago Press, 1988; *The Petrine Revolution in Russian Imagery.* Chicago: University of Chicago Press, 1997; *The Petrine Revolution in Russian Culture (forthcoming).*

5. Cracraft, "Did Feofan Prokopovich Really Write *Pravda voli monarshei?*" *Slavic Review* 40, no. 2 (Summer 1981): 173–93.

6. N.I. Pavlenko, *Petr Velikii (Peter the Great)* (Moscow, 1994). This work has not been published in English, as has another study by a leading Russian specialist: Evgenii Anisimov, *Vremia petrovskikh reform (Era of the Petrine Reforms).* Leningrad: Lenizdat, 1989; see Evgenii V. Anisimov, *The Reforms of Peter the Great: Progress Through Coercion in Russia*, trans. John T. Alexander. Armonk: M.E. Sharpe, 1993.

7. See Lindsey Hughes, *Russia in the Age of Peter the Great.* New Haven and London: Yale University Press, 1998, which contains an exhaustive bibliography of works in English, Russian, and other languages.

9

Prisoner of the *Zeitgeist*

Laura Engelstein

When people ask me how I got into Russian history, they sometimes assume there must be a family connection. They ask if I come from a Russian background—a "what-is-Russia?" question in a nutshell. My maternal grandfather served as a clerk in the tsarist army during World War I. He was proud of his excellent Cyrillic handwriting. But he left Russia—by then Soviet—not for political reasons, but because he was unable to get a decent Russian education and move up in the world and because things had changed for the worse. My mother was born in Tiraspol, Bessarabia, in 1920. Not a fortunate time and place. After ten years of anxious waiting across the border in Rumania, the family made it to New York. The home language was Yiddish. In my childhood, I heard this Yiddish, speckled with words and phrases that later turned out to have been Russian, but I had to learn Russian myself. So when asked if I come from a Russian background, I say, "No." Yet the people excluded from the general culture and subjected to discrimination and sometimes to violent attacks were also part of Russia, and of course I feel some kind of (complicated) pull.

In the United States, my mother swiftly acquired the native language (now English) and the higher education my grandfather had wanted for himself. My parents abandoned the Yiddish and Hebrew of their childhoods, but never their admiration for the languages and cultures of the old world. Like other New Yorkers of their generation and background, they considered the October Revolution the great event of modern history, but, unlike some, they were disappointed in its results. In choosing Russian history, I obviously chose to investigate the source of family emotions—attachment, loss, disappointment, and yearning. In the 1960s, moreover, revolution was not just a family myth or a nightmare. We read about *mai soixante-huit*, about the invasion of Czechoslovakia, but the events at Columbia happened in front of our eyes. At City College, campus buildings were occupied by militant black students. The mythically intense days when our fathers sat in the City College cafeteria arguing about Stalin and Trotsky until returning to Brooklyn for the night were a thing of the past. By my time, that excitement was over, but new issues had taken their place: civil rights, the war in Vietnam, the demand for new forms of personal expression.

I did not go to graduate school, however, in order to recapture a family legacy, clarify a political dilemma, or pursue "a brilliant career." I needed to leave New York, finally, but had no definite ambitions. I certainly had no idea where I was headed—to placid, albino Palo Alto, in direct proximity to untamed wilderness and filled with expensive cars. But the *Zeitgeist* was waiting. Feminism, Cambodia, the new social history. In class, we discussed the French Revolution as though it too were unfolding around us. In the field of imperial history, Terence Emmons impressed us with the range of his learning; his intimacy with Russian culture inspired envy and awe. Raised in a spirit of contentiousness (capitalism is defective, so is what took its place; religion fails the test of reason), I was ready to challenge a professor's every word, but Emmons's reasonableness offered no provocation. His sympathy for moderate solutions, evidenced in books on the Tver nobility and the political parties, did not prevent him, however, from acknowledging the spirit of the times.[1] His seminar on 1905 became the grain of sand in my oyster. It made sense, with "revolution" in the air, to find out how it worked.

Off I went to Paris (the opposite of Palo Alto) to figure out what to do next. I thought of abandoning anguished Russia for sensuous France, also with no shortage of revolutions, but I couldn't relinquish the fascination. Another student in the Stanford seminar had written a paper on the Moscow armed uprising of December 1905. It was an alluringly combustible subject. The French were interested in *guerrilla urbaine*. I read old newspapers (*Birzhevye vedomosti*, The Stock Exchange News) in flat cardboard cartons in the newspaper room of the Bibliothèque nationale on the rue Richelieu, and took the commuter train from the Gare St. Lazare to Nanterre–LaFolie to work at the Bibliothèque de documentation internationale contemporaine (BDIC). Nanterre was a hideous concrete-and-steel wasteland, with grimy halls and students intent on their coffee and cigarettes—a breeding ground for political dissatisfaction. There I read 1920s Soviet studies of the Moscow working class, with their Menshevik-style idealism. I applied to the International Research and Exchanges Board (IREX) for study in the Soviet Union and took my interview long-distance, standing in a post-office phone booth near the Quai d'Orsay. Edward Keenan asked me to define "revolutionary consciousness." I said a few words in Russian, and that was it.

It is interesting from the perspective of the professional generations to recall who was in Moscow in 1973–74, the year of the Yom Kippur War and Solzhenitsyn's expulsion from the Soviet Union. In the same wing of Moscow State University were Kenneth Bailes, Lewis Siegelbaum, Diane Koenker,

Toshi Hasegawa, Neil Weissman, Paul Bushkovitch, and Jeffrey Brooks; Dan Orlovsky was in Leningrad. Inside the forbidding Stalinist hulk, the dormitory was cozy; the bread, cheese, kefir, Jonathan apples, and honey were abundant. We thought my roommates were probably spies: the first a flirtatious beauty queen, the second a ruminoid from Ufa who ate Cream of Wheat at all hours. The Lenin Library did not allow me to xerox lists of Moscow factories published in 1905—on security grounds, they said—so I copied the lists by hand. In the archives, the supervisor announced that 1905 was not a woman's topic—*ne zhenskoe delo*—by which she meant she had no intention of giving me anything of any interest. My director of studies was Evgenii Dmitrievich Chermenskii, who had written on the role of the bourgeoisie in 1905, but he had no interest in me or my work.[2] On one memorable occasion, a friend brought me to visit Nadezhda Mandelshtam, the poet's aged widow, who lay in stately ugliness on a couch. She too pronounced that 1905 was not *zhenskoe delo*.

The guardians of Soviet orthodoxy were not wrong about me, from their perspective. I was bound and determined to say something that went against the grain. The book on 1905 was my Rosa Luxemburg moment: uneasy with ideology, I was drawn to the thrill of confrontation. Luxemburg had criticized Lenin for his undemocratic insistence on party control; she believed the workers' movement was a creative force that would come to political maturity through the experience of conflict. To me, the revolutionaries seemed rigid and doctrinaire, their language monotonous and aggressive. I found satisfaction in piecing together the events (bit by bit from the old newspapers), evoking the effaced street names (wandering Moscow, Baedeker in hand, photographing the Victorian brick factories, once Einem bisquits, now Red October), mapping residences and strike routes—reconstructing a lost world. I loved the physical Moscow, and I wanted to believe the humble followers had dignity and purposes of their own which frustrated the intentions of their leaders. I accepted the romance of popular revolution. Later, the book was reviewed in a Soviet journal. They said I was a falsifier of Soviet history, but from excess of liberal naiveté, not ideological malice like a certain Mr. Richard Pipes.

I wrote the thesis in Berkeley, where I met Reginald Zelnik, known for his research on the workers' movement, who encouraged me just enough to make me feel the project was worth completing.[3] Bound in Stanford-red covers, the bulky mass was stuffed with chunks of pseudo-statistics, plotting strike movements, neighborhood profiles, and incidents of violence compiled from newspaper accounts and police reports. At Reggie's urging, I finally submitted the manuscript to the late Jess Bell, then at Stanford University Press. Jess had a reputation for tough-minded no-nonsense. In this case, he asked:

what was the point of this, anyway? The point, as I was forced to figure out, was to understand the self-education supplied by the political process (the voice of Rosa), the dangers of ideology, the ability of meanings to take off on their own, creating proletariats of the imagination, which lure people into the fray. I saw the workers as included in something larger than themselves.[4]

The *Zeitgeist*, of course, needs resistance to get the craft moving. Inspired by the general interest in revolution, I had nevertheless looked for something to argue against. In seeking evidence of how ordinary folk managed to define their own goals, and thus refuse the authority of others, I ended by focusing on the interaction of classes and the fabric of neighborhoods in which the social movement took form. The power of the revolution stemmed not only from the drama of conflict, it seemed, but also from the urge to participate and the sense of belonging. My conclusions went against my own psychological grain.

Immersion in the leaden rhetoric of the class struggle left me weary of the Social Democrats' lack of imagination, craving a less confrontational, more personal avenue into the past. It was at this point that the *Zeitgeist* struck its second blow. At Cornell, where I began teaching in 1976 (for the record, the second woman ever hired by the History Department; there had been no full-time women faculty in the Stanford department when I was there), I encountered people who were thinking about how to think about sexuality and gender (not yet quite called that) as part of the historical project. I remember wondering why Russian radicals had no apparent interest in sex and no personal self-awareness. In 1975, anthropologist Gayle Rubin's ambitious essay "Traffic in Women" made a vivid impression.[5] She showed how the concepts of the great social theorists (Freud, Marx, Lévi-Strauss) could be marshalled to think about the place of women. At that time, I must also have encountered the first volume of Michel Foucault's *History of Sexuality*, which appeared in English in 1978.[6] I read every word and every footnote of Richard Stites's monumental study of women's liberation in old and new Russia (also 1978), thinking, here's a man with judgment *and* imagination.[7] In assembling a mass of information about literary works, social movements, political ideology, and personalities, Stites saw the connection between the private and the public, the sexual and the political, in a manner consistent with the time in which he wrote but novel to historical scholarship. Nancy Frieden's work on the zemstvo physicians, showing that medical doctors had a social as well as a professional conscience, appeared in 1981.[8] These were the rustlings of the *Zeitgeist*.

The gender pioneers thought of themselves as methodological rebels. They were charting a new course. It turned out that Russia had its own "sexual question," to which only Richard Stites, the hippie from Harvard, had paid any heed.[9] Like him, I wanted to keep sex and politics connected (a sign of our times). But if the wind was blowing in this direction, the destination was not clear. I had only a shred of Foucault to cling to—the elusive, yet elegant idea that power structures were embedded in ways of thinking.

I began with the question of sources. In Helsinki, where I first spent time in 1984, I made my way through the professional journals in the Slavonic Division of the Finnish National Library, where they were conveniently displayed on the open shelves. Among my chance discoveries was an essay on "sexual crime" by Vladimir D. Nabokov, the novelist's father, a distinguished legal expert. When Nabokov, Sr. emerged as the hero of my story—tolerant, law-abiding, clear-thinking—I searched for his papers. A brief correspondence with the remaining Nabokovs in Switzerland uncovered no leads. Later I checked the Prague archive in Moscow; Nabokov was present only in his role as a member of the Provisional Government. His early career had seemingly left no trace. On a trip to Berlin I photographed his gravestone in the old Russian cemetery, but got no further than that.

His colleagues in the legal profession (as well as their cousins in medicine—some literally: the forensic anthropologist Praskov'ia Tarnovskaia and V.D. Nabokov were related) captured my sympathy. Unlike the needy workers and doctrinaire radicals of 1905, their opposition to the established order was couched in measured tones. Combining discipline with passion, they cared about the social good and were loyal to professional and ethical values. Their very idealism involved them in constructive institutions. Excavating their world and tracing their achievements, I myself ended up in a bastion of the academic establishment, not as an outsider but as an invited guest. Thanks to a fellowship at Radcliffe's Mary Ingraham Bunting Institute in 1985, I was able to explore Harvard University's Langdell Law Library. In those days, nothing was "on-line." The tsarist-era treasures were housed beneath a locked, windowless reading room, zealously guarded by keepers of the grail. The keepers were lovers of scholarship, who admitted us to the basement stacks, where I educated myself in imperial legal history. In Langdell's international collection I retraced the reading my Russian subjects had done. The Library of Congress stacks were still open to scholars in those years, and there, too, I made discoveries I could not have predicted. The proceedings of ministerial commissions, published only for in-house use, are hard to locate unless you can go through the volumes one at a time.

As I moved from the restraint of the disciplines to the melodramas of the post-1905 cultural scene, I eavesdropped on the debate over civic values. The spectrum of expression ranging from religious conservatism to sexual exhibitionism had fallen afoul of Soviet orthodoxy no less than un-Bolshevik views of the workers' movement. In one library or another, I xeroxed

Anastasiia Verbitskaia's *Keys to Happiness* and all of Vasilii Rozanov's works, down to the last outrageously anti-Semitic pamphlet. Verbitskaia's torrid page-turner, wildly popular on the eve of World War I, combined commentary on current events and social themes with a romantic plot of female yearning and disappointment in love. I borrowed her title. Rozanov wrote about sex and religion (including the Jews) in stunning modernist prose.[10] Neither had been republished since 1917. Both are back in the bookshops today. Since the Soviet collapse, Russians have returned to the kind of debates that occupied readers and writers after 1905: how to define public values, how to balance liberties and constraints, how to integrate the personal and the social. One of Verbitskaia's novels was titled *Spirit of the Times* (*Dukh vremeni*).

In 1990 I returned to Russia, having missed the perestroika years. Almost all of my own *Keys to Happiness* had been completed. Trying vainly to find "pornography" in the Lenin Library, I discovered nothing more exciting than the amateurish snapshots of semi-draped girls in sentimental poses. I saw the famous *Livre de la Marquise*, illustrated by Konstantin Somov, in the Leningrad Public Library, where I photographed the images by standing on a chair next to the window. The new-style friendliness of the library staff was an amazement. Compared to the suspense and anxiety fifteen years before of begging for permission to copy selected pages, the ease with which requests were initialed and orders filled was astounding. I no longer had to wonder what secret formula would unlock the ideological gates: chocolates? a patron in high places? flirting with the female archivists (if you were male)? Now only money needed to change hands.

The militant resistance to Western incursions into national themes was a thing of the past, but if the resistance was no longer ideological, it was still palpable. In 1990 I also attended a conference in Leningrad on the crisis of the early twentieth-century intelligentsia. My topic, the "sexual question" (*polovoi vopros*), made the colleagues from the Institute of Russian History uneasy; the one who introduced me said I would be speaking about the "field question" (*polevoi vopros*), a slip of the tongue that made the audience titter. The sexual question had made it into journalism by now. For that very reason it seemed not only unthinkable but disreputable in scholarly circles. Yet I had been included in the conference. My book was published in 1992, then translated—badly—into Russian a few years later.

The tale of contracts, negotiations, delays, and obfuscations is worthy of Gogol. The director's secretary assured me her boss was not in town, when he was down the hall, but in any case always busy. The translation was under way, it seemed, but delayed. No means were provided for me to check it. The date of publication seemed always to recede. Visits to the office, calls on the phone, nothing seemed to move the press to action, as its quarters periodically changed address and goons loitered in the hallways. However, the new-fangled publishing tycoon, initially tempted by the sexual theme, then disappointed in the distressingly academic product, delivered in the end. Hard to find in any bookshop, the Russian version has been meaningful mostly to younger scholars, or to those who have come to see questions of psychology (*mentalité*), culture, and the experience and actions of individual persons as important historical themes.

In the United States, the book clearly belonged to the new genre of cultural history; it was the moment for histories of sexuality, of the body, of representation rather than "reality," as it was now called in quotation marks. The ideas of Michel Foucault had been noted by Soviet scholars in the 1970s but did not enter Russian intellectual life for another twenty years. In the West, by contrast, Foucault was the subject of lively dispute. Reviewing *The Keys to Happiness* in the *Times Literary Supplement*, Simon Karlinsky praised its attention to sexual themes in the context of modern Russian culture (the discussion of which he himself had pioneered), but he deplored the influence of Foucault on its conception. Foucault's concept of sexuality had indeed provided the starting point for the project. In the modern period, according to his view, new kinds of scientific knowledge provided a system of norms that replaced the moral categories of religion as the basis for public order and individual self-understanding. This transition, Foucault maintained, accompanied the shift from monarchical regimes to the advent of civil society.

In thinking about Foucault's idea, particularly as it pertained to changing attitudes toward sexual identity and comportment, I wondered whether similar mechanisms might not have been at work in nineteenth-century Russia. There, the autocracy both impeded and fostered the production of scientific knowledge and the development of civic consciousness. I wondered whether the discourse on sexuality, which Russian physicians and legal professionals shared with their colleagues abroad, functioned in the Russian setting as Foucault believed it did in the West. My purpose was to explore, not ratify, his theory. Like any theory, it aroused the imp of contradiction. Did workers show class consciousness? Not really. Did power flow from discourse? Not exactly. If discourse in this sense produces social and political results, then finding the same thought systems in a different national context might illuminate the limits of the concept itself. As a social historian, I persisted in seeing discourse less as a force in its own right than as a product of specific groups and institutions.

In departing from Foucault, both in starting with his idea and in differing from his methods, I engaged with but also dissented from a scholarly trend. Karlinsky's response convinced me, however, that I had not yet made my point. Trying to clarify the issues at stake, I wrote an essay on Foucault's relevance to Russian problems. It was intended for a conference on Foucault and the writing of history at the University of Chicago.[11] In it, I objected to Foucault's critique of the Western legal order as a luxury only a bourgeois Westerner could afford, and I used the Soviet case as an example of the dangers of denigrating legal values. I was echoing Bogdan Kistiakovsky and other liberals of the Russian *fin de siècle*. Sheila Fitzpatrick understood me as advancing yet another version of Western triumphalism and charged me with returning to a Cold War style of thought.

Between Karlinsky, on the one hand, and Fitzpatrick, on the other, I was causing distress at both ends of the ideological spectrum. Not unhappy to find myself in what seemed like a middle position, I was soon confronted with values and beliefs that tested my self-professed tolerance and moderation. Raised in an entirely secular spirit, I had not given much thought to religion, yet the *Zeitgeist* began to push me in that very direction. Its instrument was Vasilii Rozanov, the bad boy of Russian philosophy, who appears in *Keys to Happiness* as the antithesis of the liberal world view. Defending the sanctity of sexual expression, he attacked Christianity as a repressive and puritanical creed. While praising the Jews for their allegedly sensual understanding of religion, he denounced many aspects of what he imagined to be Jewish culture. His disregard for intellectual consistency was daring, if repulsive, but refreshingly frank. Unafraid to explore the irrational yet compelling impulses behind the pervasive anti-Semitism of his day, he never shaped them into a coherent scheme. He demonstrated, rather, that hatred was a form of emotional attachment. He showed that logic was a way to keep one's distance from the stuff one didn't understand—like pain, loss, fear, and confusion.

Sex was, of course, one of those messy subjects, but I had managed to write an entire book about sex focused on rational discussion and with barely a mention of religion. Reading Rozanov, who was obsessed with sex and religion in conjunction, I learned of the so-called Skoptsy, or self-castrators, who went to the furthest extreme to ensure their marginality to the human condition.[12] These simple peasants believed the Orthodox faith pointed them in the direction of self-mutilation as the best guarantee of salvation, and they stubbornly resisted the persecution of church and state. Against my better judgment, I could not tear myself away. The spirit of the times, post-Soviet in Europe, post-liberal here, had brought the question of belief back into focus. Here I was, choosing a topic designed to upset the hardiest reader, perplex and disturb my colleagues, and return me to my own lonely corner of the scholarly map (there she goes again with her curious topics). Yet my topic was topical after all. Heaven's Gate, the rise of fundamentalism, the return of the Orthodox Church and of myriad new faiths in post-Soviet Russia all provided a context for the study of this awkward group. And so did the new familiarity with trans-gender choices. Prisoner of the *Zeitgeist* once more.

I struggled with how to frame the problem presented by the Skoptsy. Was it social marginalization? Was it an example of Foucault's "techniques of the self"? Was it about gender? The Skoptsy clung to conventional gender roles and apparel; they were not individualists; they were as patriarchal and misogynistic as the rest of the common folk. Aside from the pathos of their self-inflicted deprivation, which induced an anxious sympathy, they were not easy to like. At the Woodrow Wilson Center, where I enjoyed a year of research at the Library of Congress, the policy mavens among my fellows considered my research another example of degenerate academia. But I myself was not sure what my project was about. I was used to writing the history of a problem. What was the problem here?

A skeptic and non-Christian, I myself had to come to terms with the fact of religion and with the fact that I had written two books on Russian cultural and political life based entirely on secular sources (the chapter on Rozanov being the one, partial exception). In pursuit of the Skoptsy perspective, I began work in the Russian State Historical Archive (RGIA) in St. Petersburg, exploring the holdings of the Ministries of Internal Affairs and Justice and the Holy Synod. The breakthrough came in a chance encounter with Heather Coleman, who had been researching the history of the Baptists in the archives of the State Museum of the History of Religion (GMIR) in the Kazan Cathedral. Following her footsteps, I explored the material that Vladimir Bonch-Bruevich had collected on the Skoptsy. Hoping to win the peasant dissenters' trust, the old Bolshevik had solicited materials which in Soviet times became the center of an archival collection.

Now, the cathedral had been returned to the Orthodox Church, which occupied the ground floor. The Museum's infamous Soviet-era atheist exhibit featuring the Spanish Inquisition had been dismantled, but the archives were still housed atop a winding staircase under the cathedral dome. There I met Nick Breyfogle working on the Molokane, another dissenting sect. It was a trend. Irina Viktorovna Tarasova, the archivist in charge, showed me the greatest courtesy and assistance. We sat on opposite sides of her desk in a cubby between the dank stone walls as I made my way through the boxes, discovering evidence the Skoptsy had offered about themselves: notebooks, letters, family photos. I had found a communal self-portrait, or, at the least, the record of the cultural aspirations of the few believers who could read and write. Beginning with what seemed like a series of family snapshots, we discovered the carefully compiled testimony of one individual life, which became the center of my story.

So what was it I had to say about this character and about the Skoptsy?

I wanted the book to reflect on the way historical sources are created and how they can be used. I refused to impose a conceptual scheme or suggest a final interpretation. I wanted the community's terrible choice to remain as a challenge to understanding. I was trying to resist my own impulse to systematic thinking, to the organizing compulsions of analysis. I let myself enter the imaginative world of the religious believer, not wishing to reduce this (to me) deeply foreign impulse to some more readily accessible something else. I did not want to provide a comforting intellectual framework or a protective screen of critical judgment. I had moved as far away as possible from the ready-made categories of the Marxist world view and backed away from the formulations associated with the new cultural history—the discourses and practices that seem to answer intractable questions if they are not examined very hard.

As I confronted my subjects' experiment with writing and the experience it conveyed, I myself experimented with writing in a new way. Using the strategies of microhistory, I focused on narrative and personality. When Stephanie Sandler suggested we organize a conference centered on the theme of "self and story" in Russian history, the idea made sense. The conference, sponsored by the Social Science Research Council (SSRC) in 1996, included both imperial and Soviet examples and invited a dialogue about culture among colleagues from different fields.[13] It expressed in form and content the challenge to chronological and disciplinary boundaries that was about to result in the reorganization of area studies and of the SSRC itself. Seeing the world more and more as an arena in which cultures interact and societies impinge on one another, we are less likely to stay in our professional or geographic corners.

My story as a historian is the product of interaction with colleagues, texts, and the political issues of my generation. (For the record, Princeton has just appointed its first female president, a woman my own age.) Yet at each turn I was inspired not only by the arguments and preoccupations of the moment, academic and political, but as much by the urge to take issue with the assumptions they contained. As a famous German philosopher famously insisted, resistance is dependent on the framework it pushes against, both for the provocation and the structure it offers. The *Zeitgeist* blows against our sails. Where we head is up to us.

Notes

1. Terence Emmons, *The Russian Landed Gentry and the Peasant Emancipation of 1861* (London, 1968); *The Formation of Political Parties and the First National Elections in Russia.* Cambridge: Cambridge University Press, 1983.

2. E.D. Chermenskii, *Burzhuaziia i tsarizm v pervoi russkoi revoliutsii*, 2d ed. rev. (Moscow, 1970).

3. Reginald E. Zelnik, *Labor and Society in Tsarist Russia: The Factory Workers of St. Petersburg, 1855–1870*. Stanford: Stanford University Press, 1971.

4. Laura Engelstein, *Moscow, 1905: Working-Class Organization and Political Conflict*. Stanford: Stanford University Press, 1982.

5. Gayle Rubin, "Traffic in Women," in *Toward an Anthropology of Women*, ed. Rayna R. Reiter. New York: Monthly Review Press, 1975).

6. Michel Foucault, *History of Sexuality*, vol. 1, trans. Robert Hurley. New York: Pantheon, 1978; French ed., 1976.

7. Richard Stites, *The Women's Liberation Movement in Russia: Feminism, Nihilism, and Bolshevism, 1860–1930*. Princeton: Princeton University Press, 1978.

8. Nancy Mandelker Frieden, *Russian Physicians in an Era of Reform and Revolution, 1856–1905*. Princeton: Princeton University Press, 1981.

9. Barbara Engel was pioneering the study of women at this time, but the issue of sex was not her concern: Barbara Alpern Engel, *Mothers and Daughters: Women of the Intelligentsia in Nineteenth-Century Russia*. Cambridge: Cambridge University Press, 1983.

10. For more on both, see Laura Engelstein, *The Keys to Happiness: Sex and the Search for Modernity in Fin-de-Siècle Russia*. Ithaca: Cornell University Press, 1992.

11. Laura Engelstein, "Combined Underdevelopment: Discipline and the Law in Imperial and Soviet Russia," *American Historical Review* 98, no. 2 (1993); rpt. rev. in Jan Goldstein, ed., *Foucault and the Writing of History*. Oxford, Cambridge: Blackwell Publishers, 1994.

12. Laura Engelstein, *Castration and the Heavenly Kingdom: A Russian Folktale*. Ithaca: Cornell University Press, 1999.

13. Laura Engelstein and Stephanie Sandler, eds., *Self and Story in Russian History*. Ithaca: Cornell University Press, 2000.

10

Of Outcomes Happy and Unhappy

Bruce W. Menning

The Russian military historian Aleksandr Georgievich Kavtaradze once observed more as fact than profundity that "every family has its own history."[1] I suspect that every historian's foray into the Russian archives also has its own history. I suspect, moreover, that the sum of these forays recalls the famous dictum in Tolstoy's *Anna Karenina*, that is, "Happy families are all alike, while every unhappy family is unhappy in its own way." The realities of research suggest an even more extended metaphor, in that most archival experiences probably resemble families, combining elements of both the functional and dysfunctional. The following remarks draw on personal research experiences that witnessed difficulty at the outset, achieved genuine progress through the "salad years" of archival access during the early 1990s, then abruptly turned into something less than happy. Inspiration flows from my recent completion of an article for *Kritika* surveying post–Cold War developments in Russian and Soviet military history.[2]

Appropriately enough for a military historian, the story begins on the eve of something few of us understood was happening, the end of the Cold War. As a U.S. Army Reserve officer on training assignment at the Pentagon during the summer of 1988, I was serving with the European Division of J-5 (Strategy, Plans, and Policy), The Joint Staff. In anticipation of formal military-to-military contacts with the Soviets, Admiral William J. Crowe, then Chairman of the Joint Chiefs of Staff, requested a memorandum on the viability and nature of such contacts. Drawing from a reservoir of experience dating to 1975 and interrupted by the Soviet invasion of Afghanistan, I outlined the history of previous contacts and charted an ambitious program, including exchanges of military historians. The following spring, as a military historian and civil servant who spoke Russian, I found myself in Moscow and Leningrad, participating in an official visit of military historians under then Brigadier General William A. Stofft, U.S. Army Chief of Military History. In the Soviet Union we did many things of which we had never dared to dream, including conferring with officers of the General Staff and visiting the headquarters of the Leningrad Military District, housed in the previous quarters of the Imperial Russian General Staff. We talked openly with Soviet military correspondents, and the subsequent appearance in *Red Star* of an article entitled "Who are You, Dr. Menning?" reminded me that the Cold War still raged in some quarters.[3] More importantly, we established a solid professional relationship with Colonel General Dmitrii Antonovich Volkogonov, then serving as the director of the Soviet Institute of Military History.

For those of us who had studied the Soviet military, Volkogonov was something of an enigma. He was a political officer who had risen through the ranks of the Far Eastern Military District to become Deputy Chief of the Soviet Army's Main Political Administration. He was also a hardy Siberian, the offspring of Ussuri Cossacks, who had lost his parents in the purges of the 1930s. Stalin's legacy had left a deep impression on Volkogonov; over the years he had evidently used his position to gather materials for a revisionist biography of the dictator, the appearance of which nearly coincided with the disintegration of the Soviet Union. Later, Volkogonov was sometimes denounced as a "military reformer," although he generally remained aloof from the reform fray, preferring to devote his energies to writing and advising the Yeltsin government. His biography of Stalin and subsequent works on Lenin and Trotsky won him few friends at home or abroad. In post-Soviet Russia, military officers loyal to the old regime labeled him a turncoat. In the West, he was viewed with suspicion and disbelief; some questioned the nature and motivation of his transformation, while others doubted the value of his history. How could the same man who had once written vituperative attacks on the West now emerge as a leading critic of the regime which he had once so zealously served? Worse for Russian academicians, Volkogonov aspired to the twin titles of doctor of history and philosophy. More insidiously, for anyone who felt nostalgia for the Soviet past, Volkogonov's scrutiny of Stalin and the nature of the Soviet victory in the Great Patriotic War challenged the very legitimacy of the Communist heirs. In the end, the political officer–cum–Chief of the Military History Institute understood all too well the political uses of history. And curiously, for a man in many ways unlike the traditional line officer, Volkogonov inspired almost fanatical loyalty among his subordinates.

In the spring of 1990, when General Volkogonov arrived in the United States for a reciprocal visit, there was every reason to hope for further development of contacts with his Military History Institute. His host was

Brigadier General Harold W. Nelson, the new U.S. Army Chief of Military History, who was also a Russian historian. After touring a foggy Antietam battlefield, we settled into lunch at a nearby roadhouse, at which point Volkogonov turned to Nelson and asked, "Why don't you send Menning over to my institute for a year as a visiting fellow?" Thus began a scholarly odyssey that in some ways continues to this day. I had to take leave of an office that was just beginning to experience the organizational pains of a dawning new era in Soviet/Russian–U.S. relations; to apply for a Secretary of the Army Fellowship to support a research leave in Moscow; and to begin making arrangements to take my family with me. Additional complications included the necessity to complete a book-length manuscript and to work out a research topic that would be acceptable to both the U.S. Army and the USSR Institute of Military History. Because the Army was concerned with the realities of alternately receding and expanding Soviet military force structure, the topic of my research became the history of Russian and Soviet troop mobilization.

When I arrived in Moscow in October 1990 for a ten-month stay, I began to relearn the art of improvising which had served me so well during two previous tenures as an IREX participant.[4] First, because Volkogonov's institute technically could not accept foreigners as visiting fellows, I was "seconded," to use a military term, to Georgii Arbatov's Institute of the USA and Canada. Next, I had to work the gray zone in the Moscow housing market to find an apartment suitable for my family. A hair-raising but successful visit to the district section of visas and registration (OViR) to explain how I was subletting an apartment on Leninskii Prospekt is a worthy subject in itself for a Chekhov-style short story. My two children's year-long tenure at School No. 17 is another. Then there was Margaret, my wife of some twenty-five years and a true convert to Russian culture, whose love for things Russian exceeded my own. The family secret was that even then she was suffering from incurable adult leukemia, a disease that would eventually take her life in 1998. Still, she insisted on going to Moscow, "for one last round," as she put it.

The next bit of improvisation occurred when I visited with then serving Colonel Robert Aleksandrovich Savushkin, who was to serve as my research supervisor while Volkogonov, my nominal director, was busy as a general officer and writer. Savushkin and I had met the previous spring in the United States, and we had hit it off at once. He used to say he liked me because my paternal grandmother's maiden name was Smorawski, which made me at least an honorary Slav. Never mind that she was from West Prussia and that her native language was German. Meanwhile, I was more than a little nonplussed when Savushkin confessed that he was a mystic who believed in flying saucers (takes all kinds to make up the Soviet military, I thought). Disconcertingly, when I explained my research topic, Savushkin's response was, "If I had known that was your topic, I never would have recommended your coming here." After mulling over the situation, he came up with the idea that there was enough open-source material for me to study "the theory of troop mobilization." In ensuing discussions it became clear that Savushkin possessed a unique command of the military history of the Soviet inter-war period. In fact, he was living testimony to Michael Howard's assertion that military history must be studied in depth, breadth, and context. Volkogonov had given me the opportunity to sit at the feet of a master.

With little hope of gaining access to Soviet-period military archives on a topic that we in the United States had naively thought was not overly sensitive, I commenced the limbo-like existence of earlier IREX fellows who waited interminably long times before receiving their permissions. This situation was not altogether bad; as a historian of the Imperial Russian Army, I had much background to digest about the Red Army before 1941. Days and weeks were spent bringing myself up to speed in the Lenin Library and in the library of the Military History Institute. I retraced decades-old footsteps to the pre-1917 military archive (TsGVIA) on No. 2 Baumann Street, where to my surprise I found the collection now completely open, along with free access to documentary indexes. I busily set to work on troop mobilization and war planning for the late imperial period. Meanwhile, anti-Soviet disturbances in Vilnius and Tbilisi came and went, as did the Gulf War. The Soviet regime teetered on the verge of extinction, and I had a ringside seat, not far from the section reserved for the military. Once-forbidden travel zones became open, and I took my family to the foothills of the Urals for a visit with old friends in Izhevsk, a center of the Russian and Soviet arms industry. Back in Moscow, with M.T. Kalashnikov's autograph safely tucked away, I kept mining available research materials, all the while wondering how I would explain research results based on imperial Russian realities and only Soviet theories to my U.S. commanding general.

Then, a few rays broke through the overcast. Some came from materials that General Volkogonov shared as a by-product of the Stalin biography. Added light came as a by-product of advice from the American publisher Kent Lee, who encouraged me to seek additional patronage. Consequently, I paid a late-winter visit to Major General Viktor Ivanovich Filatov, then editor of the *Military Historical Journal*. I explained my project, and a few phone calls later, I found myself working in the Library of the Soviet General Staff. Access expired within several weeks, but the mercurial Filatov suggested that I apply with General Volkogonov's support for access to the

Central State Archive of the Soviet Army (the old TsGASA, now RGVA, or Russian State Military Archive). In the spring of 1991, after several false starts, TsGASA finally opened its doors to me, along with Mary Habeck, Mark von Hagen, and other foreign scholars. Over the next several months I was able to complete enough research to justify my leave of absence and fellowship support. I will never forget those first few weeks in the archive; like a kid in the proverbial candy store I ordered many materials—on the Kronstadt uprising of 1921, the suppression of peasant disturbances that came to be called the Antonovshchina, the purges, and so on—just to run my hands over the documents and feel the maps. On another trip to Russia and Ukraine more than a year later, I felt the same emotions when I visited the naval base at Kronstadt and the submarine anchorage at Balaklava. These were places I had expected to visit only in my dreams!

The story did not end with the spring and summer of 1991. At the time, James F. Collins, who later became the U.S. Ambassador, was Deputy Chief of Mission at the American Embassy. A historian by training and a diplomat by profession, he understood the importance of military-to-military contacts and mutual confidence building, even (and especially) as the Soviet regime was collapsing. He allowed me to co-sponsor a dinner for Soviet officers and military historians in his apartment, and he arranged for General Volkogonov to appear in late spring with Robert Tucker at a special seminar on Stalin held at Spasso House. There, I recall meeting Marshal Akhromeev for the second and last time, the first having been in 1989 during the Moscow visit of U.S. military historians. I was impressed that two years after the fact Akhromeev remembered me by face and name, even though our original meeting had been brief and I had been only one of several participants in the exchange. Shortly after the Spasso seminar, General Volkogonov's dream of a new history of the Great Patriotic War collapsed. In May 1991, Defense Minister Dmitrii Iazov shut down the project, and its chief editor, Colonel Savushkin, abruptly resigned from military service in the wake of especially acrimonious criticisms from the Soviet High Command. My advisor was now no longer in service, and my sponsor was increasingly viewed as a pariah. Branded in my memory was a shouting match over the phone between Volkogonov and Iazov, which I had overheard during an office visit with General Volkogonov. When I took leave of Moscow and General Volkogonov in early July 1991, he voiced worries over the possibility of a military coup.

Of course, an anti-Gorbachev coup attempt actually occurred in August, with an aftershock of a distinctly different nature little more than two years later. By 1992, the failure of the first coup appeared to have opened the floodgates of archival access, with all manner of collections, some military, now open to public perusal. By 1993, researchers even gained limited but indirect access to the Central Archives of the Ministry of Defense (TsAMO) at Podolsk, not far from Moscow. The sudden availability of materials caused me to alter both my topic and manner of conducting archival research. Because troop mobilization had always been a slender reed on which to hang a larger military-historical study, I now changed focus to engage in a general study of Russian and Soviet preparation for war, including strategy, war planning, troop mobilization, and rail transit. Rather than camping in Moscow for a full term, I now appeared for a series of three-week forays, during which I duplicated as many unclassified materials as possible, before dropping additional requests for declassification and duplication. This situation persisted for about three years, after which a growing political conservatism, coupled with archival reorganization and resurrected obstacles to access, again imposed almost Soviet-like limitations on research, especially on materials related to 1941, the Great Patriotic War, and the Cold War. In retrospect, the imposition of these limitations corresponded with the political uncertainty that dogged the Yeltsin regime during the years after the abortive coup attempt of October 1993.

After having missed the attempted coup of 1991, I was in Moscow during the clash of October 1993 that occurred between Yeltsin and dissident Duma deputies, with some support from like-minded military officers. On October 3, during a pleasant fall Sunday afternoon, word of a possible coup leaked out by radio while I was attending a performance of the Moscow Circus. By the end of the day, both the White House (the parliamentary building of the Russian Federation) and the telecommunications complex at Ostankino were under siege. Once initial apprehensions faded and events unfolded favorably for the Yeltsin regime, I came away from the complex events of October 1993 with two powerful impressions. One had to do with the apathy with which Moscow residents greeted the possibility of a coup. I lay awake late that first night listening to "Maiak," the only radio station left on the air, and incidentally a reminder of my IREX days and nights with Moscow University's ubiquitous single-station receivers. Sometime around two o'clock in the morning of the next day a news bulletin announced that President Yeltsin had secured the support of the Defense Ministry, the General Staff, and the chiefs of all the Russian military districts. Loyal troop units were on their way from nearby cantonments to assist in securing the Kremlin and Ministry of Defense. Later, I would learn that General Volkogonov was instrumental in goading the military into action, and that the colonel who brought units to the center of Moscow from Teplyi stan' was the same officer who two years before had accompanied me on my first visit to RGVA. Meanwhile, in my room I heaved a sigh of relief, got up to turn off the radio and the light, and looked out the window at the neighboring apartment blocs. Lights burned in only a handful of the several hundred or so apartments visible from my vantage point; most Muscovites in my district had turned in, evidently not caring who might be in power when they awoke the next morning. The next day when I showed up at the archive everyone was at work, although the halls were abuzz with speculation over the consequences of the events of the previous twenty-four hours. In picking our way across town, all of us had instinctively calculated which places to avoid.

By Tuesday morning, the reality of the situation had begun to set in, with shadings of the surreal. I received an early-morning phone call from the U.S. Embassy with instructions as a civil servant to remain in my apartment until the local situation became more stable. Consequently, for the next several days I settled in to watch the drama over local television. It was carrying live broadcasts from the U.S. Cable News Network via a St. Petersburg station that continued to transmit, since it was independent of the now-defunct Moscow-based Ostankino communications complex. On Wednesday I watched in near-disbelief as tanks began firing on the White House to reduce the last pockets of resistance to the Yeltsin government. These events transpired not more than four or five miles from where I sat, yet one glance out my apartment window showed pedestrian and automobile traffic moving normally along Michurinskii Prospekt. Muscovites were out and about their daily business as if nothing out of the ordinary was occurring. I nearly had to rub my eyes to assure myself that what I was witnessing bore any relationship to the larger realities of life in post-Communist Russia. Or was I merely the victim of some Kafkaesque hallucination? Life in Moscow, sometimes verging on the fantastic, had suddenly assumed the character of the surreal. This was the second large impression that the coup attempt of October 1993 left with me.

Yet the gravity of the situation, or as the military colloquially labels it, "ground truth," had its own way of returning me to reality. I recall meeting several days later with then retired Colonel Savushkin, who after the fact asserted that if the coup had been successful, both he and Volkogonov would have been dead. Such were the risks that these two officers ran in the name of politics and history. Of course, by that time Volkogonov was already suffering from the cancer that would take his life in December 1995. I recall meeting with him for the last time in the spring of 1995, at his office in Staraia Ploshchad', where he received visitors, since he was no longer chief of the Military History Institute. We talked briefly about issues of security and military reform, then turned to military history. He asked me about my research, then mused over the work that remained. We agreed that restrictions were beginning to make work more difficult, but all in all we had enjoyed a good run. I think that in her own way my late wife would have agreed with him.

After the fact, there are those who would criticize General Volkogonov for personalizing and politicizing the process of archival access. To be sure, there were scholars, both Russian and non-Russian, who in some part owed admission to previously inaccessible archives to Volkogonov's generous intercession. To the General's credit, he unselfishly extended assistance to many scholars, Russian and foreign. At the same time, two facts suggest that it is possible to exaggerate the importance of his influence. First, the proverbial sword cut two ways: In more than one instance I discovered that invocation of my sponsor's name evoked a negative response. At one military archive, I was bluntly told never to mention his name again. Second, the reality was that General Volkogonov's coattails extended only so far. At yet another archive, I discovered what should have been obvious: that a personal call from General Volkogonov to the director was effective when it was reinforced by a formal letter of introduction from a reputable U.S. academic institution. Consequently, I would appear with two sets of formal documentation, one from my place of employment (the U.S. Army Command and General Staff College) and one from the University of Kansas, where I held adjunct professor status. Local mood and circumstance determined which set of credentials (or both) I would submit along with a request for admittance to an archive.

Whatever the circumstances of admission, it was clear for a brief period, running perhaps from the spring of 1991 to mid-1994, that a new and heady atmosphere of freedom reigned in the archives. With Soviet-style barriers to research melting away, academic researchers and archivists alike tested what at first seemed like the waters of unrestricted access. However, the situation soon came to resemble not a spring thaw with assurances that summer would follow, but an infantry advance through barbed wire after an uneven artillery preparation. Progress was wildly uneven. In some places, like the old TsGVIA, now renamed RGVIA, the disintegration of the Soviet Union had blasted the wire to oblivion. Unlike the situation during the earlier Soviet period, foreign scholars now encountered a collegial atmosphere and the possibility to engage in genuine professional consultations with archivists and fellow scholars alike. Still, I clearly recall at least one curious reminder of a Cold War past that died hard: a review in 1995 of pre–World War I intelligence estimates from the Vilnius Military District revealed that they had been fully declassified only in 1994!

The story was somewhat different at RGVA, where the tide of scholarly advance at first seemed unstoppable, then by degrees once again became partially tangled in the wire of renewed restrictions. At first, following the collapse of the Soviet regime, it appeared that the entire collection would be thrown open to systematic scholarly scrutiny. The limits of access seemed bounded only by the speed of the declassification effort and the archivists' own levels of access to sensitive materials. However, some jurisdictions, including the latter-day inheritors of the Soviet military tradition, soon moved to limit and discipline access to materials from the inter-war period, especially those related to military intelligence and war planning. These developments at first did not seem particularly disturbing to me, for I had little interest in military intelligence per se, and I had discovered early on that for some reason RGVA was not the main repository for the war plans for the inter-war period. By the middle of the decade, however, restrictions grew to encompass other supposedly sensitive materials related to military-industrial development, the purges, Soviet participation in the wars of the late 1930s, and developments leading up to the debacle of 1941. Along with other researchers, I soon found myself barred from materials to which we had previously gained admission. Again, the situation did not seem especially alarming, at least in a personal sense, because my wife's increasingly precarious health and eventual death from cancer precluded serious research between 1997 and the end of the decade. When once again I returned to RGVA in 2000, restrictions had grown more numerous and intense, with the result that many collections were simply off limits, while some archivists themselves abruptly left their positions, evidently for greener and less-troubled pastures. Still, the overall situation was not entirely bleak, for scholars retained access to perhaps the majority of RGVA's incredibly rich collection on the inter-war period. Meanwhile, the general declassification effort continues, albeit at a snail's pace, promising an incremental remedy for the larger problem over the longer term.

Within the larger context, one of my greatest regrets was that during 1992–95 we Western scholars failed to generate more support in the quest for access to the modern Russian military archives. In retrospect, these were the years holding the greatest likelihood for even more substantial gains, but for various reasons we were unable fully to exploit the initial success. Surely, part of the problem was that the pace of political change in Russia outstripped our abilities to adjust and to muster resources and time. And, surely, another part of the problem lay in the fact that we did not represent a constituency with measurable political clout.

Still another part of the problem stemmed from a mixture of apathy and sporadic financial support from Western institutions. The brief history of the Cold War Military Records project, jointly sponsored by U.S. Department of Defense and the U.S. Army Center of Military History, constituted a case in point. For a brief period between approximately 1993 and 1995, this project served as a means of mobilizing international support for preserving and making available the documentary legacy of the Cold War. With funding from the Legacy Resource Management Program, the intent was to encourage international cooperation and exchanges among military historians and archivists from the former adversarial East and West blocs. For this purpose,

Dr. Ronald Landa, a historian from the Office of the Secretary of Defense, and Dr. John Greenwood, a historian from the U.S. Army Center of Military History, enlisted my support in attempting to foster greater access to Cold War materials within the Russian military archives. With the assistance of the Historical Archive and Military Memorial Center of the Russian General Staff, we visited TsAMO and RGVA several times between 1993 and 1995. Although our proposals to engage in joint microfilming projects of Cold War materials largely fell on deaf ears, we were able in March 1994 to bring about substantial Russian participation in an international conference held in Washington, D.C. on Cold War military records and history. As a possible promise of things to come from the Russian military archives, I was given an entire file of newly declassified documents on the Berlin crisis of 1961 from the perspective of the Soviet General Staff. On the basis of this file, I was able to fashion a paper on that subject for the conference that went well beyond anything that we had expected might become available. When pressed on the limits of possible further cooperation, Russian officials advised us "to begin at the beginning," that is, with a joint program initiating systematic coverage of the Cold War in 1945, then proceeding forward by increments as the fiftieth anniversary dates for significant events unfolded. My eyes temporarily lit up as I envisioned a second major conference four years hence to examine the Berlin crisis of 1948 in half-century perspective.

The key word here is "temporarily," for it was not long before larger realities overtook the Cold War Military Records project. In truth, it would have been difficult under almost any circumstances to swim against the tide of retrenchment that was soon to engulf the Russian military archives. However, the difficult became impossible by 1996, when funding for the project dried up. Without consistent support, there was little hope of ever getting much beyond the talking and planning stages, especially with regard to the Russian archives. Still, the project did deliver more than an empty promise: since 1994 a number of East European military archives have made microfilm materials available to researchers under various arrangements with the U.S. Library of Congress. The IREX exchanges of the Soviet era had long since taught me that half a loaf was better than none.

In the end, a sense of partial success accords well with my perspective on research in the Russian military archives through much of the 1990s. We had made tremendous strides since the late Gorbachev era, when scholars were still barred from access to research materials on the war plans of imperial Russia. Still, in an odd twist on the old Leninist dictum, contemporary researchers often find themselves taking two steps forward and one back. Thus, while materials on the imperial period are now completely accessible, many once-accessible materials on the Soviet inter-war period have been reclassified and made inaccessible. During the spring of 2001, while conducting research with pre-1941 documents in the Naval Archive (RGVMF) in St. Petersburg, I even encountered a new category of materials under the rubric "limited access." Although no longer technically classified, these materials are closed to outside scholars. If 1941 can remain at least a partial enigma, what would it take to approach the conundrum of the Cold War?

As these remarks indicate, my research experience over the last decade in the Russian military archives has combined elements of the fortunate and unfortunate. Because the historian's stock-in-trade is perspective, how these elements weigh in the balance often depends upon an understanding of the larger context. In retrospect, the 1990s afforded a wealth of access and experience. While some access has been limited and while some possibilities never lived up to promise, the decade was always at least half-full. It presented new research vistas, provided fresh opportunities for scholarly dialogue with Russian colleagues, and offered a variety of ventures and adventures scarcely imaginable during the Soviet era. As for the negatives, even Tolstoy would probably have admitted that nothing in life is immutable, save perhaps death. It is entirely possible that one day in the not-too-distant future the archival flood gates will open, when the custodians of truth suddenly realize that withholding the past neither saved the old regime nor holds much promise for saving its successors.

Notes

The views expressed in this chapter are those of the author and should not be construed to represent those of the U.S. Department of the Army or the U.S. Department of Defense.

1. The following reminiscences extend coverage of my research in archives of the Soviet and early post-Soviet era treated in Bruce W. Menning, "Observations and Experiences of an American Scholar in the Russian Military Archives," in William W. Epley, ed., *International Cold War Military Records and History* (Washington, D.C., 1996), pp. 203–10.

2. See Bruce W. Menning, "A Decade Half-Full: Post–Cold War Studies in Russian and Soviet Military History," *Kritika: Explorations in Russian and Eurasian History* 2, no. 2 (Spring 2002): 341–62.

3. "Kto Vy, Doktor Menning?" *Krasnaia zvezda* 3 (May 3, 1989); the thinly veiled reference is to the title of a famous Soviet motion picture, "Who Are You, Doctor Sorge?" Richard Sorge was a Soviet spy in wartime Tokyo who transmitted reliable intelligence to Stalin about Japanese military intentions. Evidently the reporter incorrectly misconstrued my historian's interest in the Russian and Soviet military as a possible indication that I was something more than I appeared to be.

4. IREX is the acronym for the International Research and Exchanges Board, the successor to the old Inter-University Committee on Travel Grants (IUCTG), an umbrella organization for U.S. academic institutions sponsoring reciprocal scholarly research visits between the United States and nations of the Soviet bloc. I had been an IUCTG fellow in 1969–70, when I conducted dissertation research in Rostov-on-Don, and an IREX fellow in Moscow during the fall semester of 1974.

11

A Journey from St. Petersburg to Saratov

Donald J. Raleigh

I trace my interest in things Russian to my childhood on Chicago's working-class South Side, whose would-be burghers, many with East European backgrounds, had an active fear of communism. Although once designated as the worst public school system in any city with a population over a half-million, the Chicago public schools deserved top marks at the time for terrorizing their young and impressionable clientele with regular air-raid drills, owing to the "Soviet threat." Our physical education teacher at Mark Twain Elementary, unfortunately named Mrs. Dickman, supplemented the drills with various fitness regimens and nagging reminders that we should "eat bread, not candy," so that we might be as strong as the Russians. Then there was Roman Catholicism, and the hundreds of hours clocked-in on my knees praying for the conversion of the atheist Communists (at least this appears to have had some effect). In short, born in 1949, I grew up in "Dr. Strangelove's America." The perceived Soviet threat was my generation's AIDS, drugs, and school shootings wrapped into one. The only antidote to the prevailing culture of fear was my maternal grandmother's non-ideological and selective admiration for the Soviet Union's success at educating its population and sending everyone to work. Rumor had it that her husband, my grandfather, had been called Joe the Bolshevik, but to this day I cannot get a straight answer from anyone regarding how he acquired this appellation.

As part of the first graduating class at Chicago's new John F. Kennedy High School, I benefited from studying history with Michael Pagliaro, an in-your-face, inspiring, hands-on teacher, to whom I dedicated my first book. During my junior year he dared to collect the pedestrian civics textbook the Board of Education had mandated that we use, because he realized it would not challenge us. Instead we conspired to spend a semester reading and discussing current issues of *Time* magazine, and the other semester learning some Russian history, which he happened to be studying at night school. I also owe a good deal to Bernard Gaywell, who encouraged me to write, and to stunning Shirley Gorski, about whom all of us teenage boys fantasized;

her inability to teach Spanish killed any interest that I might otherwise have developed in that subject. Annoyed that I had dropped the fourth-year language class, she demanded an explanation. Here's where Pagliaro's minicourse in Russian history came in handy. After I blandly assured her that I had decided to study Russian history in college, Miss Gorski proceeded to announce my indiscretion to the entire school. Honor dictated that I at least give Russian a try.

I did, at Knox College, in Galesburg, Illinois, and I was hooked. Attending Knox between 1967 and 1971 (that is, *after* accused FBI spy Robert Hanssen had graduated), I majored in Russian Area Studies, which enabled me to take every course on Russia and the Soviet Union that the college had to offer. A marvelously engaging and idiosyncratic Serb named Momcilo Rosic taught me Russian and Russian literature. I dedicated a book to him, too. A stern and demanding Lydia Voskresenskaya straightened out our accents and insisted we love Tolstoy. In addition to language and literature, I studied Russian history, Soviet foreign policy, and Marxist economic systems; took an independent studies course on Lenin; and wrote an honor's thesis on the Soviet military. During the last semester of my senior year, I won a coveted slot on the Council for International Educational Exchange's (CIEE's) new semester-long program at Leningrad State University (LGU), which at the time was the only way for college students to gain in-country experience.

The U.S. government took sending undergraduates to LGU for a semester seriously. CIEE held our orientation at the American Embassy in Paris, where the twenty-nine of us were tested, urged to appreciate the horrific ordeal Leningraders had experienced during World War II, and informed that our Soviet teachers and those who lived in the dormitory with us could not be trusted. Segregating us by gender, our instructors warned us men that the KGB would set traps and ensnare us when we let down our sexual guard or succumbed to the rubles offered by persuasive black marketeers. As could be expected, the orientation program failed to prepare us for Soviet realities, although in all fairness, I'm not sure what might have done so.

The physical hardships of living five to a room for four months, mostly without hot water, and with a monotonous, vitamin-deficient diet, proved easier to handle than the emotional strain that we were under. The program director made one student return home after she suffered a nervous breakdown. Authorities in Novgorod unexpectedly sent us visitors back to Leningrad under mysterious circumstances and without our group leader, who, we later found out, had been drugged by the KGB and found in a compromising situation. Hospitalized for eleven days with a bout of giardiasis, I wasted away to nothing as Soviet doctors insisted that the American government had sent me to the Soviet Union sick so that I might obtain free medical treatment. Despite all, my fascination with Russian culture and history only deepened. I liked the people, found them pleasingly philosophical, and realized how much more I had to learn about the country, whose realities as I experienced them often clashed with what I had read and been taught about the Soviet Union.

That fall, 1971, I enrolled in the Ph.D. program in Russian history at Indiana University, where I studied Russian history with Alexander Rabinowitch, John M. (Jack) Thompson, and Robert F. Byrnes, and East European history with Barbara and Charles Jelavich. Indiana turned out to be a good match for my interests, and Alex proved to be the ideal mentor. My long-term research interests were determined in a year-long seminar that Alex offered during my second year in the program. Attracted to social and labor history, I at first considered writing a dissertation on the Putilov factory workers, but my own working-class background ultimately worked against this. For one thing, I had had enough of workers. For another, I remained leery of what I considered the idealization of workers on the part of historians who seemed to exaggerate workers' "consciousness." Although I did not feel comfortable expressing these views at the time, I knew I needed to come up with a different topic. By then I was aware of the impact that local history studies had in forcing reconsiderations of the histories of the United States, France, England, and elsewhere. Moreover, I had devoured Ronald G. Suny's pioneering study of the revolution in Baku when it appeared the year before. With Alex's encouragement, I wrote Suny to see what he thought about my doing a local study of the revolution in the Russian heartland. Ron shot off an immediate reply, which encouraged me to pursue the topic, but warned me to select a locale on which I could complete a dissertation in the event I did not win an International and Research Exchanges Board (IREX) grant or obtain a Soviet visa.

I understood the soundness of Ron Suny's advice, but my sleuthing soon convinced me that (1) abundant sources existed for writing the history of the revolution in most Russian locales; (2) few of these sources were found to be outside the Soviet Union; and (3) I therefore needed to play Russian roulette with my career and hope to be offered an IREX fellowship and to secure a Soviet visa. Presuming that a study of the revolution in a provincial capital within the Central Industrial Region, or black-earth zone, would illuminate the events on which our understanding of the revolution was then based, I specifically sought out an administrative, trade, and cultural center that had some, but limited, industrial development. Such a city was more representative of provincial Russia than a major factory town with a sizable working class. All roads led to Saratov, which struck me as an ideal choice on several counts. In its economic relationships, it had the general characteristics I was seeking. For a variety of objective and fortuitous reasons, sources on Saratov were more plentiful and diverse than those available for most other towns (and there were enough sources available in the United States to enable me to write a seminar paper). Furthermore, the peasant problem loomed so large in Saratov Province that its capital city became one of the most important centers of Russian populism and of the Socialist Revolutionary Party. Finally, because Saratov housed a large army garrison, the town's social makeup allowed for an examination of those concerns that affected soldiers as well as workers, peasants, and members of the middle strata.

Although subsequent sleuthing substantiated my selecting Saratov on intellectual grounds, I did not know that it was a "closed" city. No one did, except Chuck Gribble, from whom I studied Bulgarian at Indiana. But the marvelous thing about youthful optimism is that it sometimes encourages us to persevere in an endeavor that we otherwise might not entertain seriously. Little did I realize that I was embarking upon what would end up as a fifteen-year battle to visit Saratov. At the time—the 1974–75 academic year—I could not realistically expect archival access and at least benefited from the centralized nature of the Soviet system: copies of Saratov newspapers from 1917 as well as rare published materials, my primary sources, were available in Moscow and Leningrad. In researching the dissertation, I was struck by the vibrancy of local public life in Saratov, both before and during 1917, for it complicated my thinking about the character of the centralized Russian state. I could not help but wonder whether local studies of the Soviet period would similarly call into question popular (totalitarian) paradigms of the Soviet experience. I wondered, too, about life in contemporary Saratov. When my attempts to visit Saratov ended in failure, I contacted the chair of the History Department at Saratov University, G.A. Gerasimenko, whose research also focused on 1917. Gerasimenko traveled to Moscow to meet me and we maintained what I thought was a friendly as well as a professional relationship. Only in 1986, by which time he had relocated to Moscow, did it become clear that his involvement with me had been exclusively official.

A spate of exciting new studies on the Russian Revolution sustained me during the writing of the dissertation, which otherwise proved to be a lonely task, in part because my fellow graduate students at Indiana who had also embarked upon the research of local history topics left the profession, and not surprisingly, for there were no jobs to be had. At the time, local history remained at a formative stage in the field of Russian studies. This was true largely because the closed nature of Soviet society had rendered the country's heartland invisible. But there was more to it than that. Publication in 1958 by Harvard University Press of political scientist Merle Fainsod's study of Soviet rule[1] based on the Smolensk Archive, which was captured by the German armies in 1941 and later fell into American hands, inaugurated serious study of Soviet local history in the United States. The appearance of Fainsod's study, however, may have actually discouraged further explorations of this sort, since his book cast Smolensk as a "typical" Soviet city and claimed to have made exhaustive use of the archive, the only one of its kind available in the West. Moreover, totalitarianism, the dominant intellectual paradigm in postwar Western scholarship on the Soviet Union before the 1970s, may also have discouraged study of the Soviet periphery since it placed so much emphasis on Moscow's ability to discipline and manipulate the population. In this regard, Western views of a monochromatic Soviet political and social landscape ironically had an uneasy correspondence with Soviet narratives of the country's history, which were equally wooden and one-dimensional, albeit for different reasons.

The totalitarian paradigm came under fire in the 1970s, but I nonetheless encountered some subtle and even obvious resistance to the practice of local history. I found it disconcerting to learn that a mentor of graduate students at Columbia advised his charges not to take up local topics. Others insisted that to justify my work, I needed to show the "typicality" or "representativeness" of Saratov, but they could not provide me with the tools to do so. This was before I had read Clifford Geertz and others, and before I understood that such efforts were misguided. What I had trouble articulating back then was the point that while the particular Saratov events about which I wrote were certainly unique, they had condensed within them more general experiences that are larger than the local. As I wrote at the time, "In a sense, Saratov was Russia." What I meant was that Saratov could have been just about anywhere in Russia, for, as Allan Pred observed, "it is through their intersection with the locally peculiar, the locally sedimented and contingent, the locally configured context, that more global structuring processes are given their forms and become perpetuated or transformed."[2] In other words, a local focus lends concreteness to interrelationships that cannot always be ascertained on a larger scale, and can be an invaluable tool in helping to define issues on the national agenda. In fact, local studies actually help create and recreate the center because the relationship between center and periphery is symbiotic and dialectical. This is an important corrective that needed and still needs greater recognition within the Russian field, which remains Moscow-centric. Moreover, at a practical level, many topics cannot be addressed adequately on a national scale, precisely because the necessary local studies have not been done, and/or because of the difficulties in digesting the voluminous archival material now available on topics with a national scope. For these reasons, local studies continue to be essential for the study of Soviet history.

But I'm jumping ahead. Saratov remained closed, and I faced the prospect of searching for a job outside the field. The *American Historical Review* had moved to Bloomington in 1976, and I found employment as an editorial assistant for the journal. Otto Pflanze kindly offered to keep me on board for as long as necessary; however, in mid-1977, with half a dissertation written, I accepted a position at the Council for International Exchange of Scholars (CIES) as the first full-time program officer responsible for the Fulbright exchange of lecturers with the Soviet Union. During my eighteen months in Washington, I traveled frequently to the Soviet Union, where I made invaluable contacts with historians and other scholars in Moscow and beyond. I published my first book review while at the CIES, after which I was invited to serve as guest editor of a special issue of *Soviet Studies in History*, a quarterly journal of translations. My work on the *American Historical Review* had paid off; following the appearance of the issue, the publisher invited me to assume the editorship of the journal. I also managed to complete the dissertation, which I defended in October 1978, just weeks before I began my appointment as assistant professor of Slavic history at the University of Hawaii, a position I accepted without having visited the fiftieth state.

My wife Karen and I enjoyed working, living, and eating in Honolulu, where Peking duck is considered fast-food fare. Moreover, I found ways to return to the Soviet Union each year, sometimes with student groups. These latter trips tested my language skills: during the first, a coed was raped in Georgia; during another, I underwent an emergency appendectomy in Leningrad. Saratov, however, remained beyond my reach, and I had to make a virtue of remoteness from my subject-area, completing my book without the benefit of archival sources or of seeing the locale of my investigation. I finished the monograph, translated E.N. Burdzhalov's study of the February Revolution in Petrograd,[3] and began editing the diary of a Russian-born American named A.V. Babine, who spent the 1917–22 period in Saratov. I also launched work on a study of the Russian Civil War in Saratov Province. As a result of détente and expanding bilateral exchanges between the American and Soviet governments, by the 1980s researchers began to obtain limited access to certain archival collections. Working in the Central State Archive of the October Revolution and the Building of Socialism (TsGAOR, today GARF) in 1986, I experienced not only great personal satisfaction but also a strange sensation of doing something risqué and forbidden, for even though I had been trained as an archival historian in a Rankean tradition, I had never before set foot in a Soviet archive. Moreover, the terms of admission imposed from above also put me on edge. For one thing, I *was shown*—and then only after frustrating delays—a mere twenty archival files (*dela*). I could not consult archival inventories (*opisi*) or catalogues, discuss my research with archivists willing to help, or inspect files in the same building in which our Soviet colleagues conducted their research. Although it did not take long for me to determine that not every archival document should have been preserved, I nonetheless brooded over the documents that I assumed existed but to which I had no access.

Since the materials in TsGAOR dealt exclusively with Saratov Province in 1918, and my chances of visiting Saratov remained remote, I decided to limit my study to the spread and consolidation of Soviet power, ending sometime in 1919, just when the archival materials I had consulted fell silent. But during a two-month research trip to the Soviet Union in 1988, I came tantalizingly close to being allowed to travel to Saratov for three days. When this initiative fell through, and emboldened by the early stirrings of glasnost and perestroika, I declared war. I first took my case to *Moscow News*, a one-time rag now turned pro-reform. The capable young reporter who interviewed me took up my cause, publishing a sympathetic piece cast as a letter that I had purportedly written to the editor.[4] The editors accompanied my "letter" with commentary by Corresponding Member of the Academy of Sciences of the USSR, N.N. Bolkhovitinov, whom I had gotten to know and respect thanks to my involvement with the journal *Soviet Studies in History.* Comparing his experiences working in Soviet and American archives, Nikolai Nikolaevich painted a grim picture of conducting research in Soviet depositories. He went on to point out that "any visitor at any library in the United States is granted unrestricted access to any register, catalogue, and the like."

Following publication of the *Moscow News* story, which coincided with my family's move to Chapel Hill so that I could begin my appointment at the University of North Carolina, I launched a letter-writing campaign. Insisting that they back my request to work in Saratov repositories, I fired off missives to the chair of the History Department at Saratov University, to those colleagues whom I could identify, and to several of the so-called informal organizations (*neformaly*) that had cropped up at the time. The president of one of them, the local studies society, who many years earlier had met an American when both were working in Africa, invited himself to Chapel Hill after visiting his American friend in Ohio. Upon his return to Saratov, I became the first foreign, and corresponding, member of the society. An editor at the Volga Regional Publishing House initiated a correspondence with me regarding a Russian-language edition of my study of the Revolution of 1917 in Saratov.[5] The bombshell fell on April 5, 1990, when a local correspondent for the newspaper *Izvestiia*, Valentina Nikolaeva, published a brilliant article about my plight, "The Saratov Sufferings of Mr. Raleigh."[6] After learning of my predicament, she interviewed cavalier bureaucrats at the Academy of Sciences in Moscow (who had actually placed obstacles in my getting to

Saratov), the Saratov University rector, and local KGB boss. Blaming Moscow for my plight, Nikolaeva hit hard. The article's appearance caused a furor at the Academy's foreign office, forced IREX deputy director Wesley Fischer to rush to Moscow to make peace, and instilled new hope that I might actually make it to Saratov that summer.

An angry Academy of Sciences administration sought revenge when I arrived in Moscow. No one met me at the airport, no one had reserved a room in the Academy Hotel, and no one would tell me if I would receive permission to travel to Saratov. I set a date for my departure, maintained contact with historians in Saratov who supported my visit, and waited. A train ticket mysteriously appeared in my room on the ninth day for that evening's train. I caught it, despite the fact that I did not have a visa.

Dorothy Atkinson, then general secretary of the American Association for the Advancement of Slavic Studies (AAASS) invited me to share my experience in Saratov with readers of the association's *Newsletter*.[7] I wrote that I liked Saratov and its people both because of and despite the fact that Nikolaeva's *Izvestiia* article had added a certain moral tone to my presence and guaranteed a rare reception. There were television and radio appearances (some broadcast nationally) and newspaper articles; endless public lectures and presentations; and numerous informal talks. I met the mayor, deputy mayor, archbishop, university officials and colleagues, local studies enthusiasts (*kraevedy*), publishers, students, local entrepreneurs eager to make a deal, and plenty of Ivan Ivanoviches. Every evening I was the beneficiary of Russian hospitality, and paid the price in terms of physical and emotional exhaustion and a swollen liver.

Yet there is no denying that the trip rewarded me professionally. Members of the Historical Society welcomed me with open arms. The State Archive of Saratov Oblast (GASO) gave me everything I requested, and because duplicating facilities were lacking, four university students spent the month copying documents for me. The university library microfilmed rare books found only in the archive. The Volga Regional Publishing House finalized an agreement to translate and publish my *Revolution on the Volga*. Colleagues invited me to take part in a variety of collaborative projects. People hungry for contact greeted me with enthusiasm everywhere.

The trip also broadened my perspective on the course of perestroika and glasnost, confirming my view that there was a bias in our academic writing about and media coverage of the Soviet Union, which sought to understand the vast country from the perspective of Moscow, Leningrad, and a handful of other towns. Entrenched notions about provincial Russia undoubtedly had to do with many factors: the extreme centralization of political power and decision making in that country, both before and after 1917; the substantial material, cultural, and professional advantages to living in the capitals; and the lamentable fact that, thanks to Soviet power, many cities had become more provincial than they had been before the revolution. Something else needs to be addressed: much less tangible but perhaps as crucial in explaining attitudes toward provincial Russia were popular beliefs about life outside the center. And these were much more pernicious than what New Yorkers think about Omaha. It was not uncommon for those from the capitals to regard "provincials" with an element of smugness and condescension, which, at its worst, easily dissolved into contempt and scorn. One was considered to be provincial not because of the parochial or unsophisticated views one might hold, but because of where one happened to reside. And this had been a political issue in the Soviet Union, since the authorities controlled population movement by issuing living permits (*propiski*).

Permission to visit and work in Saratov repositories came at a critical moment in my research: I had actually begun to draft my book when I finally reached the banks of the Volga. The access I received to GASO not only forced me to rethink my project but, in effect, to start it over, in part because local sources made it possible to document the entire course of the Civil War and to address questions that heretofore had remained elusive. I now would seek to show how Russian political culture (which I define as the subjective aspects of social life that distinguish one society from another), Bolshevik practices, and the circumstances of civil war molded diverse elements of society into an organic experiential whole. Obviously, I would need to go back to Saratov to complete my research, and it remained a closed city. The way out of my dilemma came in the form of a proposal from the self-selected translator of my book, O.A. Lomako, to return to Saratov the next year as the houseguest of an acquaintance of his so that I might dig more deeply in the archives and edit the translation of my book. Although I was rightly suspicious about accepting an invitation from someone I did not know, I was a decade younger and more foolish than I am now. Moreover, my work in GASO had whetted my appetite.

The invitation arrived from someone recruited by the sinister Lomako, ostensibly named Viktor Ivanovich Zhirov, who turned out to be a "former" employee of the KGB. Lomako, too, I soon learned, also had ties with the KGB. I can only speculate as to why he and his associates took it upon themselves to help me to return to Saratov. For one thing, Lomako certainly harbored all sorts of zany ideas about developing business contacts with the state of North Carolina and saw me as someone who might facilitate his plans. For another, the KGB had been suspicious of my efforts to visit and work in Saratov—after all, this was their job. When I sent a copy of my book to Saratov in 1986, the local KGB insisted that only "approved" individuals could obtain living permits to reside in Hawaii and that I "had to be a spy." The political police also enlisted a graduate student to translate a chapter of the book and to write an assessment of it. His mentor at the university, who did not know English, dictated to the graduate student what to say in the evaluation. This same historian, the son of a KGB colonel, later introduced himself during my first visit to Saratov as my "ideological enemy," a role that I soon gladly filled. Indeed, I received a chilly welcome from several "Party" historians in 1990. Moreover, after my departure, KGB officials examined the archival files that I had requested and interviewed many people with whom I had been in contact. The security police even asked one historian whether I could understand how the KGB operated at the time by studying its predecessor's activities during the Civil War! All in all, I suspect that the KGB understood that Saratov would soon open to the outside world and that it sought to monitor what it believed might be a transition fraught with all sorts of negative consequences.

In any event, Zhirov and my "translator" met me in Moscow and accompanied me back to Saratov, where I was put up in an apartment across from a police station. The next morning Viktor Ivanovich dropped by to pick up my documents so that he might register me with the police. I switched on the radio as I poured water through my Melita coffee filter. The announcer's voice was cheerless, calm, soothing. Gorbachev was in "ill health." The measures "would be in force for only six months." Not meant as a rejection of reform, they were "necessary to save the economy from complete collapse." It was 9:00 A.M., Saratov time, Monday, August 19, 1991. I listened nervously to Resolution No. 1 of the cumbersomely named State Committee for the State of Emergency, harboring no doubts about what I had just heard. My thoughts then focused on my own predicament: I was a lone foreigner in Saratov; I was living in what I suspected was a KGB flat; I had no documents; and conservative elements had made a bid to set back the clock of history.

Lack of any reliable information from the outside, other than official broadcasts aired that morning and repeated over and over again, colored the first day of the Soviet coup in Saratov, creating an anxious atmosphere and guaranteeing the spread of rumors and relentless speculation. Not until evening, when anyone with a television set could, and most likely did, view the nationally broadcast press conference with the coup leaders, were Saratovites able to piece together what was going on elsewhere. Marking one of the great moments in the history of the Soviet media, the press conference discredited the putschists, made clear that they had seized not power, but merely its illusion, and suggested that Soviet society had also been closed to those who constituted it. How else could we account for the colossal ineptitude of

Russia's "Pinochets," as Soviet newspapers began calling Gennadii Yanaev and his accomplices? The next day the coup began to unfold locally. It did so spontaneously, shaped by the media and by news from the outside relayed over the telephone and teletype and fax machines. By week's end the experience had transformed people, who simply stopped being afraid.[8]

Except, perhaps, for me. With the collapse of the Communist Party, Victor Ivanovich and I had agreed to a parting of ways. He departed for the Baltic republics "to assist his comrades who needed to leave," while I mentally left politics to return to the archives. When the local reform-minded newspaper, *Saratov*, prepared a daring article about me entitled "I Was a Guest of the KGB," however, Victor Ivanovich came back to threaten me. Informants had tipped him off about the forthcoming article; during our heated encounter he unwittingly revealed that several of my close acquaintances, including my translator and editor, were in cahoots with him. Despite my reservations, insistent journalists persuaded me to allow the article to go to press on the morning of my departure. It seemed the right thing to do, because I had plenty to be angry about. It turned out that the translator of my book had enlisted the help of others, as incompetent as he, and they had managed to complete only a partial translation, which proved to be far worse than I ever could have imagined.

The episode has an ending, yet not an altogether happy one, at least for some who were involved. While I tried to figure out what to do with an unpublishable, incomplete translation, a university friend, Nina Ivanovna Deviataikina, arranged to have published a modest text based on my book,[9] which later was used in local colleges, as well as a collection of my essays, all of which were conscientiously translated by friends as a gift to me.[10] That same year I was awarded an honorary degree from Saratov University. I later found my own translators in Moscow and Saratov for my monograph, but by then the publishing house in Saratov had fallen on hard times and my editor's efforts to launch a new one ended in failure as he drank away the business's and his own resources. My university colleagues helped me identify a potential sponsor, a local businessman and politician, who ultimately agreed to put up funds to subsidize publication of my book in Saratov. By then, the political climate had changed and people advised against putting out a volume that had the word "revolution" in the title. As a result, my *Revolution on the Volga* appeared in Russian as *The Political Fate of a Russian Province: 1917 in Saratov*.[11] Unfortunately, I could not invite my sponsor to the reception that university friends organized when the translation came out, because he had died under mysterious circumstances which gave rise to nagging reports that he had been murdered. Rumor also had it that my one-time Saratov translator had been arrested for raping a minor. My would-be editor died in 2000 of alcohol poisoning.

The repercussions of the August coup had affected me directly, for the collapse of the Soviet system made Communist Party archives available to scholars, opened up closed cities such as Saratov, and allowed me to complete the research and writing of my book, *Experiencing Russia's Civil War: Politics, Society, and Revolutionary Culture in Saratov Province, 1917–1922.* I am determined that my next project will be less logistically demanding. After the 1991 coup attempt, I needed to travel to Saratov eight more times in order to exhaust files in GASO, to work through materials in the former Communist Party archive (TsDNISO), the Saratov Regional Studies (Kraevedcheskii) Museum, and the Saratov University Research Library. In addition, I benefited enormously from obtaining access to private holdings.[12] The ongoing opening and declassification of archival files throughout the decade also necessitated return trips to Moscow, where documents from the so-called Prague Archive, among others, underwent declassification. During the decade I likewise visited the branch of GASO in Balashov and worked in the Khvalynsk Regional Studies Museum. Exceeding my expectations, the vast holdings in Balashov unnerved me once I realized that I would have needed to add years of additional research to my project in order to study them systematically. The humbling experience convinced me not only that one could write a dissertation based on records stored in regional (*raionnye*) depositories, but that it was time to do so.

Documents from state archives cast valuable light on the Saratov soviet's independent political course during the Civil War, the mood of the population as perceived by the province's political police (*Gubcheka*) and as revealed through monitored correspondence, the use of force to implement the Party's ideologically fueled political and socioeconomic programs, crime, rivalries among local Bolshevik leaders, the wrenching consequences of the Party's economic policies, and the impact of civil war on Saratov as a community or set of social relations. Communist Party documents offer a multi-dimensional representation of the Party, its members, its organizations, and its affiliates, blemishes and all, as well as of the Bolsheviks' relations with their socialist rivals. For instance, access to Party archives enabled me to retrieve from the dustbin of history the so-called Revolutionary Communist Party, an off-shoot of the Left SRs, who remained in the ruling coalition with the Bolsheviks until late 1920 in Saratov and numerous other provinces and without whose support Saratov would have fallen to the Whites. The archives also allowed me to document a near-universal uprising against Soviet power in March 1921, the course of the horrific famine that seized the Volga in its grip until 1924, the Soviet government's relations with foreign relief agencies, and how workers and peasants developed a form of consciousness that found expression in resistance to and circumvention of many Bolshevik practices. Further, access to diaries found in the archives and held privately permitted me to consider the experiences of Saratov's other class, the much maligned, yet needed, bourgeoisie. Disclosing how human geographies become infused with politics and ideology, these diaries and memoirs record a cultural history that otherwise might have been forgotten by official historical memory.

The rich archival record compelled me to reconsider the Civil War's relationship to the subsequent course of Soviet history. Before researching this book I subscribed to the view that Stalinism marked a departure from Leninism and that the fledgling Soviet system entering the 1920s sustained less authoritarian alternatives to the path that Russian history ultimately took with the launching of Joseph Stalin's grandiose industrialization drive at the end of the 1920s. I am no longer so certain. To be sure, I distance myself from authors who pin the blame for this on ideology alone, and instead complicate our understanding of this crucial period in Soviet history by considering the interplay of ideology and many other factors during circumstances of sustained crisis and emergency in a country with an authoritarian political culture. Reaching this conclusion forced me to reassess my understanding of subsequent periods of Soviet history as well.

The right to use archives has affected other historians similarly. Indeed, as my own case makes clear, the opening of Russia brought about an archival revolution of sorts, making it possible for historians to visit and work in provincial centers heretofore off-limits to foreigners. The studies resulting from access to provincial Russian repositories have sparked new interest in local history, as a spate of international conferences on the subject during the past several years demonstrates. I take some satisfaction in observing and participating in this phenomenon. To be sure, the professional journey I took between my language-training experience in St. Petersburg in 1971 and my research trips to Saratov was a circuitous, extended, and often not particularly comfortable one, yet it was filled with serendipity, adventure, and endearing friendships, and ultimately took me to destinations that I had come to view as unattainable. Even though it is time for me to move on to new topics and venues, I will always remain attached to Saratov, whose opening can be seen as the metaphorical opening of the former Soviet Union and at least some of its secrets.

Notes

1. *Smolensk under Soviet Rule.* Cambridge: Cambridge University Press, 1958.

2. Allan R. Pred, *Making Histories and Constructing Human Geographies: The Local Transformation of Practice, Power Relations, and Consciousness.* Boulder: Westview Press, 1990, p. 15.

3. *Vtoraia russkaia revoliutsiia: Vosstanie v Petrograde* (Moscow, 1967), which I

published under the title *Russia's Second Revolution: The February 1917 Uprising in Petrograd*. Bloomington: Indiana University Press, 1987.

4. "The Trials and Tribulations of Professor Raleigh," *Moscow News*, no. 33, August 4, 1988.

5. *Revolution on the Volga: 1917 in Saratov.* Ithaca: Cornell University Press, 1986.

6. The title contains a play on words in Russian: Folk laments from the Volga region are known as *stradaniia*, which translates as sufferings. The word also has an obvious religious connotation.

7. My essay, which the AAASS entitled "The Triumph of Glasnost in Scholarship: Raleigh Reaches Saratov," appeared in the September 1990 (vol. 30, no. 4) issue of the publication.

8. I published a memoir of my experience during the coup, "A View from Saratov," in Victoria E. Bonnell, Ann Cooper, and Gregory Freidin, eds., *Russia at the Barricades: Eyewitness Accounts of the August 1991 Coup.* Armonk, NY: M.E. Sharpe, 1994, pp. 131–46. I also wrote an interpretive essay about the meaning of the coup in provincial Russia, "Beyond Moscow and St. Petersburg: Some Reflections on the August Revolution, Provincial Russia, and *Novostroika*," *South Atlantic Quarterly* 91, no. 3 (1992): 603–18. It was republished in Thomas Lahusen and Gene Kuperman, eds., *Late Soviet Culture: From Perestroika to Novostroika* (Durham and London, 1993), pp. 307–22, and in two different translated versions: "Vdali ot Moskvy i Sankt-Peterburga: razmyshleniia ob avgustovskoi revoliutsii, provintsial'noi Rossii i 'novostroike,'" *Zemstvo: Arkhiv provintsial'noi istorii Rossii* 1, no. 1 (1994): 74–89; and "Vdali ot Moskvy i Sankt-Peterburga: Otzvuki avgustovskoi (1991) revoliutsii. Rossiskaia provintsiia," pp. 60–74, in Donald J. Raleigh (D. Dzh. Reili), *Saratov ot avgusta 1914 do avgusta 1991: Rossiia glazami amerikantsa* (Saratov, 1994).

9. *Saratov i guberniia v 1917: Sobytiia, partii, liudi* (Saratov and Saratov Province in 1917: Events, Parties, People) (Saratov, 1994).

10. *Saratov ot avgusta 1914 do avgusta 1991: Rossiia glazami amerikantsa* (Saratov from August 1914 to August 1991: Russia Through the Eyes of an American) (Saratov, 1994).

11. *Politicheskie sud'by rossiiskoi gubernii: 1917 v Saratove* (Saratov, 1995).

12. A Saratovite, for instance, presented me with a thirteen-volume diary kept by a Saratov woman between 1914 and 1953.

12

Romancing the Sources

Nancy Shields Kollmann

When you work with sixteenth- and seventeenth-century documents, "adventure" isn't the first word you associate with research. *Sitzfleisch* might sooner come to mind, as well as "dogged determination" and picky, picky attention to detail. So ferreting out information from very old sources, however recondite, constitutes adventure, but at a rather slower pace, more like a romance, one might say. In that spirit I offer a tale of a scholarly career engaged in manuscripts and archives, a tale that reflects on methods I and my colleagues use to mine Muscovite-era documents and on changes in conditions of research over the years of transformation in Russia.

Let me start by sketching out the processes by which this Russian historian has worked from the sources on up to shape the directions of her work. My research has focused consistently on the intersection of political power and social structure. My first major project aimed at figuring out how the boyars—the tsar's counselors and the highest military/political officials in Russia from the fifteenth through the seventeenth centuries—received their rank. I suspected that kinship and marriage ties had as much to do with it as service and merit-based promotions. So I've spent a fair amount of time combing chronicles and documentary sources to construct life histories of boyars and studying their genealogies. After that project I broadened the focus to look at boyar families' practice of honor (*mestnichestvo*) and found myself drawn into studying the concept of honor as it applied to all social ranks. I read a great number of "dishonor" (*beschest'e*) cases, litigations by which people sought redress in court from verbal insult. There I argued that the existence of the right to litigate over personal and family honor in Muscovy challenges us to revise what we mean by "autocracy." And from that project I've moved on to investigate how the autocratic state functioned at the crucible of its social power, that is, in the court system. In particular I'm looking at the criminal law, and reading lots of juicy murder and assault cases in the process.[1]

In all this research, I've found that the sources say more than one would think, if one listens for their voice. To do the early modern history of Russia, or any premodern society, one has to develop a receptivity to the sources, because we have relatively few of them (although of course there are some categories in which we have ample surviving documents—petitions and litigations by service people in the seventeenth and eighteenth centuries, for example). In some genres we have none at all. Any early modernist can rip off a litany of sources Muscovy did not produce at all, or only in a few idiosyncratic works, or not until quite late in the seventeenth century: diaries and memoirs, personal correspondence, political philosophy, history writing of the non-chronicle genre, secular literature and poetry, newspapers and broadsheets, demographic records, family archives, Biblical exegesis, business archives, income tax rolls, and so on. Such a source basis means that the situation is more akin to medieval than to early modern European historical research. What I've found in research on social and political history is that the sources can yield rich data, but it requires disengaging from historiographical and modern-day preconceptions and scrutinizing the sources with a fine-tooth comb. So research in our field is in a way a true "medieval" quest.

In my work on kinship and politics in the 1970s, for example, I was exploring the significance of kinship in politics. In so doing, I was bucking the trend of the scholarship. Prosopographical study of the Muscovite elite was a growing field—A.A. Zimin, V.B. Kobrin, Gustave Alef, and Ann Kleimola, among others, were compiling lists of source references to all boyars and service princes; Robert Crummey was at work on seventeenth-century boyars. But these scholars, while recognizing the importance of marriage and kinship ties, gave the emphasis to service careers. I wanted to tilt the scales the other way, to look at kinship as structuring the boyars' world. I was put on to this approach by the publication of M.E. Bychkova's study of genealogical books (*rodoslovnye knigi*) as sources.[2] She showed that from the 1530s on, the court was compiling genealogies of the leading military servitor families, side by side with military muster rolls (*razriadnye knigi*). Yet until her book appeared, military musters had garnered the lion's share of attention. Armed with Bychkova's extensive references to published and archival genealogical books, I decided to explore why genealogical books were so important at court. So I started by examining the earliest genealogies, with interesting results that I'll discuss below.

Other fascinating perspectives on the relationship of kinship to power in Muscovy emerged as I tried to look at sources on their own terms. For example, in the 1530s the Muscovite court was visited by Tatar dignitaries, princes, and princesses, who were entertained by the grand prince and grand princesses and their suites of boyars and "boyars' wives." The lists of the boyars' wives who attended such banquets had been published in the nineteenth century but were never much appreciated or studied. Yet they are tremendous sources. The women's identities were recorded with bureau-cratic precision, indicating that contemporaries found attendance at such events important and providing us with a snapshot of the pecking order of their husbands at court. These sources also provide new data about mar-riage alliances, since some of the women were identified by their father's as well as their husband's names. Similarly rich and underappreciated are the rosters compiled in the early sixteenth century of marriage ceremonies for the grand-princely family. Royal weddings were tightly orchestrated dramas in which the tsar's closest kin and associates were assigned roles, from best man to matchmaker to bearers of candles and cakes in the wed-ding procession. Rather like twentieth-century Kremlinology, we can pos-tulate relative power among the boyars by the roles they played. With these sources I found it helpful to supplement the published data with the further information provided in archival versions. Most of these are housed in the Manuscript Collection of the Library of the Academy of Sciences (BAN) in St. Petersburg (then Leningrad), a venerable building in the heart of the campus of what was then called Leningrad State University; it was rela-tively easy to receive permission to work in the BAN manuscript division in the 1970s, and research conditions were good. These wedding rosters indicate that marriage was at the heart of faction building in Muscovy, and give us a sort of "thick description" of court politics. Russell Martin has rectified their relative neglect in his recent dissertation.[3]

Sources such as these, once discounted because they had to do with seem-ingly non-political events such as women's banquets, weddings and family ties, can reveal a great deal if one sees the document from the perspective of its time. It can also work the other way around: sometimes what sources say in passing can yield gems. Take, for example, Giles Fletcher's account of the court in late sixteenth-century Muscovy, one of the most readily available sources about Muscovy to Western audiences in Fletcher's time to this day. Fletcher had two principal targets of complaint about Muscovy, its benighted religion and its despotic political system, and it is his image of Muscovy as the antithesis of a free, orderly, pluralistic society that has taken hold in the Western mind. But Fletcher was a good observer and he said more than he realized. Noting that Muscovy did not have a parliament, for example, he described what it did have, and un-self-consciously he chronicled a political system where kinship was a key structuring principle. He didn't miss the point that the leading boyar at court was the tsar's in-law: "the emperor . . . referreth all such matters pertaining to the state wholly to the ordering of his wife's brother, the Lord Boris Fedorovich Godunov." Nor that patronage fanned out along kinship lines: "One other there is of the house of Glinskii that dispendeth in land and pension about 40,000 rubles yearly, which he is suffered to enjoy because he hath married Boris his wife's sister." Fletcher also astutely observed that political enemies were disposed of by tonsuring them or refusing clans permission to marry: "many of their heirs are kept unmarried perforce that the stock may die with them. . . . Some are put into abbeys and shire themselves friars by pretense of a vow to be made voluntary and of their own accord, but indeed forced unto it."[4] Denial of marriage and forcible tonsure were expedient strategies to end a clan's reproductive capacity. Fletcher intended to tell us about Muscovy's institutional weaknesses; he ended up revealing how affinitive principles made court politics strong. Searching for evidence in medieval sources, then, requires reading against the grain.

I encountered a good example of that when I was trying to piece together boyar factions during the struggles of Ivan IV's minority (1530s–40s). Published chronicle sources make it clear that the two warring factions were the Belskiis and Shuiskiis. The broader composition of the Belskii faction is easy to establish by plotting out their marriage alliances, which made several of the boyars at a given moment Belskii in-laws.[5] I found evidence of those marriage alliances in published sources—genealogical books, scattered references in deeds, wills, memorial books, and chronicles—and in archival sources such as marriage rosters. But the composition of the Shuiskii faction was less evident; chronicles and other sources did not reveal so much. So when I was doing a close reading of sixteenth-century chronicles, I found a few scraps of evidence that were particularly exciting. They had to do with prisons. One chronicle related that when Prince Ivan Fedorovich Belskii was arrested in October, he was imprisoned in the Mstislavskii clan's Kremlin home. Released in 1540, he was arrested again in 1542 and imprisoned in the home of Ivan Ivanovich Tretiakov; other associates of the Belskiis were imprisoned in the home of Tretiakov's cousin, Ivan-Foma Petrovich Golovin. Was this information on jailers significant?

Matching it with marriage alliances suggested close political ties. The Mstislavskiis, for example, who had emigrated to Russia from the Grand Duchy of Lithuania in the early sixteenth century, made a spectacular match around 1529, when Prince Fedor Mikhailovich Mstislavskii married a direct cousin of Ivan IV, Anastasiia. In June 1538, a few months before Belskii's arrest, the leading Shuiskii, Prince Vasilii Vasil'evich, married Anastasiia's sister. So when the Mstislavskiis imprisoned Prince Belskii in their home, they were in-laws of the Shuiskiis. Similarly, the Tret'iakov-Golovin clan, who lent their homes as dungeons in 1542, had close kinship ties with the Shuiskiis: Ivan Ivanovich Tretiakov's sister was married to Prince Vasilii Vasilevich Shuiskii's brother, Dmitrii; Ivan Petrovich

Golovin's sister married into a collateral Shuiskii line, and her daughter in 1547 married the son of Prince Fedor Mstislavskii and Anastasiia, mentioned above. This brings the Shuiskii kinship connections full circle. It would be great to have a diary or eyewitness informant for these political machinations, but lacking that, combing and combining sources like this sketches out a very tight-knit family faction.[6]

A final example gets to the heart of the methods early modern Russian historians use in their quests for data, and raises the issue of the conditions of work in Soviet archives under the old system. Historians of the early period often depend upon the arcane skills of "source study" (*istochnikovedenie*)— paleography, watermark analysis, de visu examination of manuscripts—to reveal qualitative information. Such methodology provided the key when I was trying to establish the origins of the earliest collection of boyar clan genealogies, a set of articles appended to a late fifteenth-century chronicle. I wondered who compiled this group of princely and boyar clan rosters. I never found a name, but a context emerged. From the evidence of the text itself, it is clear that the clan rosters were compiled in the 1490s and probably before 1502, because one individual mentioned, Ivan III's grandson Dmitrii, was referred to as "grand prince," a status he lost in disgrace in 1502. No one particular clan stands out in the rosters with a more elaborate genealogy, so it is hard to say which family benefited the most from the compilation of these essays. Formal analysis of the manuscript did, however, yield an interesting clue to where the items were written, but it took a little legwork and moxie to find out.

Here's the story. The collection is found in a book together with the Typography chronicle.[7] The binding is seventeenth-century, but the twenty folios on which the genealogical articles were written are marked by their paper, handwriting, and illuminations as separate from the chronicle, simply bound together at a later date. Scholars had studied the chronicle manuscript (dating it to the 1520s or later), but had ignored the genealogical section. So I sought permission to look at the manuscript in the State Historical Museum. This requires a digression. This occurred in 1976–77, when I was a graduate student (*stazher*) on the official exchange of scholars between the U.S. Department of State and the Soviet Ministry of Higher and Specialized Education, administered by the International Research and Exchanges Board. (IREX). It was the only way American scholars could gain access to archives for scholarly research in those days. We scholars from the "capitalist countries" (*kapstrany*) labored under significant handicaps. We were required to submit in advance our theme (*tema*) and our identified archival sources; archives could then use these items to limit the scope of our research. Archives could, and often did, refuse to admit us or deny us access to catalogues and finding aids.

By the terms of the exchange we were limited to 200 shots of microfilm of archival documents. We lived on separate floors with other *kapstran* scholars at Moscow State University; like other Western foreigners we had to arrange visas for travel, which we did through the "Foreigner's Section" (*Inostrannyi otdel*) at the university (my husband can still recall a favorite IREXer's anthem about "Inna of Inotdel," set to the tune of "Alice's Restaurant"). We generally felt we enjoyed less ready access to archives, were stymied in research more often than students from the *sotsstrany* (socialist client states of the USSR), and generally were given a harder time of it.

Certainly that was the case with access to the State Historical Museum. I requested permission to work there, but the Manuscript Division was declared "closed." Fortunately, after numerous interventions from the Cultural Affairs Officer at the U.S. Embassy (our official advocate), I received permission to work there for two designated afternoons, to consult only that one specified manuscript. But what a goldmine! Once the director of the Manuscript Division, the redoubtable Marfa Viacheslavna Shchepkina, gave me the manuscript (and skeptically hovered around to see if I knew what to do with it), I zeroed in on the manuscript pages containing the genealogical articles, particularly on their watermarks (which can reveal the date of production of the paper). Two could be discerned, one a nicely preserved "Shield of the City of Paris" (a shield with fleur-de-lis) and the other an eight-pointed sunburst. I compared the images to the classic reference works on watermarks found in Russian manuscripts (which books were right there in the Reading Room) and found a nearly exact duplicate of both in N.P. Likhachev's handbook.[8] And I mean exact, even though watermarks are infamous for their subtle variations. Likhachev dated the paper to 1504. To get a firm date was great, but I was even more astonished at the document that Likhachev had used to get the date.

He had found these two same marks on the paper of a 1504 charter issued by Ivan III to his son Iurii. This brought the paper used for the Typography genealogical articles into very exalted company; clearly the court and the copyist of the Typography genealogical articles bought their paper from the same supplier, and more than likely worked in the same, or close quarters, that is, the tsar's or metropolitan's scriptorium in the Kremlin. This would fit with what we know of the next generation of genealogical books, which were compiled in court circles. So it seemed to me one could argue that from the very beginning genealogical compilation was an official court function, and kinship was at the heart of politics.

But I wanted to check for myself, so I went across town from the State Historical Museum in Red Square to the Central State Archive of Ancient Documents (TsGADA), where the charter of 1504 was located. Access was not so hard; TsGADA in my experience always had a more open, professional attitude than some of the smaller manuscript divisions. But still it took a bit of persuasion to see this document; because it was part of the grand-princely archive and thus very rare and valuable, they wanted to show me a microfilm, not the original. So I explained to the woman who ran the reading room what my purpose was and why I had to see the original charter. Here another digression. In the archival complex where TsGADA and other major archives were located, a small room at the head of the main stairway had been set aside for the *kapstran* foreigners. We were not permitted to work in the main Reading Room. There were some amenities in our little enclave: a teapot, relative quiet, a chance to get to know scholars from all over America and Europe. Rather than a considerate favor to us, however, this was a means of surveillance and intellectual isolation, of which more later. Let me finish up my story of the watermark first. The reading room attendant, who was a functionary more than an archivist, listened to my explanation of why I needed to see the original. I showed my notes, cited the reference books I'd used, explained how it related to my "theme." She said she'd look into it. The next day she said permission had been granted, and I did get to look at the original. It was indeed a beautifully written and presented grand-princely document. It was a thrill to touch something that Ivan III may have touched, and certainly that N.P. Likhachev had handled; the latter was probably more impressive for me since at that time I'd been reading every word that prodigious scholar ever wrote. I painstakingly copied the watermarks and compared them with my notes from the Typography manuscript; sure enough, the watermarks on the charter were as close to exact duplicates of the ones on the Typography manuscript as I had ever seen. So I felt excited that I'd brought my genealogical articles home to the grand-princely court.

The story has a comic touch too. As I was sitting in the TsGADA reading room with my precious document, I was copying the watermark as exactly as I could. Another American scholar on the exchange that year, Tsuyoshi Hasegawa, who works on the twentieth century, happened to walk by and glance over my shoulder. He stifled a laugh and said, "So this is what you medievalists call research—you get to draw pictures?" He chides me to this day about it. Yes, Toshi, medievalists take their evidence where they can find it; and yes, sometimes drawing pictures of watermarks in archives can constitute a great "adventure in research."

I cannot conclude my tale of romancing the sources without using that watermark episode to exemplify the changed conditions of research in Russia. My experience is probably a microcosm of the experience of every historian who weathered the divide between Soviet power and post-Soviet openness. As I suggested, we labored under a catch-22 situation in the 1970s and 1980s. Because in TsGADA, the major repository of Muscovite-era documents, we were sequestered in our own room, we were often traveling blind. We had no access to the real Reading Room, down the hall, where all the in-house, unpublished catalogs and inventories of the collections and other finding aids were housed. We could only order those archival materials that we learned of through other scholars' footnotes, or, if we were lucky, there would be a published description, such as the late nineteenth-century *Opisanie dokumentov i bumag MAMIu* or the *Letopis zaniatii Imp. Arkheograficheskoi kommissii.*[9] Several American scholars, such as Valerie Kivelson, Peter Brown, Brian Davies, and Kira Stevens, to name only a few, did great work on local and bureaucratic records relying on the *Opisanie*; I wrote my book about dishonor litigations largely based on archival references I found there.

But all this began to change in the late 1980s; when I returned to TsGADA in the 1990s many barriers had fallen. The old foreigners' reading room was crammed with microfilm readers and I was shown into the real Reading Room. What an exciting moment! I was like a kid in a candy shop. The walls were lined floor to ceiling with volumes of inventories (*opisi*)—fat books, slender books, handwritten nineteenth-century ledgers, typescript Soviet productions. And there were more in the stacks that you could summon up, and typewritten registers describing the organization of the collections could be had from the accommodating front desk staff. What these inventories disclosed was a world of government paperwork and litigation from central and provincial institutions stretching from the late sixteenth century to the 1760s, and covering all the Muscovite lands, including steppe frontiers and Siberia. The massive Land Chancery (*Pomestnyi prikaz*) archive is here (over 43,000 items), where Valerie Kivelson has found a fascinating and neglected source in real estate maps (*chertezhi*);[10] its inventories take up a couple of shelves. The seventeenth-century Irkutsk and Iakutsk provincial offices (*prikaznye izby*) (together almost 7,000 items) chronicle Russian administration in Siberia. Two tremendous collections of documents from the old Novgorodian North (*Prikaznye dela starykh let* and *Prikaznye dela novoi razborki*) contain over 22,000 documents; there are about thirteen volumes of inventories for the two collections. The endless Armory archive (*Oruzheinaia Palata*) (12,000+ items; three volumes in ten parts of inventories) has treasures, including materials Isolde Thyrêt is mining for a study of relics. None of this was readily available to foreign scholars before; now it opens up worlds of possibilities, particularly for microhistory and local history, and for anyone wanting to contrast theory and practice in such fields as the law, landholding, conditions of enserfment, religious practice, and so on. The shape of Muscovite history done by Western scholars can change fundamentally.

And we can do our work better because the changes in intellectual life, despite the hardships under which archivists and librarians work in post-Soviet Russia, have allowed the very professional staffs of these institutions to do their job in a responsible way for all patrons. A little anecdote completes the circle on my watermark adventure. When I first went back to TsGADA (now called the Russian State Archive of Ancient Documents—RGADA) in 1991, I was greeted cordially by the liaison for visiting scholars, Svetlana Romanovna Dolgova. She introduced me to some of the archivists working with materials I was interested in. One, whose name I now forget, made a revealing remark. She'd worked at RGADA for years and when I started to explain who I was, she said, "Oh, we know who you are. You've been here before. You were the one who wanted to see that grand-princely charter." This was fifteen years later! And she explained that back in 1976, the director and the various archivists had had to decide whether I deserved permission to see such a valuable document, and they decided from observing how seriously I worked that it would be alright. She wasn't the only archivist who indicated that she'd been noticing me in the reading room off and on over the years, and was glad to have the chance to step forward and talk face to face.

That openness exemplifies new conditions among scholars in the post-Soviet era. In the 1970s and 1980s I made contact with established scholars —A.A. Zimin, A.L. Stanislavskii—who cordially greeted me in formal interviews arranged in their research institutes. Some reached out to develop a closer collegial relationship, including M.E. Bychkova and R.G. Skrynnikov. But as a rule contacts were formal and we *kapstran* scholars were painfully aware that it could be politically risky for Soviet scholars to associate too closely with us. Those times have changed and it is much more possible to be close colleagues and friends with Russian scholars now that we can interact freely at conferences, in reading rooms, in e-mail discussion groups, and the like.

Let me conclude by citing a few examples from my recent work to suggest how the new conditions of research promise to improve the quality and range of research on the Muscovite era. First, new access can shift the focus of research. For example, when I started my next major project after the boyar endeavor, I intended to study precedence, or *mestnichestvo*, an institution for the boyar elite. I knew that there were laws about "dishonor" for lesser classes, but I didn't know of any litigation over it, and I thought of "honor" as a primarily elite phenomenon. But as I studied the RGADA holdings as described in the *Opisanie* and in the archive's unpublished inventories, I found a world of dishonor litigations involving all social classes, even peasants and slaves. Soon precedence took a back seat to dishonor, and my project changed from a narrow study of a rarefied elite legal institution to a broad-gauge study of the social and political function of honor society-wide.[11] This is good, since the Muscovite field has traditionally privileged political history and needs more social history. This change of emphasis occurred because the sources led me that way and because of the new access I enjoyed to the collections and their finding aids.

Interestingly, Russian scholars have warmed to my topic as they themselves have been exploring the prodigious work on early modern social history that flourished during the years of Soviet power. In 1986, when I explained my topic on honor (with a particular emphasis on women's honor), I was treated to condescending smiles. "Isn't it sweet that the bourgeois historians have time for such lightweight issues as dignity and women?" By the 1990s, inspired by the new social history in the West, these colleagues are themselves engaged in research on honor, gender, and mentality.

Second, new interactions with archivists can help scholars formulate more precise and fruitful projects. For example, when I started work in earnest on the criminal law in late Muscovy, I wanted to find one or two regions where the sources were particularly rich over a long span of time. I did my homework in advance, using published descriptions and unpublished inventories. Armed with a list of likely regional foci, I asked a Russian colleague, Aleksandr Kamenskii, whom I'd come to know when he was at Stanford on an exchange program (another benefit of post-Soviet opening up), how I should proceed to narrow the list down. He introduced me to the head of the section on local (*mestnye*) collections in RGADA, Svetlana Ivanovna Smetanina. She really knew her archives. She quickly ran through my list, noting that some of the collections that I'd targeted were actually richer "on paper" than in fact, and observing that some regional collections were particularly dense in the sorts of materials I wanted. With her advice, I narrowed down to Beloozero, an old town in the North, and Arzamas, a relatively new Muscovite town. These two very rich collections have offered me far more than I can realistically cover in my study of the practice of the criminal law; I've never second-guessed that expert advice, and I might never have received it were it not for collegial connections and a spirit of professional cooperation toward foreign researchers.

In a similar example, an archivist was instrumental in helping me find data, whereas in the old days that was not the attitude. I once called upon Smetanina and her colleagues for help in tracking down an elusive reference. In the late nineteenth century the great historian M.M. Bogoslovskii published several studies of local government in the Russian North, using sources from the Ministry of Justice archive in Moscow. That archive is now the basis for much of RGADA's holdings for local records, and I knew that the collections he'd used were there. But he used a different numbering system than is used today, and I could not locate a particularly tantalizing case he referred to. This was one in which a local community seems to have lynched a group of criminals when they felt the local governor was dragging his feet on the execution. So I showed Bogoslovskii's reference to Svetlana Ivanovna and her eyes lit up with the spirit of the chase. Two days later she triumphantly came to me in the Reading Room—she'd located the collection Bogoslovskii was working in and selected three fat manuscript books from the appropriate year (1626) as likely prospects. She left me to page through hundreds of folio pages. Imagine my satisfaction when I came upon a trial transcript with allegations against a corrupt governor and reports of an unruly mob. Bingo, I'd found Bogoslovskii's case—all 400+ manuscript pages of it! From an archival collection of over 20,000 items, she had found for me the three likely items, and I found one of the most fascinating cases I've ever read. I wrote about it for a volume in honor of Hans-Joachim Torke,[12] using this case of local initiative in the criminal process to analyze concepts of justice, official corruption and competence, and the complex relationship between center and periphery in seventeenth-century Russia.

I can't say enough about how much more exciting historical research in Russia is in the post-Soviet era than before, because historians and archivists are much freer to collaborate, to share information, to network, and to shape each other's work. This makes research more of an adventure, but I hope I have likewise shown that the tried and true old methods of research—paleography, watermarks, close readings of texts—also can create adventurous moments in the uncovering of the past.

Notes

1. *Kinship and Politics: The Making of the Muscovite Political System, 1345–1547*. Stanford: Stanford University Press, 1987; *By Honor Bound: State and Society in Early Modern Russia*. Ithaca: Cornell University Press, 1999; "The Extremes of Patriarchy: Spousal Abuse and Murder in Early Modern Russia," *Russian History* 25, nos. 1–2 (1998): 133–40.

2. *Rodoslovnye knigi XVI–XVII vv. kak istoricheskii istochnik* (Moscow, 1975).

3. Russell Martin, "Dynastic Marriage in Muscovy, 1500–1729," Ph.D. dissertation, Harvard University, 1996.

4. Lloyd E. Berry and Robert O. Crummey, eds., *Rude and Barbarous Kingdom: Russia in the Accounts of Sixteenth-Century English Voyagers*. Madison: University of Wisconsin Press, 1968, pp. 134, 144, 140.

5. *Kinship and Politics*, fig. 9.

6. For a chart of Shuiskii marriage connections, see my *Kinship and Politics*, fig. 10, and the discussion of the minority on pages 161–80.

7. *Polnoe sobranie russkikh letopisei* 24 (Petrograd, 1921): 227–34.

8. *Paleograficheskoe znachenie bumazhnykh vodianykh znakov*, 3 vols. and Addendum (St. Petersburg, 1899), nos. 2943–2944, 2941–42.

9. *Letopis zaniatii Imp. Arkheograficheskoi kommissii*, 35 vols. (St. Petersburg and Leningrad, 1861–1928); *Opisanie dokumentov i bumag, khran. v Moskovskom arkhive Ministerstva iustitsii*, 21 vols. (St. Petersburg–Moscow, 1869–1921).

10. Valerie A. Kivelson, "Cartography, Autocracy and State Powerlessness: The Uses of Maps in Early Modern Russia," *Imago Mundi: The International Journal for the History of Cartography* 51 (1999): 83–105; and " 'The Souls of the Righteous in a Bright Place': Landscape and Orthodoxy in Seventeenth-century Russian Maps," *Russian Review* 58, no. 1 (1999): 1–25.

11. *By Honor Bound*. Ithaca: Cornell University Press, 1999.

12. "Lynchings and Legality in Early Modern Russia," *Forschungen zur osteuropäischen Geschichte* (forthcoming).

13

Russian History from Coast to Coast
Elise Kimerling Wirtschafter

After three children and as many books, I have come to understand the power
of privileged alienation. One teacher described my upbringing as "the origins of the Russian intelligentsia," and to be honest, I have thrived on the
incongruities of my life. As a southern Jew, I always had felt slightly removed from the white gentry environment in which I lived and went to school.
"I may live like them but I'm not of them," my father used to say of southern
polite society. For years I was happy to say the same of academia. I began
graduate school at Columbia University in the fall of 1977. Living in New
York City, for the first time in my life I felt integrated into the general population. But the feeling of comfort was only partial. Southernness rather than
Jewishness had become the alienating quality, along with my determination
to have a family and a career. During my years at Columbia, almost every
woman I knew who wanted children either left the history program or obtained a master's degree in library science. Women faculty seemed not to get
tenure, and it was difficult to see how I could be a wife, mother, and scholar.
In those days the biological clock stopped ticking at age thirty-five. Time, I
gathered, was of the essence.

As things turned out, I've had my cake and eaten it too. Indeed, I've been
energized by my ability to defy what I regarded as the prevailing feminist
message of the 1970s and 1980s. Conditions are changing, but for years I
seemed to be one of the few academic mothers of three and probably the
only one completely lacking in feminist consciousness. I am post-sixties (high
school class of 1973), post-Vietnam, slightly conservative (or classically liberal), and attentive to manicures and other feminine frivolities. After marrying I left a tenure-track job for no job in order to live in Los Angeles. I do not
bake cookies; however, I did proudly follow my man to his hometown. I
assumed, as I always had been taught, that in marriage compromises are
necessary and that of course wives—who will spend much of their youth
bearing and fretting over children—compromise when it comes to career.
Yet despite my traditional (retrograde to some) attitudes, I managed to remain

a highly productive scholar. Of course, my mother had been a rebel in her own right—working her way through college, marrying only after graduation, returning to graduate school as a mother of four, refusing to wear a hat to synagogue, and never afraid to express her own well-informed opinions and independent ideas in intimidating patriarchal settings. My father, too, had become liberated—not that he had much choice given the combined effect of three energetic daughters and a son with a heart of gold. His epiphany came sometime after my sixteenth birthday when our family visited the Vatican museum in Rome. There in a glass case a Torah scroll lay perched on display. "Oh, so that's what the inside of a Torah looks like!" I exclaimed. I had become a Bat Mitzvah at age thirteen without, however, being allowed to read from the Torah. Instead of seeing God's words in the *shul* of my childhood, I had seen them in Vatican City, home of the Inquisition.

Such were the conflicting messages and images of childhood that student experiences would only reinforce. As both an undergraduate and a graduate student, I experienced no gender bias and perhaps as a result felt no affinity for feminism. Because for the first time that I can remember being a Jew did not make me feel different, the culture wars of academia had little impact on my thinking. Filled with southern liberal guilt about segregation and racism, I identified with the ideals of nineteenth-century Russian populism. I found especially moving Peter Lavrov's injunction to educated people that they pay back their debt to the laboring classes on whose backs they acquired education and enjoyed the fruits of civilization. In the Alabama of my childhood—the Alabama of the civil rights revolution—I had known people who could be called Lavrovists. My parents always were actively involved in community service, forever going out at night to attend meetings. Aside from my loved ones, the "Lavrovist" I most admire to this day is a labor lawyer and Harvard Law School graduate who had clerked for Supreme Court Justice Hugo Black and had known Justice Louis Brandeis. He returned to Birmingham to give something back to the people, and he did so by representing steel workers in civil-rights lawsuits. He is a man in whose presence one feels hope for the progress of humankind—a man who makes one feel good about being human. But I lacked his virtuous calm and commitment, just as I lacked my parents' sense of extended family and community. I did not want to live in the South or man the barricades. I accepted the definition of the intelligentsia put forth by Vladimir Lenin and other Bolsheviks: constitutionally and structurally, the intelligentsia belonged to the bourgeoisie. For me, education and a career in Russian history became a selfish form of purely individual self-expression. However much I liked the idea of populism, I was bourgeois to the core.

To have work that one loves is a gift, and in Russian history I found the freedom of self-expression that the highly structured southern society of my childhood failed to provide. Ironically, I found this freedom, at least in its early phases, in the manner of my southern childhood—by adapting my subjective experiences to the unfriendly structures of the outside world (in this instance, the decidedly unfree reality of Soviet life).

My earliest research experiences were those of social-science history, and precisely because of this orientation, I was able to conduct successful archival research in the former Soviet Union. My early interest in the social condition of the common soldier fell neatly within the boundaries of scholarship approved by Soviet ideology. The social history of the common soldier was a topic readily understood by the archivists and historians responsible for supervising my access to manuscript sources.[1] It was both politically safe and in the interests of historical scholarship for Petr Andreevich Zaionchkovskii, my first academic advisor (*nauchnyi rukovoditel'*) at Moscow State University, to help me fulfill my research plan. The year was 1980–81, the year the United States boycotted the Moscow Olympics, but even so Petr Andreevich regularly called an archivist at the Central State Archive of Military History (the current RGVIA) on my behalf to inquire if new material would be delivered to the reading room on the appointed day. The answer invariably came back, "Yes, it will be" (*budet*). I also carried another feather in my cap: I came from an established line of Columbia graduate students and professors who had successfully carried out archival research in both Moscow and Leningrad, and even in the provinces. I had good academic lineage and respected personal connections.

Nor, from the perspective of administrators, was I one of those troublesome Americans eager to experience the full array of Russia's artistic offerings by associating with Moscow's cultural intelligentsia. Every morning I arrived at the reading room of the Central State Archive of Ancient Documents (the current RGADA) the moment its doors opened, and I remained until closing time. The kind archivist who watched over the reading room for foreigners kept us fueled with cups of tea and an assortment of candies. Usually, I also brought a lunch of boiled eggs, plain pasta, bread, and cheese, which I ate in the hall. In the evenings, after grabbing some indigestible food somewhere along the way, and on weekends, I worked at the Lenin Library. I had my fun and friends as well, but I was not out and about like some exchange students sponsored by the International Research and Exchanges Board (IREX). My teachers and Columbia peers had warned me about proposals of fictitious marriage. Thanks to my southern upbringing, moreover, I intuitively knew how to conduct myself within the prevailing system, whether or not I identified or even felt comfortable with its rules and realities. In the Soviet Union, I behaved appropriately and with discretion, according to official expectations. To all concerned I appeared to be a quiet, courteous *devushka* (young woman).

Like the Russian intelligentsia in Soviet times, I also assumed that it was better to accomplish something productive—in this case the writing of a dissertation and eventually a scholarly book—than to question the system and be barred from archival sources. My teachers had helped me to choose a "pioneering" topic, which meant that almost any material I received would be new and useful. There was no need, then, to pester archivists with requests for specific documents. I could be grateful rather than demanding, and I could make use of whatever archival documents I received. Thanks to the support of Petr Andreevich Zaionchkovskii, the Military Historical Archive delivered significant piles of previously unexamined documents, particularly military statistics, inspectors' reports, and court-martial records from the first half of the nineteenth century. I received these materials on a weekly basis, on Tuesdays if I remember correctly, and not once during my entire ten-month term of study (*stazherovka*) was I left empty-handed. In Leningrad, though only on one occasion, I even enjoyed the privilege of consulting a forbidden catalogue of archival documents (*opis'*). This allowed me to choose exactly which documents I wanted to read and thus to work with greater effectiveness.

Whatever uneasiness I might have felt about colluding with the Soviet dictatorship I repressed in the name of useful learning and international peace. For a few Soviet citizens I could provide some much-appreciated clothing and food products or access to forbidden books. More importantly, I could serve as a conduit for communications with their relatives in emigration. In addition, as an aspiring social historian, I sincerely believed in my ability to transcend ideology in order to attain knowledge and understanding. Indeed, I practiced what I preached: I was a Jew with a Zionist upbringing who befriended Palestinians at Moscow State University. One, whose Algerian wife had become my friend, frankly told me that if ever he faced me on the frontline in Lebanon, he would shoot to kill without hesitation. But I remained unperturbed, reveling in the thought that I could communicate, in Russian, with supposed enemies. I did not yet understand that enemies cannot be wooed but have to be defeated.

Nor was I afraid of the so-called Russian informers housed among the foreign students from capitalist countries. I could relate to people in different formats, as I had in the South, and without revealing or needing to express my own authentic self, I even could enjoy the relationships. Life in the Soviet Union had its moments of paranoia, but it seemed more akin to the self-delusion of Tennessee Williams's glass menagerie than to an evil prison. Of course, I also understood for the first time in my life that liberal political

freedom was a concrete treasure, but this did not prevent me from accommodating myself to an oppressive regime from whose wrath I was by and large
protected. Today, in middle age, I have enormous admiration for those brave
souls who dared to pursue Jewish, Ukrainian, and other sensitive topics, and
who often paid the price by being denied not only archival sources but sometimes even library books.

Having accommodated myself to the Soviet regime while working in the
politically acceptable field of social history, I was able to conclude my first
lengthy research experience in Moscow and Leningrad, as well as the writing of a dissertation. I emerged from the process less alienated than comfortable in the identity of a Columbia-trained social historian of Russia. But
personal choices soon dislodged me from any sense of intellectual or professional security. I departed from the path I had followed as a graduate student
in two ways, or so it seemed. I chose the personal destination of marriage
and motherhood over the possibility of a "brilliant career" and the geographic
destination of Los Angeles over the academic milieu of the East coast.

I arrived in La-La Land in the early 1980s—a southern bride with an East-
coast education. I came with the usual prejudices and assumptions about the
commercialized culture and lack of serious Culture or intellectual life in southern California. I was appalled when guest speakers came to town and faculty
went out to dinner in the company of graduate students. I was equally appalled to find that graduate students were on a first-name basis with distinguished senior professors quite early in their careers. (My mentor had called
me "Miss Kimerling" until I became a married woman, which occurred more
than a year after my defense.) I cringed when people talked about the celebrity they had passed on the street or the famous person who lived in the house
down the street. I avoided telling academic colleagues and friends that I lived
in Beverly Hills. But love and childbearing prevailed, a local teaching position materialized—one that, ironically, allows me to teach students from the
working and immigrant classes—and life moved along. Books and grants
followed in due course, computer technology made research trips to New
York and Russia less necessary, and the California community of Russianists
acquired an enduring congenial presence.

Within a few years after marrying I had become a soccer mom and
Beverly Hills matron, but I also remained a professionally trained lover of
Russian history. My ability to travel to Russia and to conferences was limited by three budding beings, all born within a five-year period. My university was a people's university with a heavy teaching load and little interest
in my research accomplishments. How was I to make a career at a marginal
university in a marginal field? (Truth to tell, within the larger field of European history, Russian history to this day remains of marginal concern.) At

first I tried to ignore my professional ambitions by escaping into mother-hood and wifedom. At the same time, however, I used every spare moment to write and pursue research. Clearly, after so many years of training and hard work, I had no intention of just giving it all up. I regularly deposited my bright-eyed beauties with their grandparents in Birmingham, Alabama—the place where I had first learned about the social hierarchies of birth and about the consequences of serfdom/slavery. The annual summer trips to Birmingham created space for retreats to the New York Public Library. In New York I was housed and fed by two sisters, and in conversations with friends, colleagues, and former teachers, I felt able to preserve the career thread begun as a graduate student at Columbia. I was especially reassured by the warm hospitality of my former teacher, Marc Raeff, and his wife Lillian. With supportive parents and a husband who left his work at the office, I managed to swim rather than sink.

Even though my move to Los Angeles violated many expectations for a woman in the field, and might well have short-circuited my academic career, the city itself proved fertile ground for developing ideas about the historical problem of social categories—the problem that had occupied my scholarly attention ever since I wrote a M.A. thesis on the category "soldiers' children" (*soldatskie deti*). After settling in Los Angeles, I began to look beyond the walls of the university system at the urban metropolis that had become home. I began to hear the voices of actors, writers, directors, and producers—most of them not big names—and I realized that I lived in a place filled with creative people. I began to relish the melting pot of immigrants that southern California had become, the sounds of the multiple languages spoken all around (forty-six officially recognized at Beverly Hills High School alone), and the sights of Christian, Jewish, Moslem, Hindu, and Buddhist religious cultures. I began to see that my children distinguished their peers not by skin color but by language and religion. Did he speak Persian, Hebrew, Russian, Spanish, Portuguese, Chinese, Vietnamese, or Korean? Did he celebrate the Chinese New Year or observe Ramadan? What kind of food did he bring to the class party? "Why do you call him black?" my son asked one day when I men-tioned the adopted child of a Hollywood celebrity who attended religious school with my daughter.

In Los Angeles multicultural politics and moral relativism are *de rigueur* among self-consciously enlightened people. The diversity of the city and surrounding areas demands social and cultural attitudes that are at once tol-erant and permissive. At its best, the result is not to eliminate rules or stan-dards of behavior from everyday life but to foster individuality and creativity. Indeed, the air of freedom and the influence of the virtual realities created in Hollywood have encouraged this historian to see history writing as a form of art which, like art, requires not only imagination but also technical mastery and careful observation. A passing perspective captured in print and usually produced by a single scholar, the writing of history is the equivalent of painting on canvas.

About a decade after my first experience of Soviet reality, momentous events changed the course of world history. My personal liberation from the assumptions of social-science history coincided with Russia's liberation from Communist rule. I had begun archival research at a time of widespread optimism about the "new social history," with its goal of writing "history from below." I quickly learned, however, that my effort to understand the social consciousness of ordinary people, who rarely expressed themselves in writing, had produced valuable information about their relationship to law and administration but scant knowledge of their actual thoughts and feelings. Comfortable with the realization that judicial testimonies represented not authentic popular expression but interaction with the state, I began to focus on how people used official social categories and legal-administrative institutions to protect and promote their interests. I learned that the meanings and definitions of social categories, and the relationships the categories described, were multiple even in a single context, suggesting that the relationships themselves might be changeable and indeterminate. From these "discoveries" I concluded that in my search for social consciousness—for what people thought about the social relationships of everyday life—I had analyzed the official conceptualization rather than the lived experience of "society."

This was not so different from my earliest experience of Soviet society. Had not one of my unofficial friends described to me the psychological price of living a dual life—his official life as a journalist and his private life as a closet dissident? Moreover, as a child of the 1960s deep South, it seemed quite natural to me that social consciousness, social structure, official society, and civil society had turned out to be quite disparate and in many respects subjectively constructed phenomena. The polite society of my childhood had not at all reflected the "real" family dramas or racial attitudes that lurked beneath. Indeed, it was not necessarily what people "really" thought that defined social relationships. It was the human capacity for deception, including the ability to adhere to the idea of how people should behave, that allowed "society" to function and sometimes even led to progress.

Thus at the very moment that Russian archives became open to foreign researchers in unprecedented ways, my belief in the efficacy of archival research began to fade, or rather I began to feel that in order to broaden myself methodologically and intellectually I needed to explore a different kind of source material. Even earlier, while still working with the legal-administrative sources, I had begun to question the categories and social-science assumptions that previously had informed my archival research. In a study devoted to Russia's "people of various ranks" (*raznochintsy*), I focused attention on the indeterminate changeability that characterized the official categories of Russian society—categories adopted for analytical purposes by generations of historians.[2] This tack appeared iconoclastic and poststructuralist to some critics. To me, however, the ambiguities of the social categories did not imply that truth was endlessly malleable or objective research impossible. Historians can know only that which the sources make knowable, and people who do not express themselves in writing reveal only so much. Precisely for this reason recently I have turned to eighteenth-century plays in an effort to reconstruct the social thinking of Russia's educated service classes.[3] In all of these endeavors I have remained devoted to the problem of how people understand the social relationships that define their everyday experiences.

But the literary sources also refuse to replicate social consciousness and once again it has become necessary to focus on the difference between the idea of society and the reality of social experience. After twenty years of research devoted to legally defined social categories, I have learned much about the conceptualization of society. I unconsciously have accepted the basic premise of *Begriffsgeschichte* (the history of concepts), a method I discovered intellectually only after already employing it in practice. The premise is that historical relationships and structures are best understood by examining the language, categories, and concepts that contemporaries employed to describe themselves, their experiences, and their surroundings.[4] This is especially true for a foreigner studying Russia; even today our Western liberal categories of thought are not automatically understandable to Russians. When at a recent workshop in Italy I rhetorically asked Russian historian Evgenii Anisimov how he was enjoying his new freedom—by which I meant democratic politics, civil rights, and the freedom to travel abroad—he answered that "a civilized person must control himself." Anisimov had completely missed the political intent of my question, and I had imposed on him my American preconceptions by assuming that freedom (*svoboda*) is a political concept. His was an individual moral response to a social-science question.

Perhaps in order to understand the organization of Russian society, it is necessary to think of history as moral science.[5] Perhaps the social experience of Russian modernity is best understood in terms of the individual's moral relationship to larger social entities rather than in terms of broad social and political structures. These are the questions brought home to me by the opening of the Russian archives.

If this opening of the archives has not become the panacea of new information and/or the harbinger of new interpretation that some people expected, this is not for lack of hard work or creative thinking. In addition to the corruption, logistical problems, and faltering infrastructure that continue to plague research in Russia, there are cultural barriers to historiographic progress. The collapse of the Soviet Union has allowed a truly international community of Russian historians to emerge. Yet while we work together on many levels by sharing information, ideas, and moral support, we do not necessarily speak a commonly understandable conceptual language. Nor do we necessarily share the same appreciation for the value of specific topics. Why, another Russian scholar recently asked me, would a young man want to work on the "dead literature" of the eighteenth-century writer M.D. Chulkov? Liberated from the strictures of Soviet ideology and Cold War politics, historians in Russia and abroad continue the search for effective analytical vocabularies—vocabularies that describe Russia in Russian terms and that make sense to Russians and foreigners alike.

As I have aged and turned to research methods and sources less dependent on conditions in the archives, I have come to realize that my early understanding of Russian history was limited as much by my own unwillingness to confront the historical record in moral terms as by the repressiveness of the Soviet system. Evgenii Anisimov has written often about the "police state" created in the early eighteenth century by Peter the Great.[6] Repeatedly, Anisimov is accused of transposing the Soviet dictatorship back onto the early modern context, where states were administratively weak and people enjoyed extensive de facto freedom. Such criticisms are justified, but I think Anisimov's voice should be heeded precisely for its *contemporary* moral message. The key to writing high quality, scientifically sound history is not to pretend that moral judgments can be avoided. But neither do moral judgments represent open-ended subjectivities that undercut objective research. Moral judgments render historians human and history writing relevant. We cannot avoid such judgments, but we can be honest about how they affect our thinking. We can reveal how personal experiences color scholarly objectivity by being aware of our underlying assumptions and definitions. We can make these assumptions clear in the same way that we make methodological and historiographic choices clear. We also can be clear about where Russian history violates our own liberal-democratic expectations. Historians today struggle judiciously to focus on the presences as opposed to the absences of Russian history.[7] How can we integrate Russia into the spectrum of European history without imposing on Russia European categories and normative models? But why, I ask, in making comparisons with European countries further to the west, must we assume that drawing attention to what is missing in Russia somehow denigrates the country's history and people?

Given that our Russian colleagues have embraced the achievements of liberal modernity—the rule of law, material progress, civil society, capitalist market relations, and democratic constitutional government—as desirable goals for Russia, do we not deny them the benefits we ourselves enjoy by refusing to hold Russia to a Western standard? In contrast to social-science historians who want us to see the Soviet experiment as one stage in the continuum of Russia's march toward liberal modernity and civil society, Evgenii Anisimov wants us to understand what the march of Russian history has meant for individual human beings. Both perspectives are needed; however, for those of us who began our Russian history adventures in a social-science mode, it is time to confront our own (and Russia's) moral duplicities and complicities.

Truth to tell, unlike many, I led a comfortable existence as a researcher in the former Soviet Union. A stranger in a strange land—first as an unmarried southern girl, then as a "widow" from my husband, and finally as an "orphan" from my children—I found the imposed structure and the absence of any need to make choices comforting. Dictatorship allowed me to work in peace and quiet because I had been chosen or somehow properly classified as a friendly guest worthy of receiving archival materials. This good fortune continued in post-Soviet times, but when I first returned to the new Russia in 1993, everyday life had become more complicated. It was February, and I had not worn a winter coat or boots for several years. My ride from the airport had forgotten me, and so I had to join a group of American oil workers who were being transported to a nearby hotel before shipping out to Siberia. The next day, after paying an expensive hotel bill, I had to find my own taxi into town. There I soon discovered that my expected housing arrangements also had not been made. Instead of getting to work straightaway—time still was of the essence—I had to spend a couple of days renting an apartment. Of course, nice people helped me at every step of the way, but I did not like the need to rely on personal, informally defined relationships. At least the old system had been predictable, or so it seemed, given that the authorities had approved of my research projects. A bus and escort would pick up the group at the airport, transport us to our assigned quarters, and that was that—off to work we would go. Yes, we struggled to eat and to make phone calls, but basically our lives were arranged for us, and there always were seats, lamps, and microfilm readers available. In the new Russia of the 1990s, seating, lamps, and light bulbs for microfilm readers seemed to be in short supply. To be sure, we now can consult the coveted catalogues (*opisi*), freely share information with colleagues, and visit the provinces. We can purchase archival access, research assistance, and copies of documents. But I cannot say that I am fully at home in the changed, economically driven research environment. Shamefully, I even feel a bit of nostalgia for the pre-capitalist system of research where private arrangements and wily negotiations were not required.

Comfortable or not, I've had no choice but to continue my Russian research adventures. At the moment, however, perhaps because my children are entering the crucial teenage years, I seem to find answers to unanswered and unanswerable questions closer to home. As a practicing historian, I have begun to look to Hollywood creativity for inspiration and enlightenment. Like the directors, actors, and writers running around Los Angeles and Beverly Hills, I have begun to see my scholarly career as an individual creative journey. The purpose of this journey is not to have a lasting word on an important historiographic question. The purpose is to explore interpretive possibilities—to master a body of sources and present empirical information through the prism of an informed analytical perspective. That the perspective of any individual scholar can be but one tentative perspective among a multitude of others—that one person's interpretation can never be unique, original, or definitive—does not mean it lacks objectivity or scientific value. It simply means that a single human brain can comprehend only so much.

Notes

1. This research produced my first book, *From Serf to Russian Soldier.* Princeton: Princeton University Press, 1990.

2. *Structures of Society: Imperial Russia's "People of Various Ranks."* DeKalb, IL: Northern Illinois University Press, 1994. I continued to explore social categories in my first synthesis book, *Social Identity in Imperial Russia.* DeKalb, IL: Northern Illinois University Press, 1997.

3. This research will be published as *The Play of Ideas in Russian Enlightenment Theater* (forthcoming from Northern Illinois University Press).

4. For an introduction, see Harmut Lehmann and Melvin Richter, eds., *The Meaning of Historical Terms and Concepts: New Studies on Begriffsgeschichte.* Washington, D.C.: German Historical Institute, 1996.

5. My interest in history as moral science was stimulated by reading Tzvetan Todorov, *Genres in Discourse*, trans. Catherine Porter. New York: Cambridge University Press, 1990; and *The Morals of History*, trans. Alyson Waters. Minneapolis: University of Minnesota Press, 1995.

6. Most recently in "'Malenkii chelovek' v Tainoi Kantseliarii XVIII veka," a paper given at a workshop in Gargnano, Italy, on "Man in Eighteenth-Century Russia" (September 2001). See also Evgenii Anisimov, *Vremia petrovskikh reform.* Leningrad: Lenizdat, 1989.

7. Gary Marker recently posed the question of presences to me at the Gargnano workshop.

14

Friends and Colleagues

Eve Levin

In the post-Soviet era, joint projects between Russian and American scholars have become commonplace. But when Natalia Pushkareva and I began our collaboration during the last act of the Cold War, it was not so. Both our academic communities expected us to espouse different, mutually exclusive, interpretations of the Russian past. The Soviet government placed numerous constraints on interaction between its citizens and foreigners from "capitalist" countries. Nonetheless, most exchange scholars formed enduring friendships with Soviets, as Natasha and I did. But that we were able to acknowledge publicly an intellectual kinship was quite unusual before the era of glasnost. Natasha and I became *sputnitsi* (traveling companions) not only in our research, but also through the fascinating, unfamiliar terrain of each other's cultures.

When I set out for Moscow on the program sponsored by the International Research and Exchanges Board (IREX) in 1981, I did not expect to find a kindred spirit. It was the grim era of Ronald Reagan and Leonid Brezhnev, when governmental suspicions were running high. In our dormitory at Moscow University, an anti-American propaganda display adorned the bulletin board. At a briefing at the U.S. Embassy, an official warned us to watch out for even seemingly friendly Soviets. "They are going to be reading your mail. They are going to bug your rooms and your telephone calls. They will be looking for weaknesses. There is going to be an incident with one of you, mark my words." A veteran of Vietnam-era peace marches, I felt like asking whether the CIA was going to read our mail too. I didn't though. I took to heart the advice we got at the IREX orientation before departure: do your work seriously and don't look for trouble. I knew that with my dissertation topic—the status of women in medieval Novgorod—a lot of people on both sides of the Atlantic would dismiss me as a scholar. Women's history was just starting to win intellectual respectability then. All of us in this embryonic field faced derisive comments about not being "good" enough to do "real" history. I did not expect Soviets to be any more receptive.

Meanwhile, in Moscow, Natalia Pushkareva had become a lone crusader for women's history. She had chosen women in medieval Russia as the topic for her undergraduate thesis. An old friend of her family, the eminent medievalist Vladimir Pashuto, had first suggested it to her. Her parents, Lev Nikitich Pushkarev and Irina Mikhailovna Pushkareva, both established historians, endorsed the project. But other professors discouraged Natasha. A.A. Zimin, another family friend, told her sadly, "Natasha, don't. It can't be done; there aren't any sources." Natasha had trouble finding an advisor at Moscow State University. Faculty members informed her that her project had "no political significance": women did not constitute a social class in terms of Marxist theory, and so did not merit study. Finally, Valentin Lavrentevich Ianin took pity on her and agreed to serve as her graduate advisor. His own work bore no relation to the study of women at all, but as the preeminent expert on the history of Novgorod and a corresponding member of the Academy of Sciences, he had the stature to endorse a seemingly outlandish project.

Natasha learned of me some months before I found out about her. In the spring of 1981, Valentin Lavrentevich gave her alarming news: halfway around the world, in the United States, there was an American woman working on *her* topic!

"No! It can't be true!" Natasha cried.
"It is," Ianin responded. "And she is coming here."

Indeed, I had requested Professor Ianin as my Soviet advisor. I had no way of knowing that he would be sympathetic to my dissertation topic, but he had a reputation for being a gentleman and a scholar, and his knowledge of the history and archeology of Novgorod was unmatched. At my first, nervous meeting with Valentin Lavrentevich, I found him genial and receptive. "Birchbark documents," he murmured, glancing through my *anketa* (research questionnaire). "I have one here that relates to your topic." He lifted a slender fragment of ancient birchbark from its glass frame and laid it in my hands. I was stunned—to hold the actual document I had studied from the published reproduction. I burst out, "I thought Americans weren't allowed to see birchbark documents!"

"*Nu, chto!*" Valentin Lavrentevich laughed. I realized at that moment that I had lucked into an ideal academic advisor, who would promote my research agenda instead of trying to limit or redirect it as so many Soviet advisors did to their American exchange scholars.

At this first meeting, Professor Ianin told me about his student, Natasha Pushkareva. "Call her," he said, handing me the telephone number. "She will help you with your plan of study." The *nauchnyi plan*, older veterans of exchange programs will remember, was the essential first step in undertaking research in the Soviet Union. In it, foreign researchers redesigned their projects to fit Soviet norms of scholarly endeavor and requested access to libraries, archives, and consultations. The plan had to be approved by one's advisor, the department chair, the dean, the rector, and the Ministry of Higher Education. At that point, it became an official part of the Five-Year Plan. So some future scholar researching late Soviet higher education might someday run across the *nauchnyi plan* of *stazher iz SShA Levina Eva* (plan of study of exchange scholar from the USA Levin Eve).

I called Natasha. We agreed that she would come to my dormitory room at Moscow State University the next day. We both anticipated someone considerably more intimidating. Instead, we both found someone quite like ourselves: young, slender, petite; both self-assured and hoping to please. I offered Natasha cake and coffee, and we sat down to talk about medieval Russian women. And in that very first conversation, we made a remarkable discovery: despite the great differences in our scholarly backgrounds, we had compatible understandings of our topic.

Natasha invited me to the apartment she shared with her parents and husband to work on my plan of study. To the other IREXers, this was a coup: less than a week in the Soviet Union and already I had an invitation to a Russian home! Natasha explained the format of the *nauchnyi plan* and we started to design one for me. Then her mother offered a meal, which I accepted appreciatively. After dinner, I asked Irina Mikhailovna if I might help with the dishes. Clearly her image of American women did not involve housework. She stared in surprise for a moment, and then smiled, "*Da, mozhno* (Yes, you can)," and handed me an apron.

From that time on, I became a welcome guest. Natasha's birthday fell a couple of weeks later and I was invited to join the celebration. When my mother and teenage sister came to visit, the Pushkarev family feted them. I took Natasha with me to the fabled International Trade Center, built on the model of a Western hotel/convention hall. It was usually closed to Soviets, except those with special authorization, but foreigners with *valiuta* (convertible currency) were welcome. Natasha dressed up in my American clothing—fortunately, we wear the same size—to slip past the doorman. In the early spring, Natasha and her husband daringly smuggled me along on a daytrip to the Novyi Ierusalim monastery—a location well outside the twenty-five–mile travel limit for foreigners.

I wondered, sometimes, whether Natasha might run into difficulties with the Soviet authorities over her friendship with me, but figured that Professor Ianin's stamp of approval on the association would exonerate her if any question arose. Years later I asked her about it, and she told me that there had never been any problem because I clearly was exactly who I claimed to be—a graduate student. But there were limits; when Natasha asked about coming with me to movies at the American Embassy, her mother expostulated, "Natasha!"

In the spring, it became my turn to present a paper at Professor Ianin's Novgorod seminar. Natasha advised me on the format and the grammar. When the day came, she served as the formal *opponent*, or commentator. My paper was well-received, generating quite an extensive discussion. Afterwards, Natasha and I found an empty classroom to talk privately. "Now I want to ask my *real* questions!" she said. The first: did I think the status of women had improved or declined in the course of the five centuries under study? The orthodox answer based on nineteenth-century historiography was negative: women's status had declined as a result of the misogynistic influence of the Russian Orthodox Church, or because of the Mongol conquest. But my research indicated otherwise, and I told Natasha bluntly, "I think women's status improved." "So do I," she replied. We went through her entire list of questions, and on each point, we found ourselves in complete agreement. "What better proof is there that we are right," Natasha observed, "than the fact that two scholars, working from different premises in different parts of the world, arrived at the same conclusions?"

Professor Ianin agreed and made us an unrefusable offer: we should co-author an article on the status of women in medieval Novgorod and he would sponsor it for publication.[1] We accepted enthusiastically. We outlined the whole and divided up sections for each of us to draft. Then, in many pleasant hours at Natasha's desk, we merged the two. From the beginning we thought of the possibility of publishing an English-language version as well (which materialized in 1986 in *Soviet Studies in History*) and designed the article to be accessible to both Soviet and Western audiences.[2] This plan necessitated some small compromises. When I wanted to include Biblical quotations, Natasha excised them; it might reflect badly on her in those days of official atheism. Natasha included the ritual invocations of Marx and Lenin, which I nixed, lest I be labeled a Communist.

When I left Moscow in June 1982, Natasha and I pledged that we would remain in touch. Natasha assured me that she would be free to correspond with me; our co-authored article established us as recognized collaborators. It wasn't easy in those days before e-mail and direct-dial telephoning, but letters and gifts went back and forth nonetheless. We talked about our dissertations and shared the momentous events of our lives. A year after leaving Moscow, I reported the good news that my dissertation was ready to defend and I had found a good position at Ohio State University.

Natasha described to me the joys and struggles of new motherhood, and the frustrations of her job search. Providing the necessities for a baby had become very difficult in the era of post-Brezhnev "stagnation." Could I send a pacifier, a snowsuit, baby shoes? Because she needed her parents' help with child care, she was reluctant to seek a position outside Moscow. But in Moscow appropriate places were few, and male candidates received preference. ("Discrimination!" Natasha later commented. "A man with a lower-ranked degree and no publications was chosen ahead of me, and at a higher salary.") Natasha had to wait for several years for a slot to open up in her preferred institution, the Institute of Ethnology of the Academy of Sciences. Among ethnographers, the study of women's customs had some merit, but historians in the Russian establishment were slow to see the value of gender history.

Natasha and I had a series of exchanges concerning the future directions of our research. We agreed that the world didn't need two similar books on the status of women in medieval Russia, and so for publication we should diversify. After reading my dissertation, Natasha made a suggestion that permanently altered my research agenda. She noted that she could pursue the study of women's legal status and economic roles more easily than I could because she had wide access to archival materials. I should instead look further into the question of sexuality, the topic of one short chapter in my dissertation, because, she wrote, "such a book can never be published in the Soviet Union." Natasha's prophecy proved wrong, but in 1984 the liberalization of the Gorbachev era could scarcely be anticipated. I concurred with Natasha's advice, and we pursued complementary projects through the 1980s. We provided each other with hard-to-get publications, as well as citations to useful sources. In 1989 we both published our first books: Natasha's *Zhenshchina drevnei Rusi*, focusing on women's legal position, economic roles, property rights, and physical image; and my *Sex and Society in the World of the Orthodox Slavs, 900–1700*.[3] In addition, Natasha and her family adopted my graduate students as they made their way to Moscow to do their dissertation research—a practice that has continued to the present day.

Although we had exchanged letters, gifts, and photographs over the years, Natasha and I had not seen each other again until I returned to Moscow on a research trip in September 1990. By that time, the Cold War was over, and glasnost and perestroika had transformed Soviet society beyond our previous imaginings. The old Communist-era restrictions on expression of ideas and association with foreigners had evaporated.

In 1990 Natasha and I talked about politics for the first time. I was surprised by her sympathy for Ronald Reagan, and she by mine for Mikhail Gorbachev. Being feminists, we discussed the influence of first ladies.

"We like Nancy Reagan," Natasha told me.

"How can you like Nancy?!" I questioned.

"Well, she is so friendly and she dresses so well."

"That's why we like Raisa Gorbacheva," I responded.

"How can you like Raisa?!"

In 1990 Natasha felt free enough to introduce me to her relatives in the military—people whose very existence had remained secret in 1981–82. Her cousin, a lieutenant-colonel, spoke frankly about the army's ethos of non-involvement in politics. "The Army does not back an individual or a party," he said. "The Army defends the country and serves the people." During the coup attempt in the summer of 1991 I remembered his words, and I was not surprised when the military withheld its support for the hard-liners.

Although the official restrictions on foreigners' travel were still in place, enforcement had become lax and I was able to take a number of trips with Natasha and her family. Natasha and I went to Lithuania to visit with a friend of her family and to see historical sites. Rakhil Samoilovna Margolis, a survivor of the Vilna ghetto, took us on a walking tour of its location. She pointed out nondescript buildings with horrifying histories: "I watched from here while a huge group of Jews was marched to the forest and shot." "Here is where we kept our secret stash of weapons." "This was the underground bakery, where people who had money could buy extra bread." She told us the story of her escape in the last weeks before the final liquidation of the ghetto:

The ghetto had a small back gate, which only the Jewish mayor and the German authorities could use. One day, the mayor brought the key to the gate into the workshop where Rakhil Samoilovna's fiancé was employed and asked him to make a duplicate while he waited. Thinking quickly, the young man surreptitiously pressed the key into a moistened piece of bread, then made the requested copy. Later, he made a second duplicate key from the impression in the bread. He and Rakhil and three dozen or so other young resistance members used the key to slip out the gate one night. But it turned out that their Lithuanian contact had betrayed them to the Nazis, and the members of the group who arrived at the rendezvous point on time were gunned down. Rakhil and her immediate companions had gotten lost, however, and so escaped with their lives. For the next several months, they lived in the forest as resistance fighters. Although Natasha knew that Rakhil Samoilovna had survived the war, she had never heard the full story. Rakhil Samoilovna had assumed that only a Jewish visitor such as myself would be interested in a personal account of the Holocaust.

The other purpose of our trip to Lithuania was to purchase supplies that had become scarce in the center. But on the eve of Lithuanian independence, we found some of the local merchants unwilling to sell to interlopers from Moscow. We developed a subterfuge: I borrowed the Lithuanian identity card of Rakhil Samoilovna's daughter, who had recently emigrated to Israel—a woman about my age and similar in appearance. But if I spoke, it would become instantly apparent that I could not have been the proper owner of the card. So I pretended to have a bad cold, Natasha did the talking, and we emerged from shops with raw chickens and bottles of tomato sauce. In other places, it helped for me to resume my proper identity. After a morning of exploring old churches in Vilnius, Natasha gained entrée for us into a crowded restaurant by announcing pompously, "I have charge of an American and I need to get her fed!"

Natasha finagled tickets for a river cruise, and we headed off to Uglich in a chilly October. Remembering the travel restrictions from the Soviet period, I was stunned that Natasha and I were permitted to travel together, sharing a cabin. All the way to the marina, I kept asking Natasha what we would do if there was trouble. She brushed off my worries and left me to guard our luggage while she took our passports to claim our cabin assignment. Just a few minutes later she reappeared with our key and a funny story: Natasha had presented her Soviet passport and my American one, and pointed to our names on the list.

"*Devushka* (young lady)," the clerk admonished sternly, "you may not share your cabin with a man who is not your husband!"

"What do you mean, a man?" The clerk pointed to the name on my passport, Levin, a Russian name, but in the masculine rather than feminine form. "But she's a woman," Natasha protested. "Look at the photograph."

The clerk agreed that the picture did seem to be of a woman. "But why does she have a man's name?"

"It's an American passport," Natasha pointed out. "They do strange things with names."

We had to laugh over the official prudishness, especially when we observed a foursome of two young men and two young women who surreptitiously exchanged bunkmates.

The highlight of the cruise was a visit to the church dedicated to St. Dmitrii of Uglich, the child-martyr famed in Mussorgskii's opera *Boris Godunov.* The interior walls of the church were lavishly frescoed with illustrations of his life. Natasha and I particularly admired the painting of Dmitrii's mother, Maria Nagaia, dramatically defending her child.

During the trip, I glimpsed some of the worst aspects of the collapsing Soviet distribution system. In order to economize on provisions, the kitchen served the same beef stew at every meal, including breakfast. But then the delicacies requisitioned for the cruise began to appear for sale at the snack bar between meals: honey, canned shrimp, caviar, and good-quality tea. At each stop, local women with net shopping bags met the ship, hoping that the crew would have goods to sell to them.

Even in Moscow, the autumn of 1990 was a time of continuous deficits. I became part of the Pushkarev family's network for obtaining necessary supplies. Natasha and I shopped at the Finnish store Stockmann's several times a month, buying there with my credit card the items that could not be obtained for cash, either Soviet rubles or American dollars, at any other place. I also learned to buy up large quantities of sausage or lemons if I happened to stumble upon them for sale. One day, as I was leaving Natasha's apartment, I spotted a truck unloading white boxes at the corner grocery. I ran back to her door, puffing: "Natasha, Natasha! There's sugar at the grocery store!"

Natasha took charge instantly. "Don't take off your coat!" she ordered. She got her mother on the telephone. "Mama! Our Eva says there is sugar at the grocery store. Where are our coupons?" For at that time, sugar was rationed and could be purchased only by holders of ration coupons. "What do you mean, Papa has them? Where is he?" She turned to me. "Go stand in line," she directed, and she set off to scour the neighborhood to find her father, who had gone out walking with her seven-year-old son. Just as I got to the front of the queue, Natasha came running up with the ration coupons, and we collected ten kilos of sugar.

Our collaboration extended beyond traveling and shopping, to professional endeavors. Natasha had begun to earn extra money by writing articles on Russian women's history for popular magazines—an avocation that became an important source of income for her by the late 1990s. She proposed to the magazine *Evropa + Amerika* that she and I co-author a piece about medieval Russian sex. Public discussion of sex had recently become politically acceptable. Just a few years earlier, Natasha had had to solicit special permission from her dean to read the *Kama Sutra*; now copies in Russian translation were offered for sale in every subway station. The editor of *Evropa + Amerika* found our idea attractive, and we wrote the piece in a dialogue format, mimicking our many conversations on the topic. The editor was not the only staff member who liked our article, entitled "Was There Sex in Medieval Russia?"[4] Someone spirited a copy of the manuscript out of the office and sold it to *Megapolis-Kontinent*, who published it in advance without any permission from us.[5] And so I gained first-hand experience of how laxly Russians observed copyright laws.

When I left Moscow in early January 1991, our farewells were not nearly as wistful as they had been in 1982. Natasha and I knew that we would remain in touch, and we had begun concrete plans for her to come to the United States. Those plans came to fruition in the spring of 1992, when Natasha was invited as a guest scholar for two months at the Hilandar Research Library at Ohio State. She had a multifaceted research agenda. First, she intended to trace the sources I had relied upon so heavily in my book to inform her own further research on premodern Russian women. Second, she was to fulfill certain programs assigned to her by the Institute of Ethnology: to research bibliography on Russian ethnology in Western languages, and to collect information about the preservation of Russian customs among émigrés and their descendents in the United States. I accompanied her on some of the interviews she conducted in relation to the latter project, helping to translate as she asked informants about typical meals and wedding celebrations.

Although by that time Natasha had traveled quite extensively in Europe, the American Midwest was new and fascinating to her. Most of all, she reveled in the shopping malls, spending leisure hours admiring goods virtually unknown in Russia, "as though in a museum," as she put it. She was impressed by the courtesy of the shop clerks, who let her browse as long as she liked and thanked her for stopping in even when she bought nothing. We visited reconstructed pioneer villages—the concept of living museums was new to Natasha—and she remarked on the similarities to nineteenth-century Russian peasant life.

Two years later, we were offered another opportunity for a collaborative project. Donald Raleigh, the editor of the "New Russian History" series for M.E. Sharpe publishers, approached me at AAASS with an idea: would Natalia Pushkareva be interested in authoring a survey of Russian women's history for the series, with me as translator and editor? No similar contemporary history existed, so we could readily anticipate a market for such a work. Natasha agreed enthusiastically and began work on the manuscript as soon as her schedule allowed. By spring 1995, she sent the draft to me with a note, "You are tsar and god. Do what you think best with it."

That summer, I began the translation. I had done scholarly translations before, including several of Natasha's presentations, but this work required special handling. Natasha had written it in the lively style typical of Russian works intended for mass appeal. While I wanted the English text to reflect Natasha's vivacious personality, many turns of phrase in the original Russian would make her sound affected and overly sentimental in English. American authors don't talk about "brave princesses" and such in works intended for adults. So with each sentence I stopped to think, "How would Natasha express this thought if English were her native language?" Sometimes I had to put the idea into an entirely different form. When reviewing my translation later, Natasha exclaimed over one segment, "None of these are my words, but this is *my* idea!"

I also had to consider that average American readers, most likely college students, would not have any great familiarity with the Russian language or Russian history when they encountered this book. Thus Russian terms had to be kept to a minimum—only where no English equivalent, even a rough one, existed. In addition, I would have to contextualize many of the historical events, such as the Battle of Kulikovo or the liberation of the serfs, which Natasha had referred to in passing. From my own experience with undergraduates, I hesitated to pepper the text with editor's footnotes providing clarification; students tend not to read them. So I decided to make use of the broad authority Natasha had given me, and I integrated the necessary background into the text itself. I also inserted into Natasha's original footnotes additional references to secondary readings in English, so Western readers could seek further information on topics that interested them.

In the process of composing the draft translation, I found myself with literally hundreds of questions for Natasha. I wanted to get her approval for my additions; I was unsure of my understanding of a number of terms; and I wasn't convinced by her argument in a few places. The most efficient way of settling these matters was for us to sit down together for a couple of weeks, so I traveled to Moscow in January 1996. Once again, we sat side by side at her desk, poring over our manuscript for hours. The sections on women's costume took up much of our time. "What did this garment look like?" I would ask Natasha, and she would find a picture or sketch one. Sometimes she would need to draw a construction guide—fortunately, both of us are accomplished seamstresses—so I would know how to describe the item. In one discussion of women's underwear, Natasha pulled up her blouse and pointed to a part of her bra. "I couldn't do that with a male translator," she quipped. The colors of fabric also required a lot of visual cues because my dictionaries would give such unhelpful definitions as "a shade of blue." Natasha would look around the room and pull out a knick-knack, scarf, or book in the right shade. "Oh," I'd comment, "turquoise."

We were also fortunate enough to be able to review the copyedited manuscript together the following October. Natasha had come to the United States for a conference and stayed on for a few weeks afterward. The copyeditor was Carolyn Pouncy, the translator of the sixteenth-century text *Domostroi* and a mutual friend.[6] Carolyn proposed lively chapter titles and subtitles that we adopted enthusiastically. This raised a question: could we come up with something less prosaic than the working title, *Women in Russian History?* Natasha put her proficient, if non-colloquial, knowledge of English to work.

"Could we call it 'Women Bright and Gay'?" she hazarded.

No, I said, and I told her about the alternate definition of the last word.

"What about 'Fairy Women of Russia'?"

No, I said, and I told her about the secondary meaning of the first word.

"Does every word in English mean 'homosexual'?" Natasha asked in frustration.

Finally, we decided to stick with the working title after all.

Our book, *Women in Russian History*, came out in March 1997.[7] I was in Russia again, doing research for a new project. We hosted a lavish dinner party for a select group of Russian and American guests, preparing the meal with the same easy collaboration as we had the book itself.

Natasha's presence in Columbus in October 1996 also comforted me through a difficult period: my treasured senior colleague, Allan Wildman, was dying of cancer. Natasha also knew him well; a number of years before, he had carried a letter from me to her, and soon he and her family had become fast friends. Allan spoke with both of us about his hope that I would succeed him as editor of *The Russian Review*. Natasha shared Allan's confidence in my abilities, and particularly wanted to see a woman fill such an influential position. But she thought there would also be more tangible rewards, so she was stunned to learn that editors of American journals receive no compensation. Natasha herself had taken on editorial work at the journal *Rodina*, not only for the honor, but also for the pay.

For Natasha and her parents, as for so many Russian scholars in the post-Soviet era, the collapse of the Soviet Union meant the end to the financial security they had enjoyed under the old system. The family cobbled together sufficient money to cover expenses from a variety of sources: publications; Lev Nikitich's pension as a veteran of World War II; salaries (paid irregularly) from the Academy of Sciences; and Natasha's tutoring of high school students for university entrance examinations. As a result, they worked almost constantly. To stretch their income, they learned the skill of comparison shopping: government stores were cheaper than private ones; the Danilovskii and Teplyi Stan markets were less expensive than the nearby Cheremushskii. Unlike the Pushkarev adults, I had no obligations on Saturdays, so in the winter of 1997, Tioma, Natasha's thirteen-year-old son, and I were entrusted with the weekly grocery shopping. We'd head out about nine in the morning with our two shopping carts and navigate among the stands set up in the frigid air, checking prices and quality. Because I still qualified as a "guest," I was forbidden to pay for the staples on the shopping list. But I slipped in treats: crackers for Lev Nikitich, salted nuts for Irina Mikhailovna, cookies for Tioma, the occasional pineapple or mango. As I became more aware of the family finances, I took to picking up something—a dozen oranges or a jar of jam—every day on my way home from the archives. And I marveled that amidst the financial strain and constant turmoil of earning a living, my friends were still able to produce scholarly works of enduring worth.

Natasha and her family found the American system of peer reviewing and revising and resubmitting articles to be fascinating, and stringent. When I visited Russia again in 1997, they arranged an invitation for me to prepare an article for the leading Russian historical journal, *Otechestvennaia istoriia*, on the mechanics of publishing in the United States and the approaches to historical issues featured in *The Russian Review*.[8] Natasha and her mother, Irina Mikhailovna, helped me to write my piece in Russian. They converted my grammatically correct, but awkward prose into something sophisticated and elegant. As I struggled to find the right vocabulary to explain the postmodern approaches to scholarship, Natasha provided the necessary phrases. Because she reads widely in Western historical and feminist scholarship, she understood what I was trying to say.

Natasha and I have continued to collaborate in our scholarly work. Natasha selected excerpts of my book *Sex and Society* for inclusion in Russian translation in a collection she edited.[9] The same year, I provided a commentary to Natasha's article "The Russian Lubok of the 18th–20th Century" for the collection *Eros and Pornography in Russian Culture*.[10] And so, fifteen years after we resigned ourselves to "never" publishing the fruits of our collaborative studies of premodern sexuality in Russian, we did.

It is now common for Russian and American scholars to form long-term collaborative relationships, visit each other, publish together, and share the flow of daily life. Natasha and I, unwitting forerunners of an international trend, rejoice in the new atmosphere.

Notes

1. E. Levin and N.L. Pushkareva, "Zhenshchina v srednevekovom Novgorode XI–XV v." *Vestnik Moskovskogo Universiteta, Seriia Istorii*, no. 3 (June 1983): 78–89.

2. Eve Levin and Natalia Pushkareva, "Women in Medieval Novgorod, Eleventh to Fifteenth Century," *Soviet Studies in History* 23, no. 4 (Spring 1985): 71–90.

3. N.L. Pushkareva, *Zhenshchina drevnei Rusi* (Moscow, 1996); Eve Levin, *Sex and Society in the World of the Orthodox Slavs, 900–1700*. Ithaca: Cornell University Press, 1989.

4. N.L. Pushkareva and E. Levin, "Byl li seks na Rusi?" *Evropa + Amerika* 3, no. 1 (1992): 125–31.

5. "Byl li seks na Rusi," *Megapolis-Kontinent* 17, no. 15 (April 24–30, 1991): 12.

6. Carolyn Johnston Pouncy, trans. and ed., *The Domostroi: Rules for Russian Households in the Time of Ivan the Terrible*. Ithaca: Cornell University Press, 1994.

7. Natalia Pushkareva, *Women in Russian History: From the Tenth to the Twentieth Century*, trans. and ed. Eve Levin. Armonk, NY: M.E. Sharpe, 1997.

8. Eve Levin, "Problemy rossiiskoi istorii na stranitsakh zhurnala *Russian Review*," *Otechestvennaia istoriia*, 1998, no. 2, pp. 143–49.

9. N.L. Pushkareva, *Liubov', erotika i seksual'naia etika v doindustrial'noi Rossii (X– pervaia polovina XIX veka)* (Moscow, 1999), pp. 239–491.

10. Eve Levin, "Pornography Before Pornography," in *Eros and Pornography in Russian Culture*, ed. M. Levitt and A. Toporkov (Moscow, 1999), pp. 87–93.

15

Within and Beyond the Pale
Research in Odessa and Birobidzhan

Robert Weinberg

On the evening of Sunday, August 18, 1991, I had just sat down to inquire of a colleague whether he knew someone who could send me an official invitation to visit Birobidzhan, capital city of the Jewish Autonomous Region (JAR), located some 5,000 miles from Moscow along the Russian-Chinese border near Khabarovsk. Established formally in 1934, Birobidzhan, as the JAR is popularly called, had its beginnings in 1928 when the Kremlin set aside the territory as the national enclave of Soviet Jewry where a secular Jewish culture rooted in socialist principles could serve as an alternative to Palestine. Yiddish was intended to serve as the bedrock of a proletarian Soviet Jewish culture and community, and help foster the national-cultural consolidation of Soviet Jewry. A Yiddish newspaper has been published, albeit with a short hiatus during World War II, since the early 1930s, making it one of the few extant Yiddish newspapers. During Birobidzhan's first decade of existence, studying Yiddish, which along with Russian had been designated as an official language of the region, was obligatory in schools where Russian was the language of instruction. In addition, a Jewish theater and a library with a sizable Judaica collection were established, and in 1935 the government decreed that all official documents, including public notices, announcements, posters, and advertisements, had to appear in both Yiddish and Russian. Indeed, Yiddish remains one of the official languages of the region to this day, notwithstanding the fact that Jews number no more than several thousand out of a total population of over 200,000. Even fewer inhabitants know Yiddish.

The Birobidzhan experiment failed dismally, a fact that many observers noted by the end of the 1930s. Not only did the region fail to attract many Jews because of its location so far from the center of Jewish population, but the forbidding climate and harsh conditions also militated against significant numbers of Jewish migrants. By 1939 just under 18,000 of the region's approximately 109,000 inhabitants were Jews. Soviet Jews found moving to one of the major cities of the western Soviet Union, such as Minsk, Leningrad, Moscow, Kiev, Odessa, and elsewhere, more attractive than uprooting themselves and their families to the marshes of Birobidzhan, where educational opportunities did not exist and job possibilities were either limited or not to their liking. Moreover, the Kremlin had decided during the purges of 1936–38 to clamp down on Jewish settlement in Birobidzhan, closing virtually all the Yiddish schools in the region, dismantling agencies dealing with Jewish migration, and shutting down many Jewish cultural and social institutions. Despite retaining Yiddish as an official language and maintaining the fiction that Birobidzhan embodied the national and cultural aspirations of Soviet Jewry, the Kremlin stifled the emergence of Jewish culture and society in any meaningful sense of the terms.[1]

I had already sent numerous letters of introduction to libraries and academic institutions in Birobidzhan in the hope that someone could help me obtain a visa from the Soviet government. I was anxious to visit Birobidzhan because I was beginning a new project on the history of the JAR and wanted to supplement an upcoming trip to Moscow with a journey to Birobidzhan, a city of some 80,000 inhabitants. But by August no one had responded to my requests for an invitation.

My efforts were interrupted by a plaintive cry from my wife Laurie, urging me to come quickly to the living room, where she was watching television. As a dutiful Jewish husband, I immediately dropped what I was doing and hurried downstairs. I stopped in my tracks when the TV announcer said that Mikhail Gorbachev was under house arrest following a coup by hardliners who had also sent tanks into Moscow. Needless to say, my first thoughts went to our friends in Moscow and Leningrad, and then they turned to the letter I had been composing. I realized that the coup could possibly jeopardize my upcoming trip to Moscow, funded by the International Research and Exchanges Board (IREX), and despaired of ever visiting the Soviet Palestine, convinced as I was that the coup spelled the death knell for my hope to conduct research in Birobidzhan. I saved the computer file of the half-written letter and spent the next several days glued to the television, watching Soviet citizens heroically challenge the putschists and hoping for a peaceful resolution of the crisis.

Needless to say, I was thrilled when I heard on Wednesday, August 21, that the hard-liners had given up their half-hearted efforts to turn back the clock. As soon as I stopped gleefully jumping up and down, I turned my attention to the letter I had begun writing on Sunday. Fortunately, I never had to avail myself of the help offered by my colleague because shortly after the coup I received the letter I had been waiting for, an invitation from the State Historical Library of the JAR. Some six months later, one Sunday afternoon in early March 1992, I found myself in San Francisco boarding an Aeroflot flight destined for Khabarovsk via Anchorage and Magadan.

Ever since my first IREX-funded research trip in 1982–83 as a graduate student, I had always looked forward to the unexpected challenges that living in the Soviet Union constantly threw my way. A research visit to the Soviet Union during the waning years of Brezhnev meant a series of adventures. My fondest memories of my first extended stay in the Soviet Union are of those strange, unexpected situations in which I found myself while I was working on my dissertation on the Revolution of 1905 in Odessa.[2] I had the good fortune to have been granted access to archival respositories, and for the most part archivists were generous in doling out documents. To be sure, working conditions in libraries and archives in post-Soviet Russia are now far better than they were when I was a graduate student some twenty years ago. Yet I sometimes long for the days when you had to talk yourself blue to gain access to an archive and never even entertained the thought of asking to see the archive's catalogue. Perhaps I possess a masochistic streak, but I know from talking with several colleagues who engaged in research in the late 1970s and early 1980s that many of us feel nostalgic for some aspects of life and work in the so-called era of stagnation. Besides, tales of life in Brezhnev's Soviet Union enrich my teaching, making for fascinating anecdotes that students frequently find hard to apprehend.

At the very least, I appreciate the fact that I have been able to conduct research during both the Soviet and post-Soviet periods, if only to experience how the changes in regime affected my work in libraries and archives. In the early 1980s I bristled when a worker at the Lenin Library in Moscow shouted at me whenever he gave me the photocopies I had ordered; in 1992 the same person invited me to take a seat while he looked for the photocopies I requested. And imagine my joy when, in February 1992, a librarian at the Lenin Library tracked me down several days after she had provided some bibliographic assistance and inquired whether I had had any luck getting hold of the material in question. I had the impression that with the fall of the Soviet Union and the end of Communist rule, library professionals were able to perform the job they were trained to do and exercised their freedom to do so with relish.

Moreover, the excitement of conducting research on Odessa, particularly when handling documents written some one hundred years ago, was heightened by coming across materials that opened up new vistas of understanding and offered alternative perspectives on the events I was exploring. For example, there was the time in 1982 when an archivist at the Central State Archive of the October Revolution (now State Archive of the Russian Federation) in Moscow gave me a file that I had not requested. When the archivist delivered the folder to me, I noticed that only two other researchers had previously used the folder, which contained hundreds of pages of reports. Furthermore, both researchers had looked at the same forty pages in the folder, a fact that I easily ascertained because archive rules require that you sign your name at the front of the folder and indicate which pages you read.

Curiosity got the better of me, and I immediately went to the pages that the two previous researchers had noted they consulted. My jaw dropped and my eyes widened when I realized that the document was the police dossier of Leon Trotsky's first arrest as a young revolutionary in the mid-1890s. No doubt, the archivist responsible for giving me the folder thought she or he was doing me an enormous favor by showing me such a document. Perhaps the person assigned to fulfilling my endless requests for materials was trying to break the monotony of her or his day by having some fun with me, an unseen American graduate student. Or perhaps the archivist felt she or he was living dangerously, engaging in some sort of subversive or dissident activity by showing me the dossier. I have no way to assess the risk assumed by the archivist, and to this day I still wonder who gave me the opportunity to spend several hours copying the account of Trotsky's underground activities in Odessa. I regret that I never had the chance to thank whoever spiced up my time in the archive and taught me that countless hours in archival repositories frequently result in unexpected, exciting finds.

In March 1983 I supplemented my research in Moscow and Leningrad with a three-week trip to Odessa. I was housed in an isolated wing of the university and depended on the kindness and good graces of the woman who operated the buffet to put aside food for me every evening. This system of ensuring my nourishment was disrupted on March 8, International Women's Day, when the buffet was closed and no restaurant would seat me. In what seemed to me to be the low point of my ten-month existence in the Soviet Union, I wandered the streets of Odessa, looking for a store where I could buy some food. All I could find open was a small grocery store that was well-stocked with only candy and cookies. And so I celebrated International Women's Day in my dorm room, finding solace in a kilogram of cookies and in the knowledge that the buffet would be open the following day.

Denied permission to work in Odessa's archives, I spent most of my time reading books, journals, and newspapers in the university library. As a guest of the university, I had unfettered access to the university's holdings. But since the destruction wrought by the Germans during World War II had resulted in the loss of a significant part of the university's collection, I found it necessary to request permission to work in the Odessa State Historical Library. That was no easy matter to arrange, and it took several efforts by my university hosts, culminating in a shouting match, to persuade the State Historical Library's director to allow me access. I was given a desk in a small reading room off-limits to other users of the library, where a librarian kept a watchful eye on me. According to the library's director, my isolation was for my own benefit since no one would be able to bother me. After a week or so, I was summoned to the office of the director, who told me that he cherished the free exchange of information and ideas. He added that my presence in Odessa was testament to the Soviet Union's commitment to "peace and friendship" (*za mir i druzhba*), that ever-present Soviet mantra of the early 1980s. However, this supposedly heartfelt conviction did not prevent him from adding, without the slightest sense of irony, that he was revoking my permission to work in the library because I had already read too many newspapers.

Shut out of the public library and having exhausted the collection of the university library, I spent more time walking around the city, getting a feel for Odessa's topography that helped me to better understand the events of June 1905. For example, I knew that the central area of Odessa's harbor was connected to the city center, situated atop a bluff high above the Black Sea, by the impressive staircase that figures so prominently in Sergei Eisenstein's film *The Battleship Potemkin*. But I had not grasped from my reading about Odessa that the port district was also connected to the rest of the city by two sloping roads, located at opposite ends of the harbor. Seeing the physical configuration of the port and the city center provided insight into the tragic events of June 1905, when mutinous sailors from the *Potemkin* came ashore and placed on display the corpse of their comrade who had been instrumental in sparking the rebellion against the harsh regime aboard ship. It was not until I actually laid eyes on the topographical layout of Odessa that I better understood the macabre events of June 15 and why the harbor was awash with blood: escape was made all the more difficult by the sharp inclines and the staircase that connects the port to the rest of the city.

During the course of June 15, thousands of Odessans streamed into the harbor either to pay their respects or just to observe the scene. People filed by the dead sailor, placing flowers near him, kissing his hand, and swearing to avenge his death. In an effort to prevent those already gathered in the port and to hinder others from entering, the military had sealed off the port district in mid-afternoon by positioning soldiers at both borders of the harbor and along the bluff overlooking it. By late afternoon the mood of the crowds thronging the harbor started to turn ugly as many people, fortified by vodka and wine stolen from unguarded storerooms, began to plunder other warehouses. Despite the military cordon, looters made their way out of the port into the city center, where they proudly displayed their booty and frequently fell into the hands of the police and military.

The rioting in the port continued into the evening and acquired tragic proportions when some rioters set afire the wooden buildings of the harbor. The fires lit up the nighttime sky over Odessa and spread steadily and quickly throughout the port. Moreover, disorders in the center of the city reached crisis proportions as clashes between civilians and soldiers, Cossacks, and police broke out. As pandemonium spread, military officials finally commanded their troops to restore order by opening fire upon the rioters in the harbor and elsewhere in the city. What followed was a massacre, as thousands of civilians trapped by the cordoning off of the harbor found themselves caught in the crossfire of soldiers who occupied higher ground. By the morning of June 16, hundreds—perhaps even a thousand—had died, either from gunshots or from the fire. Apparently many individuals perished because they were so drunk that they passed out and were consumed by the fire. Prior to seeing Odessa firsthand, I did not grasp why so many people could not escape the bullets of soldiers or save themselves from the fire.

Similarly, my insight into the class and ethnic tensions that played such an important role in the labor unrest that engulfed Odessa in 1905 was heightened by visits to neighborhoods outside the city center. Home to large numbers of predominantly non-Jewish workers who lived in overcrowded tenements, these districts seethed with social and economic discontent, and fostered a deeply rooted sense of second-class citizenship among the residents. These neighborhoods were cut off from the city center by either a ravine or the steep inclines that linked the harbor to the rest of Odessa. Moreover, no public transport in the form of horse-drawn trams connected the outlying regions to the city center. Little wonder that the workers of these neighborhoods harbored deep resentment toward those Odessans who lived in the better maintained city center. As in the case of the June events, seeing firsthand the lay of the land honed my analysis of labor unrest in 1905 Odessa.

Visiting Odessa in the early 1980s contributed significantly to my overall grasp of what had transpired there in 1905; so too I longed to see Birobidzhan, a region that embodied in the 1930s the hopes and aspirations of many Jewish Communists throughout the world. My interest in Birobidzhan had begun in 1982, when I was living at Moscow State University, conducting my research on Odessa. One morning, as I was exiting the building on my way to the library, I noticed a newspaper in Hebrew. Upon closer examination I realized that the Hebrew was Yiddish, and that I was holding a copy of the *Birobidzhaner shtern* (Birobidzhan Star). During the remaining months of my stay in Moscow, I infrequently came across other issues of the newspaper, in both Russian and Yiddish, and decided that I wanted to turn my attention to the history of Birobidzhan after I finished my work on Odessa.

As I sat down and got comfortable on the Aeroflot jet headed for Khabarovsk ten years later in 1992, I gave thought to what awaited me in an unfamiliar city where I knew no one. I had just spent the month of February in Moscow, where I witnessed the first flush of excitement—and bewilderment—in the immediate aftermath of the dissolution of the Soviet Union. What would I find in Birobdizhan? Fortunately, the flight provided such interesting diversions that my mind wandered from my thoughts of Birobidzhan. Besides dozens of Russians returning home after visiting the United States, other passengers included several Christian missionaries headed for Magadan and other remote areas of the Russian Far East, where they intended to spread the gospel. I struck up a conversation with a twenty-something Californian also destined for Magadan. He was hoping to enter into a joint business venture with a Russian who was ready to help him hire workers to collect, pack, and ship abroad morel mushrooms. The previous year a large swath of virgin forest in the Russian Far East had been devastated by fire and, according to the American (who had no inkling of Magadan's tragic past as a center of Stalin's system of prison camps), morels tend to proliferate in the new underbrush of forests recently scorched by fire. But perhaps my favorite passenger was the retired American zoologist from the Southwest. An expert in tigers, he had been invited by the government of a city in the Russian Far East that had been experiencing, in his words, a "tiger problem"; that is, tigers had been straying too close to the city in search of food, and the city fathers were hoping this American specialist could develop a strategy to keep them out. When I was in Birobidzhan I saw firsthand evidence of the problem: the local museum had on display a stuffed tiger that had been killed the previous year after approaching a children's playground. Given the adventures that awaited these Americans who had no prior experience in the Soviet Union and did not speak Russian, I realized that I was at least prepared for whatever awaited me in Birobidzhan.

A librarian from the State Historical Library in Birobidzhan, along with her daughter and son-in-law, met me after I cleared customs in Khabarovsk, and we started the journey back to Birobidzhan at midnight. Birobidzhan is 100 miles or so west of Khabarovsk, and I expected the journey to take two or three hours. I realized soon after we started that the ride would take longer than I anticipated. I noticed that we had left the main road out of Khabarovsk and were wending our way down a dirt path that led to the Amur River. For reasons unknown to me, the Soviets never got around to building a road across the Amur; cars and trucks take a ferry during the months from April to October or drive across the frozen river during the remainder of the year, except during those weeks when the ice is breaking up. However, a railway trestle does carry passenger and freight trains over the river throughout the year. The Amur was still frozen in early March, and so we readily drove across the river, though I secretly wished that the car had pontoons or I had water wings.

We arrived safely in Birobidzhan near dawn, and my hosts deposited me in a room at the nicer of the city's two hotels. I paid the ruble equivalent of two dollars a day, a consequence of the incredibly favorable exchange rate resulting from the inflationary spiral after the lifting of many price controls in January 1992. In contrast to Moscow, where I saw how the beginnings of inflation and the collapse of strong political control convinced my friends and acquaintances that they were about to be inundated by social chaos, economic woes, and the like, life in Birobidzhan was comparatively calm. I did not yet observe a crisis mentality among the inhabitants of Birobidzhan, whether Jew or gentile. They did not feel that declining living standards would contribute to the breakdown of the social and political order, and Jews in Birobidzhan felt secure in their lives as both Jews and citizens of a society trying to resuscitate itself.

I spent nearly a month in Birobidzhan, working in the State Historical Library and State Historical Archive, familiarizing myself with the renaissance of Jewish culture, interviewing people who had lived there since the 1930s, and also enjoying a modicum of celebrity status. I did radio and television interviews, lectured at the Pedagogical Institute about the study of Soviet history in the United States, and was even recognized from television by the woman who took my ticket at the movie theater across from the hotel. In the best tradition of Russian hospitality, the staff of the archive never failed to bring me tea and cookies when I worked there, a far cry from the early 1980s when some of the staff at the Lenin Library occasionally snapped at me when I asked them for bibliographic assistance or submitted a book request. Furthermore, the director of the state archive gave me full access to the materials that had been seized from the Communist Party of the JAR soon after the failed August coup. In short, the time I spent in Birobidzhan was invaluable not only in terms of the research I managed to complete, but also in terms of experiencing the changes wrought by over a half decade of glasnost and perestroika.

To be sure, during the early 1990s the worlds of the Soviet and post-Soviet eras coexisted uneasily and even clashed. But events in Birobidzhan demonstrated that the Soviet-era atmosphere of suspicion and secrecy was a thing of the past. Birobidzhan in the early 1990s bristled with excitement and activity as the Jews of Birobidzhan engaged in a concerted effort to realize the original promise of the region as a vibrant Jewish cultural center. The editor of the *Birobidzhaner shtern* made sure to introduce me to others who knew about the region's history or were involved in the effort to revive Jewish life and Yiddish. Not only was the lighting of Sabbath candles televised on Friday evenings, but a Purim play—financed by the city government—was attended by hundreds of people reflecting a cross-section of the populace and was broadcast all over the JAR. It testified to the desire of Birobidzhan's inhabitants, gentile and Jew alike, to rekindle Jewish identity and proclaim their ties to Jews in Israel and elsewhere. In addition, some 150 children and teenagers (not all Jewish) were attending a Jewish Sunday school that offered classes in Yiddish, Hebrew, and Jewish history and culture. A variety of Jewish organizations had also cropped up, ranging from a Zionist youth group to the "Maccabee Sports Club." Moreover, a B'nai B'rith chapter from New Jersey had organized a Jewish summer camp, and instructors from two Israeli universities had offered classes in Jewish literature, history, philosophy, and folklore. Official commitment to the maintenance of Yiddish as a living language was revealed in the course offerings at the local Pedagogical Institute, where a Yiddish-language program had been instituted.

The Jewish cultural renaissance was complemented by efforts to familiarize residents with the history of Jewish life and culture in the JAR and the purges of the Stalin years. The *Birobidzhaner shtern*, for example, published documents from the state archive on Jewish life in Birobidzhan during its initial years. The region's museum put together an exhibition exploring the repression that targeted the political leadership, peasantry, and Jewish intelligentsia from the mid-1930s until 1953. One of the many fascinating insights offered by this exhibition concerned an accusation that the Jewish wife of the JAR's first Party chief had tried to poison Lazar Kaganovich with gefilte fish during his visit in the mid-1930s.

Of course, I still had to contend with the legacy of the Soviet period and find my way in the new society emerging from the atrophying world of communism. For example, I could not exchange currency legally in Birobidzhan for the simple reason that the banks had no arrangements to accept my dollars. Then there was the time a KGB officer paid me a visit in my hotel room and asked me a series of questions about the purpose of my visit to Birobidzhan (incidentally, all government buildings in Birobidzhan, including KGB headquarters, still had signs in both Russian and Yiddish). In one telling incident, the man in charge of economic relations between the JAR and foreign countries offered to sell me his book manuscript, along with his notes, about the history of the region from its establishment in 1928 to the outbreak of World War II. He would not permit me to read what he had written unless I paid him one thousand dollars. In exchange, he would hand over to me all the research he had amassed and permit me to claim his work as mine by replacing his name with my own on the manuscript's title page! My effort to explain my reluctance fell on deaf ears since he believed that intellectual ideas were also subject to the allure and power of market forces. He responded that a team of Finnish documentary filmmakers had offered him several thousand dollars for his manuscript. I told him to sell his materials to the Finns and headed to the library where I could read free of charge the dissertation upon which he based his manuscript. I am happy to report that he did publish his manuscript (under his own name) several years later.

The trip home was less interesting than was the trip to Birobidzhan, but it too had its moments. After the passengers on the flight cleared customs in Anchorage and while we spent an hour or so waiting for the next leg of our trip, several Russians approached me and asked me to call friends and relatives elsewhere in the United States. Not surprisingly, I found myself charging phone calls to my credit card as I spent a good half hour dialing numbers for my fellow passengers. In one case, the person I reached complained, "We told him not to come! We told him not to visit us here! We told him that we could not take care of him!" On the flight from Anchorage to San Francisco, I sat next to a young man headed for Los Angeles. He innocently asked me for advice on how he could get to Los Angeles given the fact that he had twenty or so dollars to his name and had no idea that some 400 miles separated the Bay area from southern California.

I have been traveling to Russia for the past twenty years to do research. Many friends and students quizzically ask what impels me to do so, in light of what they consider to be substandard and unacceptable living and working conditions. I respond that regular visits to Russia have allowed me to glean knowledge and understanding of Soviet and post-Soviet society and culture that I can then take into the classroom. There has been no better way to track the changes affecting Russian society—from Brezhnev to Gorbachev, from Gorbachev through Yeltsin, and on to Putin—than to experience them. Still, researching and writing about Russian history, whether during the late Brezhnev years or in the wild, wild west atmosphere of Moscow and St. Petersburg in the early 1990s, have been enhanced by the unexpected richness of the materials I have read in the libraries and archives of Moscow, St. Petersburg, Odessa, and Birobidzhan.

A colleague said to me recently that one of his graduate students was grousing about the slow delivery of materials at the Russian Center for the Preservation and Study of Documents of Recent History (a major repository of the Communist Party's materials). "Wimp," my colleague blurted out. "He doesn't remember the good old days when you were lucky to receive permission to work in any archive, let alone the Party archive." While I am not sure I would call life and work in Brezhnev's Russia "the good old days," I do share my colleague's sentiment that the virtually unfettered access to archives since the early 1990s has spoiled us. We now expect everything to come easily to us when we work in Russian libraries and archives, and take the changes in access and availability of materials for granted. I do not mean that those of us in the field who received their Ph.D.s before the collapse of communism deserve a medal proclaiming us "Heroes of Socialist Labor." I certainly do not believe that suffering of any sort is good for one's soul or improves one's character. But a sense of humility and sensitivity, not to mention historical perspective, is called for when anyone does research in Russia. Two decades of research in Soviet and post-Soviet Russia have taught me that hard work and perseverance—along with a bit of serendipity and the kindness of strangers—result in unexpected research finds and enhance the quality of my work.

Notes

1. For a history of Birobidzhan, see Robert Weinberg, *Stalin's Forgotten Zion: Birobidzhan and the Making of a Soviet Jewish Homeland. An Illustrated History.* Berkeley: University of California Press, 1998.

2. Robert Weinberg, *The Revolution of 1905 in Odessa: Blood on the Steps.* Bloomington: Indiana University Press, 1993.

16

Mysteries in the Realms of History and Memory

Cathy A. Frierson

In the early days of my archival research in Russia, the late days of the Soviet Empire, revelatory conversations typically came during long walks out of doors, beyond the reach of any listening devices. In May 1985, I was on such a walk in the English park surrounding Pavlovsk, the palace Catherine the Great ordered built for her son Paul, outside St. Petersburg. It was a Sunday afternoon and we were three women whose very acquaintance marked the decline of old Soviet ways and their yielding to a new order under M.S. Gorbachev as general secretary of the Communist Party and head of the Soviet government, then two months into his tenure. The conversation that day proved to be the first in a series of family histories Soviet citizens would tell me over the next decade. Their stories would be as critical to my understanding of Russia as the research that led me to be there to listen to personal confrontations with the Soviet past. Researching history consistently led me into the realm of personal memory as well. The first such revelation in my inaugural year of research in the Soviet Union came as a complete surprise.

Two months earlier, I had arrived in Leningrad after six months of frustration as an International Research and Exchanges Board (IREX) exchangee in Moscow. Every archive I had sought had been closed to me as a student of Richard Pipes, recently special advisor for Soviet and East European Affairs to President Ronald Reagan, who had just proclaimed the USSR the "evil empire." Unlike my fellow graduate students from Harvard on the exchange that year, I had naively listed Pipes as my dissertation advisor on my exchange forms, rather than other less notorious figures on the Harvard faculty. After providing a target for Soviet anger over the fall and winter, I had gone to Leningrad in March with no hope of doing archival research. Instead I planned to see the city, then leave the USSR two months before my term as an IREX exchangee was scheduled to end. I had promptly come down with bronchitis in Leningrad's swampy climate and was sitting with my head under a towel over a bowl of steaming water in my dorm room on Shevchenko Street when someone knocked on my door.

My husband opened it to a woman who introduced herself as Barbara Engel, history professor from the University of Colorado. She asked if I were Cathy Frierson. When I said that I was, she recounted something odd that had happened earlier in the day. She had gone to the Museum of Ethnography to try to talk her way into the archive. Instead of receiving the usual rejection at the gates by the guard, she found herself being ushered into the office of the director. After Barbara had explained her research project on women workers in St. Petersburg for a few minutes, the director stopped her and said she thought the American worked on peasants. Barbara explained that most of the women workers were former peasants who had left the village, but that she was interested in their experience in the city. The director responded, "They told me to prepare materials for you on peasants." Barbara asked who had mentioned her, because her approach to the Museum of Ethnography had been her own decision without consultation with anyone in Leningrad. The director answered, "Aren't you Cathy Frierson?" When Barbara replied in the negative, the director asked her if she knew this Cathy Frierson or where she could be found. Barbara said that she thought a Cathy Frierson had just arrived from Moscow to the Shevchenko Street dormitory. The director then concluded the unexpected interview by asking Barbara to find Cathy Frierson, to tell her, "We are waiting for her here," and that Barbara should come back, too, because the director found her topic interesting.

Barbara and I thus found ourselves seated side by side for the next eight weeks at a small desk adjacent to that of the archive's director. We understood that we were the second and third non-Soviet scholars (David Ransel was the first) to read materials in the Tenishev Fund, a coveted trove of survey responses submitted to an amateur St. Petersburg ethnographer by rural residents across European Russia in the late 1890s. Every day we sat like scribes, reading as quickly as we could, frantically scribbling notes, always anticipating that the next day might find us standing outside the guard's gate, denied further access.

I was an intellectual historian when the Tenishev materials became available to me. In planning my IREX year, I had requested only personal files of the writers whose work on the peasants figured in my dissertation on *representations* of peasants in the post-Emancipation period. I had eschewed the *reality* of village life almost completely. When Barbara and I were handed the index to the Tenishev files, I had to make rapid choices on which subjects to pursue. An earlier frustrated interest and a gap in the secondary literature shaped my choices.

My frustrated interest was a study of the *volost'* or cantonal court records as a window on rural values and attitudes toward law and justice. Four years earlier, when I had proposed this as a possible dissertation topic to Richard Pipes, he had dismissed the likelihood that any court records had survived a full century. I acceded to his judgment and turned to the question of representations. During my six months in Moscow, I had focused my research in the Lenin Library on the cantonal court as a subject of public debate throughout the post-Emancipation era. These days of making the best of my archive-deprived existence bore two key fruits: my first refereed article on the cantonal court debate and a thorough knowledge of the literature. When the index to the Tenishev files appeared, I designated responses on the cantonal court my first priority. The debate about the "peasant soul" in my study of representations had also alerted me to the passionate debates about peasants' concepts of law, justice, and punishments as features of a native Russian customary law. "Crime and Punishment" thus became my second priority.

The gap I thought these files might help me fill was the subject of peasant family divisions. Because they had figured so prominently in the articulation of the negative image of peasant women, I had searched in vain for an article to explain the basic facts of family divisions. The Tenishev index immediately revealed that local respondents to Tenishev's survey had been eager to address this question, and in welcome detail. My major challenges—in a stunning reversal of my discouraging and enervating Moscow experience— were now to get through a wealth of archival materials and to decipher the scripts of the rural correspondents. I found the latter a particular pleasure, delighting in the opportunity to learn the elegant and consistent script of local bureaucrats, the slightly more idiosyncratic and delicate gentry scripts, and the almost block-like script which signaled a peasant correspondent.

The Tenishev files led me to challenge a truism in the historiography of the cantonal court embraced both by Western authors (such as Pipes), who focused on the absence of a "rule of law" in Russian history, and by Soviet scholars and their Western acolytes, who dismissed the success of any imperial reform institution. The truism was that the cantonal courts were a failure on every count: as a channel for the penetration of positive law into the countryside, as a site to which peasants could or did turn to resolve their disputes, or even as a procedural entity. The detailed reports by local observers from the late 1890s revealed instead a vibrant institution handling a sharply increasing number of peasant disputes. I would have to wait a full decade to publish this conclusion, and then only in a British journal, because my U.S. colleagues collectively resisted my positive analysis of the cantonal court as an arena of legal socialization.[1] No sooner had I done so than Gareth Popkins wrote me from the University of Aberystwyth in Wales to tell me that his extensive archival research on the same subject in several regional archives also supported my conclusions. In March and April 1985, however, I knew only that the Tenishev files were presenting me with new understandings of the cantonal court as I gradually comprehended what the various scripts in faded ink on yellowed pages described.

As Barbara Engel and I read these rich files, the director continued her work beside us. We overheard her telephone conversations, witnessed her dealings with her staff, and learned that she was the chairman of the Communist Party cell at the museum. Her assistant would arrive around 2:00 P.M. each day, bearing pastries from a shop around the corner. We then crammed into an oversized closet for tea and conversation—the director, her assistant, the two American researchers, and various members of the staff invited to join in our discussions. These were openings into a previously closed society—open access to a protected archive, open access to the daily work of an archive director, open access to women workers in that archive, and for them, access to us as informants on the United States beyond official Soviet sources of contemporary information, albeit in the presence of their director and chief of their local Party committee.

She was a remarkable woman, this director. She was only forty in 1985, a surprisingly young director in the late Soviet gerontocracy. She was vibrant, funny, warm, passionate, an accomplished ethnographer. She was a devoted Communist who confided that her favorite old Bolshevik was Felix Dzerzhinsky, founder of the Soviet secret police, who won her affection through his own passionate commitment to the cause. Barbara's and my walk with her through the parks at Pavlovsk was our valedictory excursion. At the end of the day, as we were descending toward the bus stop outside the gates, our talk was of World War II. This was an unavoidable topic in that fortieth anniversary year of the "defeat of the Fascists," while we strolled the grounds of a palace totally destroyed by German soldiers and painstakingly restored as a monument to Soviet resilience. I steeled myself for the recriminations I had heard all spring from other Soviet citizens about the treachery of the United States and Britain in their refusal to open a second front. These were always followed by self-righteous glorification of the Soviet people's valorous martyrdom in an *exclusively defensive* victory over Hitler as the saviors of Europe and European culture.

But this was not the meaning of World War II then occupying the director's mind. Its meaning had only recently been transformed into a personal record of her own genesis, previously unknown to her. On her fortieth birthday, she first learned the truth about her birth. For the first time, she learned that her family history as she had known it had been a fabrication that had made it possible for her to have a family at all. For her father had just told her that she had been born not in the western village she thought of as her birthplace, but on a farm in Germany. She learned that both mother and father had been slave laborers there, each seized in a Wehrmacht raid on their home villages and shipped west to grow food for the Third Reich. They had met on that farm and fallen in love, and her mother had conceived and given birth to her on the eve of the Nazi defeat. American soldiers had found her parents walking on the road away from the farm, loaded them into a jeep with their infant, and delivered them to the border of the Soviet Union, where they watched them cross over. She learned that her young parents made their way back to their destroyed village somehow, and that they were alerted to Stalin's policy of sending to the Gulag as traitors all Soviet citizens who had spent time in Germany during the war as prisoners of war or slave laborers. They then assumed the identities of two young people their age who had perished during the war and began to weave a story of their wartime experiences that would keep them safe from exile to hard labor and family separation. They told her this family history as she grew up. These were the family origins she proclaimed as she climbed the ranks of the Communist Party. As she blossomed into a favored advocate of the Soviet government, her parents kept silent about a personal history that had compromised their own trust in a state that had threatened to punish them for their victimization and had forced them into falsification before their child. They remained silent as they watched their daughter grow into a fan of Felix Dzerzhinsky, founder of the very prison system that stood as a spectre just beyond the frame of the story they had so carefully constructed.

Still reeling from her father's revelation, the archive director shared it with us as an implicit explanation for why, when Barbara Engel appeared before her requesting access to a closed and officially obscured past, she decided to let us in to sit beside her, reading hundreds of files that could, as she undoubtedly knew, lead us away from the official Soviet version of Russia's pre-Bolshevik past. I would shortly publish three articles on the social history of the Russian peasantry on the basis of that research, articles that launched my tenure-track career. I have little doubt that I owe my career to this woman, to her confrontation with the disjunction between official and personal memories, and to her willingness to open the archive to me.

But some doubt there is—not about whether access to this particular archive launched my career, but about the reason I gained that access. Perhaps the archive director did not act out of generosity and amended personal memory at all. Perhaps there is another explanation altogether, one that had nothing to do with a personal confrontation with the great falsification of Soviet history (however moving a tale that makes), but instead everything to do with networks of power. For although I had spent my days during the previous six months languishing in the Lenin Library in Moscow while all my U.S. peers worked in archives, I spent at least one evening of every week in the apartment of a couple with high contacts in the Communist power establishment. The husband was a Lenin prize-winning research physician. More important was his wife's family. Her father was a Party poet, who wrote of the glories of communism. They traveled rather frequently to Paris. We got to know them through a French colleague. We knew that they reported on us to the KGB after each visit. This seemed a normal feature of our social relationships then. We soon recognized that if we dined with them once a week and told them lots of stories about our week's activities for them to exchange for an exit visa to Paris the following spring, no one followed us the rest of the nights of the week when we visited *other* private apartments. Most of our conversations were pure pablum; we used to refer to them as the "peace and friendship show." But just before we left for Leningrad, intending to terminate our stay in the USSR prematurely, my husband dropped his usual happy-go-lucky replies to their queries about our day's labors. Instead, he said, "Well, actually, we've had it and are planning to leave as soon as we've seen Leningrad."

"You're not satisfied with your work?" they asked with apparently genuine surprise.

"No, we're not," he continued. "In fact, we're sick of the way Cathy's been treated. For six months she has been treated completely rudely, unprofessionally, and disrespectfully."

As they focused with unprecedented attention, he then recounted the many indignities I had suffered, down to the TsGALI (Central State Archive of Literature and Art) director's supercilious announcement to me as I stood in my winter coat, hat, shawl, and gloves in the entryway of her domain, "Yes, Cathy Frierson, all of the materials you have requested are here. And, yes, Cathy Frierson, they would all be very useful for your work. But you, Cathy Frierson, will never see them because you will never be permitted to cross this threshold. Good day."

So off to Leningrad we went after our dinner with the daughter of a poet and her Lenin-prize husband. Barbara Engel and the archive director did indeed have their peculiar conversation. And Barbara and I did indeed enjoy remarkable access to the archive. Six weeks into our files, as Barbara and I were wrapping up our work, the archivist turned to me and asked from her desk, "So, Cathy, when will you bring your husband by?"

I answered, "Why would I do that? He has his work and I have mine."

"Well," she said, "we'd like him to see that we are not treating you 'completely rudely, unprofessionally, and disrespectfully'."

"Oh," I said. "I see."

This exchange raised several questions. Foremost among them: Why did our Moscow host and hostess intervene? They had no need to; our weekly record had already assured the trip to Paris, which took place during our time in Leningrad. Had they grown to like us? And were their networks such that they could both identify an archive I might find useful (despite my own failure even to submit a written request to visit it) and get a phone call through to gain permission for me? And how could that have borne fruit if Barbara Engel had not unexpectedly decided to brave an unannounced visit? I had visited the Museum of Ethnography upon arriving in Leningrad—not the one that housed the Tenishev Fund, however, but the Kunstkamera across the river (which holds the collection of non-Russian ethnographic materials and Peter the Great's collection of natural curiosities). Perhaps my husband had mentioned my plight to his Leningrad patron, who might have made the requisite call. But that seems a most unlikely explanation given my own lack of prior interest in the Tenishev Fund and the director's repetition of my husband's declaration in Moscow.

I felt that I was by far the least critical player in this minor archive mystery, which, to repeat, launched my career as a teacher and scholar. It was of a piece with almost all my experiences during that first year in the old Soviet Union, when everything seemed beyond any influence of my individual efforts or actions. Certainly I could lay no claim to superior skills at achieving archival access; the best I could do was to exploit to the full the materials of the Tenishev Fund when they unexpectedly landed on a desk in front of me, index included.

Four years later, another archive door swung open before me, with equal impact on my development as a scholar. This time, too, personal history may have moved the director to favor revelation over concealment. And, once again, a fellow U.S. scholar led me to an archive director who would open the door. It was 1989, and the sunny days of glasnost-era access to archives were approaching their zenith. I was now working freely in the personal files of major figures from my dissertation in archives closed to me in 1984–85. The supercilious director who had earlier physically and verbally barred my entry to TsGALI now offered me virtually unrestricted use of materials, going so far as to invite me to browse in the storage rooms. Only rarely did I go to the Lenin Library, but one day there I had a fortuitous meeting with Nellie Hauke Ohr. She told me she had just returned from Smolensk, where she had enjoyed remarkable access in the regional archive to materials related to the collectivization campaign. I had already completed the first draft of my translation of A.N. Engelgardt's letters from his estate in Smolensk Province in the 1870s and 1880s, and was preparing its introduction at the same time that I was completing my first book, *Peasant Icons*.[2] I had not dared to imagine that I could go to Smolensk to read materials; I was still adjusting to my unlimited access to his materials at TsGALI in Moscow. But Nellie encouraged me to call the Smolensk archive director, assuring me that he would welcome me.

Within a matter of weeks I was boarding the night train to Smolensk at Belorusskii station. My Lenin-prize physician friend took me to the station, as my husband was at the Academy of Sciences hotel with our two-year-old son. My friend was good enough to bribe the conductress to give me her single compartment when we discovered that the other person in my two-berth sleeper was a KGB officer, just disrobing down to his boxers. A small, but memorable indicator of the new era was the radio music coming through the speakers in my compartment. It was exclusively Western—and mostly American—contemporary rock music, unlike the Soviet fare of train travel four years earlier. As we pulled out of Moscow, I lay snug in my heavy cotton sheets and wool blankets and marveled equally at my destination and at Sting serenading my journey.

A driver met me as I got off the train and drove me thirty minutes through December morning darkness to leave my luggage at the Intourist hotel on the outskirts of town. It was frequented at that season primarily by truck drivers hauling freight between Poland and Moscow. I pushed thoughts of my return there that evening aside as we left for the archive in the middle of town. Surely there is no more romantic place in Russia to do research. I was as wide-eyed as a toddler on Christmas morning as the car turned into a cobble-stone drive leading up a hillside under a broad arch through white-washed fortress walls into the courtyard of Smolensk's eighteenth-century emerald and white rococo cathedral rising high into the winter light. Bells were ring-ing in the tower to signal morning services. With no time to take in this scene, I was whisked through the white wall, making my way into the low-ceilinged entry room for the archive. There the wiry director bustled out of his office, moving around me like a late October bee in New England—darting to one side, then the other, taking my coat, then my hat, then my bag, then my gloves, all the while interrogating the driver about the hotel. He summarily declared that it was unthinkable that I should stay out on the fringes with truck drivers, dispatched the driver to retrieve my suitcase, and announced that I would be staying in his apartment with his wife and son.

We moved to the business of the day, which for him was most immedi-ately the opportunity to speak openly with an American about glasnost and culture, to recite whole stanzas of Anna Akhmatova's *Requiem*—then only recently published in the USSR—and finally to read me some poems of his own composition. I wondered if I would actually be doing any *research* while in Smolensk. By early afternoon, however, I was deep into the materials on Engelgardt he had prepared for me.

That evening, he walked me home to his Khrushchev-era apartment block.

Those who have visited him since know his home well—two narrow, rectangular rooms end-to-end with one large window at each extreme, a bathroom, and a tiny square kitchen, all on street level. The air in Smolensk was infused with the odor of the huge meat-processing plant that dominated the dimly-lit night sky.

Over supper and afterwards, it was his wife's turn to tell stories of her childhood as an orphan of the Terror. By bedtime, she and I were sitting thigh to thigh on my bed for the night, poring over pictures of her parents— her Latvian father, the young Bolshevik who had enchanted her mother, the young Polish university student, who had joined him in the revolution as a Red Army soldier. There she was, the young Polish, Bolshevik soldier, in uniform, smiling. There they were again, the young Soviet couple on the steps of the obstetrical clinic he directed and she served as a doctor. Again, they were smiling, the fulfillment of their dreams of serving the people in a socialist state shining from their eyes.

By 1937, they were both gone, first the father, then the mother, taken away in the night, their two young daughters left alone in their apartment. Soon they, too, would be spirited away, not by Stalin's footsoldiers, but by the elderly woman across the hall. They barely knew her, but she had been watching. She gathered them for a journey to the far north, where they grew into their adolescence as Soviet citizens, one to become a young Communist, the other—my hostess—to maintain a cautious distance. They, too, learned to obscure their family history, and most importantly, the existence of their relatives in Poland. More stories followed from their refuge to the present day, concluding with a generous good-night for me as I slid between the crisp, heavy cotton sheets on the bed. These were my first introduction to the wonderful textiles in Smolensk, remnants of its imperial heyday as a center of linen production, which in turn was partially a legacy of Engelgardt's introduction of flax as a commercial crop in the region.

The next morning, I awoke to the smell of breakfast and sounds of quiet preparations for the day. As I stepped out of my rectangle room into the second one, I saw my host, standing before a window opened into the cold, black air. He raised his hands high over his head, breathing deeply, then exhaled loudly as he dropped them. Three times he did this as I paused on my way to the kitchen. He turned his head only long enough to tell me that he did this each day as an exercise inspired by India and yoga, to cleanse his lungs and stimulate his blood. Then he turned his face back to the window and lifted his arms again, pulling as much slaughterhouse, Smolensk, winter air into his chest as he could.

Somehow this image has lingered as my most emblematic memory of that glasnost year—more than Sting, more than the satisfying hours in TsGALI, more than watching the Congress of People's Deputies debate the meaning of the Molotov-Ribbentrop Pact on Moscow television, more than standing in a crowded field in Leningrad on a minus-twenty-one-degree day as one of thousands joining a spontaneous memorialization of Andrei Sakharov a day after his death. I keep returning to that moment, to that portrait of a hungry mind and an eager soul opening the window from his physical confinement to suck in the air that he had transformed through his fertile imagination into an agent of Eastern holistic health. That scene serves as my explanation for why this regional archival director would open his archive and its materials on an obscured past to me, a stranger from the other side of the Cold War. He worshiped Akhmatova and recited her words with the reverence of someone whose wife's life had long before brought Akhmatova's sorrows into the fabric of his understanding of his culture. Opening the doors wide to U.S. scholars held the promise of an airing as invigorating for the history of Russia as he imagined his morning exercise to be for his body and soul.

His generosity led me not only to materials on Engelgardt, but also to the discovery of biweekly police reports, district by district, on fires, their causes and losses. Slip by slip, month by month, year by year, district by district, they lifted and fell as I rushed through the pages of the governor's chancellery in search of police surveillance reports on the exiled Engelgardt. Eventually I paused to read them and was hooked. The consistency of their format and chronological regularity as biweekly reports convinced me that the imperial bureaucracy had decided to collect data on fires systematically. The details included in each handwritten report suggested several questions that shaped my research thereafter. Over the next ten years I followed their leads to other regional archives in Novgorod and Vologda, where other archive directors have opened the way for my research on fire and arson in rural Russia.[3]

During a trip in the early 1990s, I was working again in the Tenishev Fund, reading every respondent's report that included replies to questions about fire and arson. It was winter, as it usually was for research trips squeezed in between semesters of teaching. Each day I left my son at home with my husband and our surrogate family, whose apartment we shared. My husband was using that research trip to interview scientists and policymakers in (by then) St. Petersburg. This meant I could work each day until around 3:00 P.M., then relieve him of child care to do evening interviews. For our son, this proved a magical arrangement, for he spent his days playing in the snow in the nearby park of Sosnovka with his father, being fed hot lunches by our surrogate babushka Anna Andreevna, who then devoted her afternoon to playing hide-and-seek with him in the five-room apartment. When I arrived home, I would take him by trolley to the market of aluminum stalls that surrounded the Politeknicheskaia subway station in that early phase of the economic transition, where he delighted in buying chewing gum from Turkey, imitation Ninja Turtle toys, and Soviet-era toy cars and trucks. Each day I also bought two packs of Western cigarettes for the archival assistant who worked with me at the Museum of Ethnography. This was her request after I once brought her Lindt chocolates. As an adamant anti-smoker, I considered this a compromise of my own values, but one way to treat this assistant as an equal by honoring her request. The compromise seemed minor by comparison with the larger one I had refused to make when the post-Soviet archive director demanded that I pay him $35 a day to work there.

On this trip to the Tenishev Fund, I now worked in the storage rooms themselves, at a desk within sight of the shelves where the files lay. As in the case of the cantonal court files earlier, the files on fire and arson fundamentally informed my revised interpretation of these phenomena. One of the most important revisions came from eyewitness accounts of peasants' behaviors during village fires. Every published contemporary account had characterized the peasants as hysterical, irrational, selfish, or helpless in the face of fire. As I read report after report from the late 1890s, I began to make such small comments in my notes as, "This doesn't sound like chaos," and "This sounds like other accounts with a division of labor at a fire," and "These peasants weren't helpless or hysterical!" Peasants as capable firefighters began to take shape in my mental village, just as they had surfaced as plaintiffs and judges at cantonal court sessions. The material culture of Russia's villages and new understandings of peasant agency took form during my days in the Tenishev archive as the rewards for tromping through the winter snow and ice of St. Petersburg in January.

As before, I was often invited to break for tea and pastries. Soon the assistant, whom I had not known before, wanted to tell me her family story as well. So it was that I gave up an entire morning of research to listening, while she smoked Marlboro after Marlboro, occasionally pausing in her narration to plug in the samovar again to prepare more *kipitok* (boiled water) to heat up our tea. She, too, it turned out, had an obscured past, one dating to the very inception of the Soviet state. For, she explained, her great-grandfather had been an officer in the Imperial Army. As the Civil War spread and he learned of the Bolshevik policy of forcing such men to serve their cause under threat of kidnapping their families, her great-grandfather decided to flee. He took his young family deep into the forest, somewhere in the Pskov region. There he reenacted the internal colonization of slash-and-burn farming practiced by his distant forebears, who had similarly sought independence beyond the reach of Riurikid grand princes by moving from location to location in the sheltering woods of old Rus'.

Incredibly, or so it seemed to me, they managed to evade the Leninist, then Stalinist state, as the settlement expanded with the arrival of others fleeing the regime, the largest number appearing in the 1930s. Only during World War II did Soviet soldiers come upon them, ship the adults off to exile, and place the young ones in state homes for "children of the enemies of the people." For the archive assistant, this forcibly repressed piece of her family past had recently been revived by her cousin, who had asked her and her family to join him in making a pilgrimage to the hiding place in the forest. Initially reluctant, she had made the trip and, so she explained, was still in a state of wonderment and disbelief about her ancestry.

As for me, the American researcher, I took in this tale, like those of other archivists who had helped me, as a gift to be deployed later in teaching my students for whom Gorbachev would soon seem only a historical abstraction, to say nothing of the virtually unknown Lenin and Stalin. Their surreal qualities forced reflection over the relationship between history and memory, between the fantastic falsehoods of the Soviet historical enterprise and the equally fantastic family truths these individuals now used to define themselves.

By the mid-1990s, unrestricted access to central and regional archives had become standard, and I, as an American visitor, had become mundane. Archivists no longer told me their stories. Reading rooms in local archives began to fill up quickly each morning with citizens from the area who were researching *their* families' stories. They were seeking documentary evidence to confirm what they remembered or had been told by relatives about their grandparents' and parents' origins, and about the fate of those who had disappeared from the family circle and family reminiscences in the enforced silences of the Soviet period. My relationships with archive directors and assistants became more businesslike, completely devoid of the tension and excitement of entering new territory that I sensed in the spring of 1985 and winter of 1989, and of the revelations of the early 1990s. But the thrill of reading handwritten court transcripts and other documents from local court cases remains strong.

It seems that my work as an historian of Russia has come to resemble more closely that of my colleagues who study the United States or western Europe. It has become a more controllable, predictable, and individual experience. The likelihood of open access; the elimination of internal visas and obstacles to travel around Russia; the free provision of previously denied indexes to each archive's holdings; the ability to develop a working knowledge of the kinds of materials gathered by the imperial bureaucracy in each locality and the patterns of their filing in the archives; the ease of ordering photocopies of texts and photographs of graphic materials; and the nonchalant receptivity of local archive directors to Western scholars' requests now place responsibility on the individual scholar. Success now depends on the same skills historians of Germany or France develop. We historians of Russia are now distinguished largely by the visas we have to procure, our stamina, and our willingness to live in Third World conditions while we do our research.

My research experiences are so similar from season to season as to be a peaceful retreat from the demands of my life as an American professor. The reading room in the Vologda archive is like all the others I've visited in Russia. The mass-production, proletarian culture of the socialist economy still defines these spaces, where one always sits at narrow tables with chipping pine-veneer tops, side by side with a researcher who is likewise seated on a wooden chair with a worn, cloth-covered seat that scrapes across the floorboards. In the windows, there are always geraniums or spider plants sprouting fronds in the weak sunlight that comes through the glass. The reading-room attendant sits behind a wood-veneer desk. On her windowsill or along the shelf behind her, she always has a cracked and chipped cup or two, some mismatched saucers, a couple of tin spoons, and a stained teapot. There is likely to be a much-used heavy plastic bag, inside whose grease and crumb-smeared surfaces one might detect her "second breakfast" of bread and salami, or her afternoon tea treat of cookies or part of a chocolate bar.

It is quiet in Russian reading rooms, quieter somehow than in the reading rooms of Harvard's Widener, the New York Public, or the Library of Congress. In such a setting, Russians are very still people. One hears only the breathing of one's neighbors, the scratching of their pens, the elongated sound of a large piece of old paper turning and settling as the reader completes one page and moves to another. The radiator hums. The snow or freezing rain taps at the windows. The teakettle sometimes whistles. It is warm. It is very, very peaceful. One can escape utterly there.

In March 1985, I was on the verge of leaving the Soviet Union and the study of Russia, dissuaded by obstructionist archival directors in Moscow of any future for me as a historian of their culture. I was en route not only out of the country, but also into an attitude of angry disdain toward the Soviet people in the form of these figures who had so frustrated and humiliated me. One after another, archive directors outside Moscow drew me back. Their welcoming assistance ensured that I would return to Russia, where daily life fed my historical understanding of the texts I read in their archives. They made it possible for me to live through the "world historical events" of Soviet collapse and transition, and to write the history of late imperial Russia with late Soviet Russia and post-Soviet Russia before my eyes.

There is no way to know, really, why doors opened so wide for me, first in 1985 in St. Petersburg, then in Smolensk in 1989, and in Novgorod and

Vologda through the end of the century. Make of it what you will—archivists reconciling official lies and personal truths, the effects of Gorbachev's official policy of openness, a shared respect for scholarly labor, a powerful acquaintance's intervention, my own growing confidence in the likelihood of a positive response, or still other factors. My inability to explain with certainty what the truth is in my research history or whether all the family stories I heard were true serves as a caveat for me against being overly certain about any historical truth, as a teacher or a scholar.

Notes

1. Cathy A. Frierson, "I must always answer to the law . . . : Rules and Responses in the Reformed Cantonal Court," *Slavonic and East European Review* 75, no. 2 (April 1997): 308–34. I first presented this research in 1986 as a paper at a conference at the University of Massachusetts, Boston, on the peasantry of European Russia, 1800–1921, sponsored by the National Endowment for the Humanities. Jane Burbank was the only U.S. scholar who supported my conclusion, which she found valid on the basis of her research in the late 1980s and early 1990s in cantonal court archives in Moscow Province. She ultimately convinced me to submit it for publication.

2. Cathy A. Frierson, trans., *Aleksandr Nikolaevich Engelgardt's Letters from the Country, 1872–1887*. New York: Oxford University Press, 1993; and *Peasant Icons: Representations of Rural People in Late Nineteenth Century Russia*. New York: Oxford University Press, 1993.

3. Cathy A. Frierson, *"All Russia is Burning!" A Cultural History of Fire and Arson in Late Imperial Russia*. Seattle: University of Washington Press, 2002.

17

A Historian of Science Works from the Bottom Up

Paul R. Josephson

One November morning in 1991 I walked into the Computer Center in Akademgorodok, the Soviet city of science built from the ground up in the middle of Siberian forests in the late 1950s and 1960s. I made my way past the security guard intending to stop only if he called me back at least three times. He hailed me twice, then assumed that I knew where I was going, or perhaps he no longer cared. I found the director's office only to discover that he was in America. However, hearing of my research on Akademgorodok's scientific institutes, and without asking to see my permission papers, his secretary took me to the memorial library of Andrei Petrovich Ershov. The history of the development of cybernetics in Akademgorodok and the Soviet Union as a whole stood before me. Ershov, a pioneer in programming and artificial intelligence from the early days of computer science in the USSR, had kept all his personal papers until the day he died. There they sat in his office in well-ordered files. And there I sat, too, alone and unsupervised, reading through personal letters, correspondence with government, Party, and Academy of Science officials, and the meetings of commissions to plan the future of computer science in the USSR.

Without ceremony I had been granted unlimited access to information of the most sensitive nature, illuminating political and scientific developments in a field of Soviet science previously held under the most secret restrictions. I was having the proverbial researcher's field day in a culture renowned for frustrating inquiry of any kind. Glasnost and perestroika had permitted geographical and political penetration into archives that were off limits even to Soviet scholars.

Sitting in Ershov's office, I had come quite a distance since the fall of 1984, when I was nominated by the International Research and Exchanges Board (IREX) to undertake research in Moscow and Leningrad on the history of Soviet physics for my MIT dissertation. On that first attempt to enter the USSR as a researcher, I was denied admission to the country as a scholar in my own right by the Soviet Ministry of Higher Education for reasons still unclear. In a bizarre turn of fate, I entered the USSR that fall on a visa marked "spouse of a scholar," the scholar being my wife, an historian of Russia and an approved exchangee. Once in Moscow and Leningrad, I was granted access to materials in the Leningrad Physical-Technical Institute, the center of Soviet physics before World War II. This baffling generosity of access to materials of some importance for national security seemed all the more strange because my wife, the official exchangee, was simultaneously being denied access to many of the archives she requested for a topic with no security implications—the nineteenth-century peasantry.

Looking back on my first decade of research in the USSR, I now see that my transformation from *persona non grata* to unsupervised researcher in previously secret files depended largely on my willingness to take risks and on the generosity of Soviet colleagues, archivists, and librarians whose motivations varied, but whose assistance was uniformly crucial.

The key to my research success in 1984–85 was an excellent advisor and superb human being, Dr. Viktor Iakovlevich Frenkel, the leading historian of physics in Russia. He lived and worked in Leningrad at the Leningrad Physical-Technical Institute, the equivalent of MIT in the United States. Although I arrived in the USSR in October of 1984, I did not meet Viktor Iakovlevich until the following February. My wife and I had requested to be placed in Leningrad, so the Soviet Ministry of Higher Education sent us to Moscow. I finally met Viktor Iakovlevich when he traveled to Moscow to attend sessions at the Institute of History of Science and Technology on Staropanskii Lane. That meeting had itself been years in the making. Academician and Nobel laureate Peter Leonidovich Kapitsa had made it possible.

In the late 1970s I heard a lecture at Harvard by Sheldon Glashow, like Kapitsa a Nobel laureate. Glashow's talk was fascinating in itself, but what captivated me was his mention of Aleksandr Aleksandrovich Fridmann, the Russian geophysicist. Fridmann first proposed equations in the general theory of relativity that described a non-static universe and rendered the cosmological constant of Einstein's general theory of relativity superfluous. I ran up to Glashow after the lecture to learn more about Fridmann. Like most people, he knew only Fridmann's contributions to cosmology, but little about his life. Looking for information on Fridmann in Harvard's libraries, I found his collected works and an article in an early Soviet journal, the predecessor to *Voprosy istorii estestvoznaniia i tekhniki* (Issues in the History of Science and Technology). Finding little else, I impetuously wrote to Academician Kapitsa in Moscow with questions about Fridmann. I would subsequently understand that this was the act of a rash young man. I was grateful that Peter

Leonidovich passed my letter on to Viktor Iakovlevich, apparently without a second thought. I was later told that Peter Leonidovich realized my interest in Fridmann was sincere and that Frenkel was the best person to answer me.

Viktor Iakovlevich responded with a long letter. He explained some of the details of Fridmann's life and the need to work in Soviet archives to learn more about him. Only after I had lived in the USSR did I recognize that this was a courageous act in Brezhnev's USSR, where contact with Westerners might be considered reason to punish someone by denying him the right to travel abroad and perhaps even to fire him. But the history of physics was Viktor Iakovlevich's love, profession, and career. Like his father before him, the leading physicist Iakov Ilich Frenkel, he believed that contact with Westerners was vital for healthy scientific inquiry. In many ways, Frenkel's letter about Fridmann led me to study the history of Soviet physics in greater detail, and ultimately to write a doctoral dissertation on the Leningrad physics community from 1900 to 1940.[1]

During the 1980s I had fewer problems than many American scholars with archival access, thanks to Viktor Iakovlevich. One incident at the Saltykov-Shchedrin State Public Library in Leningrad was typical. I requested the correspondence of the physicist Iakov Dorfman, a specialist in magnetism, with European physicists. My *sotrudnik* (literally *helper* or *assistant*, but in this case an illiterate and rude man) refused, saying it bore no relation to my research interests. I appealed to the director of the library, pointing out that the *sotrudnik* could not read the English, German, or Italian letters, and so could not judge their relevance to my work. I gained permission to read the letters, but not, it turned out, due to my powers of persuasion. Only later did I learn that the library had turned to Frenkel, who convinced them that there was no reason not to show me the letters. He also insisted that I be given another *sotrudnik*. Identifying and locating Dorfman's letters in the first place had been a challenge. Until 1989, researchers were rarely allowed to see the catalogue of an archive collection. What materials did the archive hold? How could a scholar determine what he or she wanted? Encouraging one's archivist with a small gift might get a few folders delivered. But when a researcher demonstrated excessive familiarity with the field, some archivists strictly limited the number of files he or she could order. Accordingly, much time was lost, and we Western scholars were expected to be grateful for anything we received. Recognizing that securing materials would require months of cajoling, bribery, and written and oral appeals, as well as days of bickering with archival assistants over the useless folders they delivered to the scholar-supplicant, IREX required a minimum research stay for any first-time scholar of six months. Based on years of experience, they realized that six months of effort might yield six weeks of research.

By the fall of 1989, Mikhail Gorbachev's reforms were readily apparent. I returned to the USSR for four months of research through the National Academy of Sciences exchange with the USSR Academy of Sciences. My research focused on the history of postwar Soviet nuclear physics and nuclear energetics. Now the papers rained down. I was permitted to use the archives of five other physics institutes, including personnel folders; minutes of academic council meetings and party cell meetings; five-year plans and research reports; correspondence with Academy of Sciences, Communist Party, and ministerial officials; and the in-house bulletin board, or "wall newspapers," in some cases going back to the days of high Stalinism.

At one institute, though given virtually free access, I had trouble convincing the archive director to arrive on time and stay all day. She came in at ten or eleven, took tea at noon, and would leave by three. She nevertheless respected my desire to work from nine to five, and eventually gave me a key to the archive with instructions never to answer the phone or let anyone else in. No matter how hard the banging on the door, I continued to read. It took me a full month to develop a strategy for using the store of materials, which included minutes of crucial Party cell meetings and personnel folders. If I found a particularly testy discussion at a meeting, I would grab the personnel folders of the individuals involved to get a better flavor of the dispute.

This freedom to follow such leads on the spot took me further and further away from perspectives emanating from the Party center and top. It prepared me to shift my own research perspective out of Moscow and Leningrad toward institutional history from the bottom up. It alerted me to the potential value of such research materials as interviews, newspapers, and photographs in cities off the beaten path. By that cold November morning in Akademgorodok when I gained admission to Ershov's office, I had fully developed my research approach for institutional history based on regional institute archives. I believed then, as now, that one can better judge the dynamism of the Soviet system by understanding how persons at the local or regional level dealt with day-to-day and long-term pressures while pursuing their interests. Researchers who focus solely on central Party, ministry, or KGB archives get only one sense, granted a crucial one, of the relationship between the center and the periphery. I also get a sense of the concerns of central Party and government organs about the conduct of science from their letters, admonitions, and inquiries in the institute's archives. Over the last ten years, I have been fortunate to work in the archives of over a dozen scientific research institutes, in most cases as the first and only Western researcher to walk through the doors.

In 1991–92 I spent three months in Ukraine and Russia. This visit was the richest and most challenging by far. In addition to continuing research on the history of physics, I embarked on a history of Akademgorodok.[2] I needed access to formerly closed archives of the regional Communist Party organization and a wide range of Academy institutes. I was allowed to work in the Novosibirsk Party archive where I tracked the activity of each institute's Party organization. I perused the personal papers of leading Party officials. I had the impression that I single-handedly paid the archive's heating and salary payments through charges for photocopying documents. I agreed to pay a premium for photocopying, but steadfastly refused any "archive access fee," which some directors requested.

Happily, in most places archivists now willingly shared catalogues of their holdings, although the titles were not always revealing. The difficulty was in determining which files to select within the limits of time available and the daily archive quota without actually seeing the items, a problem that Kant may have been thinking about when he discussed the category of the synthetic a priori. Not being a philosopher, I adopted the 20–20 approach; that is, I requested the daily maximum number of files, usually twenty. I strove to read them all at one sitting, and whether or not I had succeeded I returned them eight hours later and ordered another twenty for the next day. I cannot be certain I avoided missing some important material, but I believe that given the limits of time I did the best that anyone could under the circumstances.

In addition to working in the archives of scientific research institutes for the Akademgorodok project, I conducted over sixty interviews with leading scientific and Party personnel. Since then, interviews have become a major aspect of my research. To encourage my respondents to be forthcoming, I decided not to use a tape recorder. In retrospect I wish I had used a recorder, for my notes in some cases are incomplete. These interviews demonstrated the impact of glasnost on an individual level. In one case, I explored my interest in the role of scientists in protecting Lake Baikal from paper-mill pollution, and in abandoning the Siberian rivers diversion project. Baikal, the largest freshwater lake in the world, was under assault from Soviet planners who undertook to build smelters and paper mills not far from its shores. These planners and their colleagues later advanced plans to divert Siberian rivers, which flow into the Arctic Circle, to European Russia and Central Asia through canals 1,500 miles long (i. e., the distance from Boston to New Orleans).

I interviewed eighty-year-old Academician Andrei Trofimuk, director emeritus of the Institute of Geology and Geophysics, a Party man and a specialist in finding and exploiting oil reserves through the wasteful technique of pumping water into wells to float the oil out. Trofimuk had personally defended Baikal in letters to General Secretary Leonid Brezhnev. He showed me thirty volumes of his personal papers on Baikal, collected over three decades, which documented the frustrations of scientists in facing down irrational large-scale programs to develop Siberian natural resources. These papers represented the same kind of striking wealth of materials as those in Ershov's office. Trofimuk told me I could see his papers only with permission of the presidium of the Siberian Division of the Academy of Sciences. He could not know that my colleagues at the Budker Institute of Nuclear Physics, located just across the street, had prepared for me seven such letters, signed by institute director and presidium member Aleksandr Skrinskii. It remained merely to type in the date, addressee, and greeting. The head of the foreign department of the Budker Institute had drafted the form letter, completely coded by random-number generator, more cleverly than I could imagine. "Dear Esteemed (blank)," it read, "Please permit Paul Josephson, a world-renowned American historian of science, to work in your institute and to use any materials relevant to the great history of Akademgorodok, which he intends to chronicle. Signed, Aleksandr Skrinskii." I returned with such a letter to Trofimuk within the hour.

Later, in Moscow, I talked with the last president of the Soviet Academy of Sciences, Gurii Marchuk, also former chairman of the Siberian Division and at one time director of the Computer Center. Before our interview, he had called Akademgorodok, discovered that I had worked in Party and institute archives, and decided to be completely open with me—and charming, I might add. After thanking him for his candor, I asked him to recall a meeting of Party activists at which he spoke in 1972, providing him with chapter and verse of his own comments. He was so pleased that he regaled me with stories of his glorious history for another forty-five minutes.

The new openness suggested other potential research materials. I sought out photographs and unfamiliar newspapers. The construction firm Sibakademstroi had built Akademgorodok. It had also built hardened silos for nuclear missiles and other classified concrete structures, so I was not sure I could get in the door, let alone view its weekly newspaper, *Sibakademstroivets* (1957–present). I found the main building of Sibakademstroi (called the "Pentagon" by local residents), walked in, discovered no doorman, and found the editorial office. I explained my interests in Akademgorodok to the editor. He shared the nearly universal respect for Americans among Russians in those days and was thrilled to contribute to my project. He showed me bound volumes of the newspaper and even let me take them home for the weekend. This enabled me to make copies at the Budker Institute.

Learning how to make copies had been another fine art requiring development from my first stay in 1984–85. Most Soviet copying machines were obsolete Western models for which it was nearly impossible to acquire spare parts or ink cartridges, let alone service. Until quite recently, they were strictly controlled by the government to prevent the flow of information. There were restrictions on hours of operation and numbers of copies, and even on times when one could place an order. Getting permission was another game entirely. In 1984–85, I spent quite a bit of time in the library of the Institute of Scientific Information in the Social Sciences (INION). For some reason, the woman responsible for accepting orders for copying and microfilms—limited to one hour per week—took a liking to me. Perhaps she thought it amusing that I referred to her as Galina Kseroksovna ("Galina, daughter of the copying machine"). She took my orders any time I showed up, filled out the forms for me, and did so without a hint that I owed her anything. Other foreign scholars at INION began asking me to help them place their orders. Galina Kseroksovna was a true friend.

As early as 1989, central government archives and universities were copying materials for me, in many cases free of charge. The advantage of working in scientific research institutes was that they possessed modern copiers, and most assistants were willing to provide unlimited services to a Westerner. Occasionally I had to provide my own paper or pay for an ink cartridge to accelerate the process. Since I was writing a history of their beloved organization, it surprised me that the greatest difficulty I had in getting permission to make copies was at the archive of the Siberian Division of the Academy of Sciences. I had to detail each item to be copied in a letter to the presidium for its authorization. But glasnost was still such a bureaucratic novelty that no one at the presidium knew who should give authorization in the absence of the presidium's scientific secretary, that is, one of the senior officials. Once I had solved that problem with two days of stomping through snow from office to office in temperatures of minus thirty degrees, I was told that each institute whose documents I wished to copy also had to provide approval. Fortunately, a colleague, Natasha Pritvits, Akademgorodok's official historian, stepped in, securing verbal permissions over the phone, an impossibility even two years earlier. Now the problem of getting copies remained, as the archive itself had no copying machine. But I had developed a good relationship with the director of the main Novosibirsk Library which houses the archive, and he agreed to have the library do it for me free of charge. I had bought the entire weekly newspaper of Akademgorodok, *Nauka v Sibiri*, from the library on microfilm, which had helped the library in a time of financial crisis, but this only partly explains his kindness.

But enough of the travails of securing copies of materials—back to 1991–92 and my research on Akademgorodok. I encountered an unexpected obstacle to my research at the Siberian Division archive, namely, the assistant assigned to me. She seemed to resent my presence. For the first few days many of my folder orders fell on deaf ears: "I can't find that," "That's not available," and so on. Then one day I walked into an entirely different atmosphere. She wore a beautiful dress, and greeted me pleasantly. There were cakes and tea on my table. All the files I had requested were on the desk. After reading for a short while, I turned to her, begged her forgiveness, and asked her what had brought about the change. She responded that she had heard a radio program about me, about a world-renowned historian of science from America who was writing a history of Akademgorodok. Now she was determined to assist me in this project. Once again, my friends at the physics institute had helped me out by planting the story on the radio.

I set out to acquire photographs of the construction of Akademgorodok, of the scientific heroes of my story, and of Khrushchev and other party officials. I noticed in the weekly *Sibakademstroivets* that one photographer had received credits for most of the photos. I tracked him down. Now old, retired, but in good health, he invited me to his apartment. Over dinner and vodka we concluded a deal for fifteen of his photographs. Another man, the official photographer of Akademgorodok, kindly provided me with photographs of leading scientists, as well as several heretofore unpublished photos of Khrushchev, Yeltsin, and others. All he wanted was a recent *Playboy* magazine. We sealed the deal by drinking a bottle of five-star Armenian cognac. This led me to quit research for the rest of that day.

The early 1990s also brought me access to an archive in Moscow that I had been trying to enter for years. The Kurchatov Institute of Atomic Energy, the site of the first Soviet reactor (still in operation), is where physicists designed the Soviet A-bomb. After completing my study of Akademgorodok, I turned to the history of peaceful nuclear programs in the Soviet Union.[3] For three years, several leading physicist friends had spoken with the directors of the institute on my behalf. They introduced me. I called several times to follow up on their introductions. I sent a copy of my curriculum vitae, a one-page description of my project, and a list of publications to the minister of the nuclear power industry, Evgenii Velikhov, who was also the director of the institute, and to Anatolii Aleksandrov, the former president of the Academy of Sciences and former head of the institute. To understand the development of civilian power reactors, the genesis of fusion, the beginnings of food irradiation programs, the creation of nuclear propulsion engines, and the spread of the nuclear enterprise, I had to get inside the institute's walls. The topic of my project clearly interested the directors as well, for they finally agreed that the time was right to work in the archive.

Only later did I realize that personal contacts had once again played the crucial role in securing access to the Kurchatov Institute archives. Just as Viktor Iakovlevich Frenkel had helped me in my initial visits, so Dr. Igor

Nikolaevich Golovin assisted me in this project. Golovin was Igor Kurchatov's deputy on the bomb project. He visited the United States at my invitation in 1991. During that visit to New Hampshire, he had insisted on helping me split and stack firewood, not what I had expected from this eighty-six-year-old physicist. Later that year, when I was working at the Lebedev Physics Institute in Moscow, my supervisor, Evgenii Lvovich Feinberg, asked me pointedly one day why I had not called Igor Nikolaievich, for "they were waiting for [me] at the Kurchatov Institute." Indeed, Igor Nikolaievich had secured the necessary permissions. I set off for the institute and began to work in Kurchatov's house, now a museum in the center of the institute's complex of buildings, reactors, and particle accelerators. The Kurchatov Museum director, Raisa Kuznetsova, made certain I felt comfortable, shared her knowledge of Kurchatov, and carried documents from the archive to my desk at the museum. Igor Nikolaievich took me to lunch, introduced me to other physicists who also kindly showed me their facilities, and gave me the phone numbers of colleagues associated with nuclear power since the early 1950s whom I would never have located otherwise. These included individuals at the center of the nuclear propulsion, fusion, and reactor programs.

While the archive had opened to me, many of the materials remained classified. This was not because there was something "top secret" in them, but rather because the declassification process had still not begun. In the economic decline Russia has experienced since 1990, there has been little money for libraries or archives. The Ministry of Middle-Machine Building, "Minsredmash," the equivalent of the U.S. Atomic Energy Commission, which funded most physics institutes, guards its secrets as zealously as the AEC does. Even so, I saw research reports on the construction of the first Soviet reactor, the first experiments, proposals for the first fusion reactors, and correspondence between Kurchatov himself and other scientists and government officials. Igor Nikolaievich also conducted me to the first reactor, the F-1, a graphite and uranium mound, still operating a few miles from the Kremlin on the institute's grounds. I touched the graphite; it was warm. In another institute I was told that I could not see any papers that had to do with Minsredmash. They failed to inform the archivist, however, and when he asked whether materials pertaining to Minsredmash were of interest to me, what could I say?

In recent years, family and other obligations have prevented long-term research stays. But the break-up of the USSR has given most institutes the ability to decide on their own whether to receive a scholar and how much access to give her or him. Through a series of shorter trips over the last five years, largely through the National Academy of Sciences Office for Central Europe and Eurasia, IREX short-term travel grants, and a sister-city organization for Portsmouth, New Hampshire, and Severodvinsk, Russia, of which I was president, I have turned my attention to institutes off the beaten path. I have avoided Moscow and St. Petersburg, only passing through on the way to Arkhangel, Murmansk, Severodvinsk, Obninsk, Kharkiv, Kiev, Odessa, and Simferopol. The culture and concerns of scientists in the provinces are different from those in Kiev, Moscow, and St. Petersburg, where all money and power seem to disappear as if into a black hole. My hosts in the provinces have been quite willing to make friendly gestures. For example, my hosts in Obninsk, home of the Soviet breeder reactor program and site of the first reactor in the world to provide electricity for civilian purposes (1954), have given me fascinating photographs. One was of the TES-3, a portable nuclear power station that moved around on tank treads. Professor Oleg Kazachkovskii, director emeritus of the institute, has shared his personal archive and photos. He also wrote a seven-page letter providing valuable critical comments on a chapter in *Red Atom*, my study of peaceful nuclear programs.

Of course, there have been failures. The Sevmash nuclear shipbuilding facility will not admit me on site, let alone to its library or archive. Colleagues in Obninsk and at the Efremov Scientific Research Institute for Electrophysical Apparatus have told me that ministerial officials will turn down my requests no matter what they say on my behalf. Eating mooseburger in the Efremov Institute with the academic secretary did not get me access to the archive or the institute's weekly newspaper, but has provided a great story. My biggest disappointment has been the fact that the directors of the Ukrainian Physical-Technical Institute in Kharkiv have let me inside their doors several times, but refuse to allow me to work in the archive. This is, to be sure, an institute involved in top-secret military research.

The break-up of the USSR has altered research experiences from the mundane to the significant, from how scholars gain access and make copies to the kinds of materials they see. The agonies of the Brezhnev era centered on stubborn secrecy and obdurate arbitrariness. Researchers had to develop a combination of detective and survival skills. We had to devote our energies to identifying and overcoming obstacles to access. Now we have quite the opposite problem. Access is virtually unlimited; the materials are overwhelming and require a completely different set of research skills to navigate through them. This path is not through the obstacle course of a paranoid and bloated bureaucracy, but through mountains of detailed, informative documents and crowds of willing interviewees, all anxious to open their culture's past to thorough and meaningful scrutiny. From famine we have moved to feast, and it is a rich feast indeed.

The high point of all of my research visits to the former Soviet Union was the weather during the week I chose to finish working in the Novosibirsk Communist Party and Siberian Division archives in December 1991. The high temperature that week was minus thirty-two degrees Celsius, the low was minus thirty-eight. A friend with a sauna invited me to warm up at the end of the workweek. After two hours of heat and three hours of beers and vodka, I took a brief roll in the snow before dressing to go home. This made me appreciate archival research in the Brezhnev years.

Notes

1. *Physics and Politics in Revolutionary Russia.* Los Angeles: University of California Press, 1991.
2. *New Atlantis Revisited.* Princeton: Princeton University Press, 1997.
3. *Red Atom: Russia's Nuclear Power Program from Stalin to the Present.* New York: W.H. Freeman, 1999.

18

Orthodoxies and Revisions

Nadieszda Kizenko

Nothing would seem more obvious for a child of Russian émigrés than to study Russian history, but my case was more deceptive than it seems. We knew the profile of the émigré *intelligent*—we counted many as friends—the first wave, of course: parents born in St. Petersburg, Yugoslavia, Paris, or Berlin; all the usual European languages; some valuable family heirlooms; a broad general culture; courtly manners; a generosity of heart and spirit; a cherished memory of life before 1917; and an intense sense of mission to keep alive something of that life for when Russia might be ready to receive it again. Because the parish to which my family belonged in Syracuse, New York, had many such members and an excellent weekly school, I could feel not only part of the Russian tradition generally, but part of the émigré tradition-with-a-mission specifically. Russian spoken in the home; nary a church service missed; Mar'ia Pavlovna smiling appreciatively as she described Peter the Great's *beau geste* in toasting his victory with "To the Swedes, who taught us how to fight"; my father's love for the old orthography—all of this created something very close to what I would recognize years later in Marc Raeff's *Russia Abroad*.[1]

So it came as a gradual and not altogether pleasant awakening to realize that my family actually departed quite sharply from the ideal type. My parents had been born not in Russia, but in the Soviet Union. They spoke Russian to us, but they also spoke (*and wrote*, as my mother proudly insisted) properly in Ukrainian, and could manage in Polish, too. My mother was born in the mid-1930s in a Siberian Gulag to mistakenly de-kulakized Belarusian farmers (it took years before I realized that this did not make them the White Russians glamorized in English and French writings). My father grew up in Kharkov in a family that got derailed on their way to the Crimea during the Civil War (1917–21) because the children came down with typhus; they remained there, only to lose their house after Lenin's New Economic Policy (1921–27). Most heretically, they had fond memories of Germany in the last year of World War II, one family in a DP camp, the other family working as drivers for the American Red Cross.

They came to the United States as latter-day indentured servants, working for tenant farmers in Maryland and Arkansas. Their families and friends worked in factories in New Jersey and New York, and played dominoes on Friday nights. Some fought in the Korean War. They were as likely to decorate their living rooms with photographs of Ronald Reagan as Nicholas II. If their children became engineers or computer programmers, they had arrived. In short, they were absolutely typical examples of the second wave, which has yet to enter Russian cultural mythology in any form.

My father's vocation as an Orthodox priest (he was of course, paid next to nothing, and moonlighted in a variety of Shakespearean occupations, from candlemaker to gravedigger) defined the nature of our contacts with both the Russian and the American communities. For the Russians, we were regular and honored guests at baptisms, weddings, and funerals, and in turn hosted visiting bishops and archimandrites from the neighboring monastery in Jordanville. To the upstate New Yorkers of the 1960s and early 1970s, our social place was less evident. My mother never wore makeup or pants, and kept her hair pinned up on her head. My father's beard and long hair made him look like a hippie; with the addition of his black cassock, he was often taken for a rabbi as well.

Thus, from the standpoint of our relations with the outside world, "Russianness" meant one long series of misunderstandings. It meant explaining to classmates that, although my parents were from the Soviet Union, they were not Communists; that we read Soviet children's books although my mother glued together the pages with references to Lenin (to block out the detested Bolshevik leader); that we threw snowballs at effigies of Stalin even as we wanted to root for athletes with names like ours in the Olympics. It meant having to wonder why my sixth-grade textbook insisted that Russian history began with Peter the Great, but, because of the Russians' backwardness and love of tyranny, Lenin had to come to power in 1917. (When I asked my father why 1917 had happened, he replied, "For our sins.")

The discrepancy between the version of Russianness I knew at home and the versions depicted in both American public-school textbooks and the first-wave press nearly drove us mad. It took going to Harvard as an undergraduate for me to realize that I did not have to be an engineer, and could actually spend my time reading about the matters that interested me most.

Those four years were both a material and an intellectual paradise. Thanks to the History and Literature concentration, what would have passed for heresies in my previous Russian studies came thick and fast. Edward Keenan questioned whether the Mongol yoke had been all that bad and whether Ivan IV had written his celebrated letters; Richard Pipes thought the pogroms overrated, reminded us that there was a right-wing tradition in Russian intellectual history, and dismissed monasteries as dens of homosexuality. Russian history seemed more elusive than ever.

By the time I started graduate work at Columbia, I realized that my education had neglected precisely the two groups I knew best—Orthodox clergy and pious women. Much the same held true for Russian historical scholarship generally, with the lonely exceptions of Theofanis Stavrou and Gregory Freeze.[2] That lack, along with a chance comment by Edward Kasinec, my former employer at Harvard's Ukrainian Research Institute (now head of the New York Public Library's Slavic and Baltic Division), led to my dissertation topic and my first research trip to Russia. I arrived in September 1991, just after the August coup, to begin working on the charismatic Father Ioann of Kronstadt (1829–1908).

The timing was right for many reasons. Father Ioann was an extraordinarily complex figure, celebrated for his miraculous healing abilities and his work among the poor—and vilified by the radical left for his supporting the monarchy. Even after his death in 1908, he remained a potent political and religious symbol, both inside and outside Russia. The Russian Orthodox Church Outside Russia had canonized Father Ioann in 1964, not only to celebrate his holiness, but also to make a strong statement against the revolution and godless rule. I still remembered childhood debates about whether the glorification was proper. Father Ioann caused far more misgivings within the Moscow Patriarchate, who reluctantly canonized him in response to popular pressure in the summer of 1990.[3] In the autumn of 1991, memories of the canonization were still fresh in Russia, as was the reignited controversy about how Orthodox Christians should respond to the holiness of someone who was not politically correct. The post-1988 wave of canonizations in Russia made saints not only historical but also newly relevant. I hoped to consult apropriate archives, to interview some of the people who had agitated for glorification, and to travel to Kronstadt to see what remained of the sites associated with the modern saint.

The bulk of archival material in St. Petersburg was in the TsGIA SPb (Central State Historical Archive of St. Petersburg), formerly LGIA (Leningrad State Historical Archive), formerly GIALO (State Historical Archive of the Leningrad District), on Pskovskaia Street. It contained, among other things, the surviving tens of thousands of letters people had written to St. Ioann, documentation of the Ioannite cult that had formed around him, and his last diary. Because it was somewhat off the beaten track, TsGIA SPb gave one the benefits of working in a small regional archive. No one else in my IREX cohort was using it, and indeed there were few foreigners there for months.

As a result, the workers were particularly friendly. They won my heart from the moment they called me "Nadezhda Borisovna." It was the first time in my life that people had used the patronymic in addressing me, and I was still young enough that it was flattering to be considered a grown-up. They had their first laugh when I was filling out the registration form and came to the category of *partiinost'* (party membership status). The explanatory text gave examples of what to write, from a specific membership category to simply "Party member for X years." I asked, not altogether seriously, if I was supposed to indicate whether I was a Republican or a Democrat. Natalia Aleksandrovna Chekmareva, the head of the reading room, snatched away the form, muttering, "How embarrassing . . . to give such things to foreigners" "And you know, Nadezhda Borisovna," she added, "our own people will not have to fill out that information any more either."

She looked over the rest of the form and took me aside. "I don't want to embarrass you, Nadezhda Borisovna, your Russian is nearly perfect," she whispered, "but you don't have to put a hard sign after every consonant." "In the new orthography, no," I replied. "But my father is so devoted to the old orthography that I use it as well." "The *old* orthography? You mean the *iat'*, the dotted i, and everything? I don't think I've ever even seen it in everyday use, outside the materials here in our archive of course. Well, if you wish."

Once the registration and the meet-the-staff were over, Natalia Aleksandrovna brought—not without some ceremony—the *opis'* (inventory) of Father Ioann's personal archive. I studied it and placed my requests as if it were the most natural thing in the world. Only later did she explain that I was one of the few people to see and use the *opis'*, as opposed to having the materials chosen for me. Even without the explanation, however, I had looked at the sign-out user's sheet: over a period of eighty years, fewer than ten persons had used it, including the archive workers who had periodically examined and resewn it. There were no foreign names, and I felt something of the joy of both the explorer and the prodigal when I wrote down my name and the date for the first time—then, and later on similarly untouched files in the months to come.

I went to all the St. Petersburg archives I had planned to use, to get an overview and then to work out a plan of attack. The decision was made for me almost immediately. Natalia Aleksandrovna warned me that TsGIA SPb would be closing for a ten-year major renovation starting January, so I should get as much done as I could before that. I felt incredibly lucky at having arrived just in time for everything to be open, and just in time before it would close again! I would spend every possible day in that archive, and most evenings in the public library in the center of town.

All historians remember their first archive and their first brush with the silent traces of their subjects' voices. What surprised me most was the quantity of surviving letters to Father Ioann—over ten thousand—and the range of topics they discussed. Although I knew the number of individual *dela* (files), I had no idea of what or how much was in them. Now I understood why Father Ioann had the equivalent of his own postal code. The letters showed that he was expected to help in virtually every type of incident that might befall people in the course of their lives, from business disputes and choosing winning numbers on lottery tickets to healing sick relatives and instructing people in the Jesus prayer.

Before I traveled to Russia, everyone had assumed that I would be writing just another biography, or at best a life-and-works. But the letters allowed me to see that the influence of a saint on his environment went both ways. People did not only appeal to Father Ioann's authority, they also used him in their relationships with the imperial administration, the church hierarchy, and their immediate families. In extraordinary letters that minced no words, they asked for healing, better work conditions, or just money; they cursed their children or their parents, and asked if leaving their families would help them find salvation. Most surprising was that Father Ioann's status as holy defender of the "little people" extended beyond the Orthodox community. Roman Catholics, Jews, and Muslims within the empire also enlisted him in their service. Whatever the letter-writers' religious background, they shared a familiarity with holiness and the notion that holiness existed to serve other people. Almost invariably, they called Father Ioann *"ugodnik Bozhii"*—someone who is pleasing to God, or God's favorite. This closeness, they wrote, allowed—indeed required—him to intercede on their behalf as well.

The letters showed the private, unmediated side of Father Ioann's widespread veneration. But there was a more public and deliberately constructed side, too. Material culture has rewarded many historians looking for information beyond the world of print, particularly when the subject is also the object of a popular cult. Through the many surviving souvenir postcards, scarves, and mugs in the former Museum of Atheism and in the Central State Archive of Phonographic, Photographic, and Motion Picture Records, I came to appreciate that Father Ioann was at the center of a publicity machine peculiar to the modern era. Thanks to visual images massively reproduced in every possible form, a broad section of the population came to know the saint more quickly than they might have even fifty years before their lifetimes. This mass scale, made possible by an ever-expanding transportation network and developments in communications, meant that Father Ioann could achieve in just a few years the empire-wide recognition that earlier saints had taken hundreds of years to attain. He was the first Russian saint to become a celebrity in the modern sense. In view of this, I could study his iconography in the largest sense—his icons, yes, but also his image as reflected in political cartoons and souvenir trinkets. In the archives of St. Petersburg, Father Ioann's image and artifacts started to take shape.

When I asked the coatroom lady what people normally did for lunch, she looked at me askance. "We had a foreign lady this summer who always went to this café around the corner," she said darkly, "but it is *very expensive*. The rest of us just bring something from home." I understood, and began bringing a sandwich, a teabag, and something sweet to share.

This marked the beginning of teatime conversations that led to a different appreciation of Russian history. Natalia Aleksandrovna was the most educated and the only one with a genuine interest in my topic, as well as the only one with engagingly idiosyncratic opinions. "I will tell you frankly," she would say as she dragged on her cigarette, "I never did find Father Ioann of Kronstadt really appealing. St. Serafim of Sarov, now, that was a real saint, the kind that restores your faith in people and in Heaven. But Father Ioann of Kronstadt . . . you know, my grandmother still remembered his funeral, even though she was only a little girl at the time. She would describe the crush of people and the nervous exaltation, saying there was something psychologically disturbing about it. I guess that's it: he is not heavenly enough for me, he reminds me too much of the kind of people we are hearing from more and more. Personally, my favorite character in Russian history is Tsar Alexander II."

The older security guards were a different lot. The war they all remembered had also been the defining experience of my parents' emigration wave, so our common memories started with that. Even the most suspiciously anti-American among them thawed when I brought in some Lindt chocolate to celebrate a holiday. She then noted with satisfaction that it was nowhere near as good as the rations she had received when she was a pilot during the war. "One bar of that," she declared, "kept you going for two days."

But above all they wanted to know what things had been like for my parents, first in Germany, then in the United States. Almost all of them had known someone who was a conscripted "Eastern worker" (*Ostarbeiter*), who had been forced to toil in Germany and had never come back; my family's account was tangible evidence that not all DPs ended up either assimilated or as only more of the poet Nekrasov's "Russian bones" in an unmarked grave.

"You understand, Nadezhda Borisovna," one told me, "we have met some descendants of those who left during the Civil War. They are very nice, but it is a different planet; whereas your family was defined by the same things we were: NEP, the first five-year plan, the horrible thirties, the war . . ." "Don't exaggerate!" suddenly barked the genteel coatroom attendant and blockade survivor with a fondness for Harlequin romances and Jane Austen. "Now everyone keeps talking about the arrests, the famine. Well, I'll tell you something. I lived here in Leningrad in the thirties, and it was just fine. I personally never knew anyone who had been arrested, and I'll tell you what,

Nadezhda Borisovna," she turned to me, "we never heard about the famine either. We never had any problems with the food supply, and sometimes I doubt whether it can all really be true, whether all those people really did die or it is something that Ukrainians or ill-wishers blew out of proportion to break down the Union."

"Ah," I said uneasily as everyone waited to see what would happen, "sometimes I do wonder whether it was a lucky thing that my Belarusian grandparents were doing time in Siberia then. You know, even in forced labor good workers got bonuses, like extra rations or a new pair of boots." "True, very true," she replied, "almost nothing is monolithic, and now they paint everything in such black colors." "But it still seems that the famine was dreadful and millions of people did die," I said. "Well, in *Leningrad*, we didn't know about it." And that was that.

Was anything left of Father Ioann's house, school, or church? Kronstadt was still officially a closed city, but I signed on for a day-trip bus tour anyhow. As we walked through the city's grid, we were shown the house of the Russian inventor who had perfected radio before Marconi, and had even designed a prototype television, "but they took away the credit from him and gave it to foreigners." The glorious Sailors' Cathedral built at the beginning of the twentieth century was still standing, unlike almost all the other St. Petersburg-area churches built in the "Russian style" and destroyed in the Soviet period. Inside, however, the space had been broken up into several stories and offices. Not surprisingly, the stick-to-the-script guide made no mention of Father Ioann, perhaps the city's best-known resident, nor of St. Andrew's Cathedral, the church where he served, which had been blown up and replaced with a park and a large central bust of Lenin. When I asked him about it in private during the lunch break, he said only that he did not usually mention it. But with the same monotonous, bureaucratic drone, he spent most of the way back reading selected passages from Father Ioann's famous "My Life in Christ" over the tour-bus radio.

A diversion more possible for a foreigner in 1991 than in previous years was belonging to a church choir. The central churches of St. Petersburg were out of the question: the singers were all professionals and I could not get used to people constantly coming in and out. My attempts to find the newly-opened "Free Church" met with no success. But not far from our residence on Maurice Thorez Boulevard was a recently reopened Gothic-style church in the suburban Pargolovo Park. Originally meant for the private Roman Catholic devotions of the French wife of a Russian nobleman, it was used only for Orthodox services after her conversion upon his death. Because the church lay miles outside the city and off the beaten track, no one official paid much attention to it. In its family atmosphere, its dedication to social work, and its isolation, it was the closest to émigré conditions of any church I had encountered.

Everyone there was an unpaid amateur, and, as in the emigration, every extra throat was welcome. Within a month, I was asked to join a "male" quartet (as the only woman, I sang first tenor) which lent its services on weekdays to churches with no set choir. The high point came when we sang one of the first services since the reopening of the church dedicated to the Russian fleet's victory over the Turks at Chesme in 1770. The church interior still reflected its recent function as a naval museum, with a painting of the sea battle instead of Christ the Savior in the iconostasis-less altar apse. Between working in the archives, tracing the routes of Dostoevsky's characters on weekends, and feeling part of a reviving church culture, there seemed no reason not to have a thoroughly happy inner life.

But I was far from the pure life of the spirit, alas. The fall and winter of 1991–92 were a turning point not only in Russia's political life, but in material conditions as well. When we arrived, people were debating whether Leningrad should resume the name of St. Petersburg, and the economy was lurching erratically from the fixed to the free market. The Academy of Sciences, our official sponsor, provided us with ration coupons and our ruble stipend. When my IREX cohort arrived, we were receiving the ruble equivalent of forty-three dollars a month; by January 1992, the amount—still the same in rubles—had shrunk to seventeen.

This was not an issue for those whose parents or spouses could supplement their incomes. For this archetypal graduate student with no other savings, however, the gradual erosion meant living in authentically Soviet-style poverty, only without the reserves of grain, coffee, soap, and sugar that every decent family had. As a result, despite the real joy of archival discoveries, my strongest memories of that longed-for year in the homeland are of mean, grinding want, and the only time I have been obsessed with food and comfort. In a weird symmetry, I found myself living a perestroika version of my parents' stories of childhood poverty.

Taxicabs were out of the question. Several of us had been placed in prefab housing on Maurice Thorez, which meant that traveling to the archives took over an hour each way. At first I disdained the tumult of boarding the No. 2 bus at Finland Station. Within a few days, however, I realized that the difference between getting a precious seat or standing was also the difference between a lyrical appreciation of the pastel façades of the imperial city and arriving at the TsGIA SPb archive in peace or thirty-five minutes of sullen elbowing and cursing. I now calculated exactly where to stand while waiting for the bus, in desperate hopes of finding myself in front of one of the doors and thus more likely to seize a coveted window seat, closest to the view and furthest away from both physical and moral pressure. (The old women and the veterans left standing vented their hostility on those closest to them, but by November I did not care who muttered what about insolent young people.)

There was no coffee in St. Petersburg that winter, no coffee and little tea. Even the elite Hotel Astoria had run out by the end of November. The empty cafés served cold non-alcoholic beverages, and the only consolation was being able to order the occasional faux champagne by the one hundred grams in ambitious restaurants.

Then there were the ration coupons. In theory these entitled us to half a kilo of macaroni, a kilo of meat, a kilo of grain, and so on, per month. But that meant first finding them and then standing in line for them. St. Petersburg in the winter of 1991–92 seemed to confound the laws of the market; it really was better to be an old pensioner with time (to stand in line) and contacts (to tip off where a supply of cookies had arrived) than an American student trying to use the hours when archives were open for research.

Once, just before the archive closed at five, one of the workers who had left early flew in with precious news: there were sausages for sale, if you had coupons, in the shop around the corner. The reading room emptied in minutes. All of us raced over to stand and wait. The sausages were pale pink shot through with red—beautiful; I can still see them now. The air was thick with competitive solidarity, broken only by a scuffle when there was an argument as to whether a woman who had left for an hour had really entrusted her place to the man behind her. Just when I was thinking most happily of how the sausages would bubble and squeak in the pan next to the potatoes, the bored voice of the cashier announced that the shop had run out of them. The last person to get his haul darted out with his magical brown-paper package and a look of secret victory, and I nearly wept. All the other stores would be closed by now, and this would mean another tedious dinner of potatoes and soup.

By December, there were days when we had to wake up at six-thirty to stand in line for bread, and I was wondering what would happen when the peanut butter finally ran out. The only bright spot came when a distant aunt, who happened to be the chief accountant at a food store in Minsk, arrived literally bent double under a load of fruits, vegetables, and a glorious grilled chicken.

The fabled winter darkness of St. Petersburg did not help. We could not phone home easily; to schedule a 2:00 A.M. call for the next day, one first had to get past the international operator's nearly constant busy signal. After several failed attempts, I felt so lonely on one commute home that I actually tried to rest my head on the shoulder of the soldier next to me. Devastatingly, but not unexpectedly, the poor man leaped back nervously and edged away as quickly as he could through the packed evening bus.

Although I could not afford to go home, I did get a surprise visit from a close American friend on winter break. My parents had loaded him up with all the things I most craved: cheese, new packages of tea and coffee, smoked salmon and sausage, chocolates and dried fruits, lemon juice, new stockings, romance novels, and, best of all, several liters of olive oil they had carefully poured into empty plastic brandy bottles. We went to a concert the next day—Christmas Eve—that turned out to be performed by tone-deaf "authentic" folksingers whose every awful number was preceded by an even more unbearably boring lecture by the bedazzled ethnographer who had discovered them.

When we came back to the flat, the door had been broken open. No one appeared to be moving inside, so we carefully tiptoed in. The place had been ripped apart from top to bottom. Every small attempt to cheer me up—all the chocolates, all the tea, my good winter boots, my warm slippers reserved for the freezing archive, the camera and tape recorder of course, even my alarm clock—was gone, all gone, not to speak of the olive oil. The kitchen was filled with spilled flour and sugar; all the cabinet doors hung open.

My closet displayed the last crushing irony. In an attempt to blend in, I had brought my oldest and ugliest clothes, with only a few bright things to gladden the heart. As I ran to the shelves, I saw the hideous things still there, but everything remotely attractive had vanished, along with the big suitcase on wheels I had purchased for the trip. (A friend in Moscow later noted wittily and not inaccurately, "You mean they edited your wardrobe.") The only consolation was that my precious notebooks—thank God I had not brought a computer for my archival notes, but instead had bought the most standard-issue Soviet school notebooks possible—were still in the desk. The only thing that had kept me going some days was the thought that I was getting good work done; if that had been lost, I think I might have broken down completely.

Even the new phone had been ripped out of the wall, so that we could not call the police. When we managed to rewire the old one, forgotten in a closet by the previous tenants, a weary officer informed me that their only car was out on duty, and that he and another officer would have to take public transport. They came two hours later to dust for fingerprints and to comment dourly, "What? You kept regular hours, and everyone in the building knew you were foreigners? Bound to happen; it was obviously an inside job. You'll never see your stuff again. Just be glad you weren't here when they showed up, and forget about it."

But of course I could not. For weeks I scrutinized every woman I saw, thinking I might spot that skirt or those shoes. I could not decide whether it was safer never to leave the flat or never to come back. The olive oil, my one link with memories of an Italian spring, kept filling my dreams. There were only two consolations. The first was that my parents had poured the oil into a plastic brandy bottle still in its liquor-store box, so I could imagine the thieves choking on it as they sat down to drinks. The second was that every Russian I knew was stricken and tried to help immediately. The archive ladies asked timidly if I needed any warm clothing or boots, and offered to take up a collection for me. Natalia Aleksandrovna told me that after she had been burgled the previous year, she most missed the pretty little cosmetic case given her by an American researcher—but she had been charmed despite herself that the robbers had taken her family's complete works of the Slavophile Pavel I. Melnikov-Pecherskii. "I mean, of all writers! This made me think that perhaps they were not the usual lot."

My American colleagues expressed sympathy, but little else. The Academy of Sciences actually suggested that it was a curious coincidence that I had been burgled only after my friend arrived. In an emergency post-crime briefing for all the IREXers, the man in charge of the exchange actually asked me in front of everyone, "How well do you actually know this boyfriend? Maybe he had an interest in the missing objects?" Only the remonstrations of his woman colleague, the shocked sniggers of the other IREX-ers, and my own stony face finally stopped him.

But that was the turning point. I moved out of Maurice Thorez. IREX had ruled that henceforth we would receive at least part of our stipend in dollars, so finally there was room to breathe. The Leningrad Theological Academy next to the St. Alexander Nevsky Lavra had rooms to let. So for a hundred dollars a month, I now had high security, a central location, easy access to well-sung services, a room of my own, and two square meals a day cooked by other people.

Being in the Theological Academy meant more and better conversations. While the Academy library had nothing I could not find at the Saltykov-Shchedrin Public Library, it did have people who cared as much about Father Ioann as I did. It felt good to be back in the company of men in black. The seminarians kept to themselves, but the priests and academicians were livelier. Over breakfast and dinner, as more of them learned what I was working on, they would share their theories or points of view. One person insisted that it was *a priori* impossible that Father Ioann could have introduced Rasputin to Emperor Nicholas and Alexandra; another tipped me off to an obscure collection that contained tantalizing hints about the saint's several reburials; another showed me the saint's old room in the Academy. It was an intellectual exchange possible probably only then and there, and I left for Father Ioann's diaries in Moscow's State Archive of the Russian Federation (then still the Central State Archive of the October Revolution) only with great reluctance.

Before I left, I had one more visit to pay. A priest friend of my father's had sent him a clipping from a newspaper article about Chernobyl. He had recognized my mother's maiden name in the surname of the military officer in charge of the cleanup and circled it. "Perhaps this may be a relative of Matushka Tamara?"

We looked at the initials and determined that they corresponded to the youngest son of my grandfather's youngest brother. A Moscow relative did some research and tracked him down; he was a lieutenant general and the head of the Leningrad Military Academy I rode past every day on the No. 2. She wrote him several times; there was no response. I tried as well, with the same lack of success. When my sister came to visit me on spring break from the University of Chicago, we decided to pop by unannounced. As we waited behind the sentry booth clutching an envelope of family photographs and some presents, having answered to the guard's question only that we were the general's visiting nieces, we started to wonder whether the visit had been such a good idea. After the outside door clanged behind us and two armed guards escorted us past a large portrait of Lenin, we grew even more nervous. And there—in a Red Army lieutenant general's uniform—stood a copy of my "kulak" grandfather, as erect and imperious and born to command. "You can go," he said to the guards, and turned to us after the door closed. "Whose daughters did you say you were?"

I uttered my mother's name feebly, and added, "We thought you might like to see some photographs." "Have a seat," he said slowly, then suddenly grinned. "So Tammy got out after all . . . well, well. Let's see those pictures."

There were some old ones from before the war of my grandfather and of my grandparents doing time in Siberia. He scrutinized them, saying only, "Of course, I barely remember Uncle Ivan, but there he is . . . my brother and sister will recognize him, they are much older. We'll phone them right now. Wait, who is this?" he asked, pointing to the most recent Thanksgiving family picture, where my bearded father sat in the center in full clerical garb.

"That's . . . Father," I said uneasily.

"I can *see* that it's a Father," he shot back. "Whose father is it?"

"That's *our* father!"

"Tamara married a *priest*? So that's true, too."

We looked each other over.

"Just do me one favor," he said finally. "My wife is from a very good Soviet family; maybe we can keep this between us for a while? Now let's call my brother and sister, your aunt and uncle; they're in Kiev and Kaliningrad. Tamara a priest's wife . . . well, well. . . ."

He arranged a ride home for us in an official black car with curtains in the back; for the one and only time in my travels in Russia, the policemen saluted as we drove past.

Moscow's adventures were different. Other than the files of the Police Department, my focus there was on one source only—Father Ioann's diaries. A tiny proportion of the edifying sections had been published during his lifetime as *My Life in Christ*. I was interested in the things that had never appeared in print, especially those that might shed light on the saint's decision to remain a virgin—even after marrying—and his complicated relations with his wife. I also wondered how and whether the tone and content might change after 1881, when Father Ioann became a nationwide, then international, celebrity. A saint's diary was a rarity, a real discovery. With the diaries, I hoped, both the saint and the historian might become household words.

As I started reading them, however, my enthusiasm wavered. The first two notebooks consisted almost entirely of copied-out excerpts from scripture. Quote after quote, beginning with the Book of Genesis: what could one do with that, other than learning how to decipher the saint's difficult handwriting? The diaries were scanty on events and experiences that were not specifically religious; the entries were not consistently dated; there was disappointingly little on politics. And then I realized that it was a matter of genre. The diaries' overwhelmingly self-critical and negative tone, depicting the author as a selfish tyrant, and their tireless chronicling of his every lapse became comprehensible when I realized they these were not diaries in the classic sense. They were instead the spiritual chronicle Orthodox priests in Russia were encouraged to keep, both of their own progress and that of their parishioners. Father Ioann's pattern of holiness was so unusual that it raised many questions. Was he consciously striving toward sanctity? Did he see this as compatible with his priestly role? After all, holy men in his religious tradition had been mostly monks. How did he reconcile the path toward spiritual perfection with married priestly service?

Gradually, the saint opened up to his diary and to his reader. He was as ascetic as any monk, keeping minute records of what he ate and how it affected him. He suffered from high-handed treatment by his clerical superiors, his wife's relatives, and the wealthy people whom he encouraged to give to the poor. Most important, however, was his chronicling of how his life had changed when thirteen people wrote to the popular newspaper *New Time* describing how he had healed them. People began to haunt his every step, hovering outside his house round the clock. They came by ship, by train, and on foot, making Kronstadt one of the biggest pilgrimage sites in the Russian Empire. His diaries described the shift from parish priest and private ascetic to public holy man. At the height of his fame, his handwriting became a scrawl and the diary served largely as an appointment book. This gradual movement from the inside out is a cautionary tale for any would-be saint—or celebrity.

Since that year I have returned several times to do research in Russia, almost always in the long days of summer and in a rented flat in the center. The money is better, and the living conditions are too. My book on Father Ioann of Kronstadt proved to be only one harbinger of the "Orthodox spring." Since its publication, many more studies of Orthodoxy have appeared. Special issues of scholarly journals and entire conferences have been devoted to Orthodoxy in Russian history; rare is the session of the American Association for the Advancement of Slavic Studies session that does not include at least one panel on Orthodoxy. On the other hand, St. Petersburg's city archive is still closed, the Central Historical Archive's legendary Serafima Igorevna Chekmareva has emigrated to Germany so as not to rot in an old-age home, and my retired lieutenant-general uncle now runs a real estate and construction company. Yes, 1991 was the worst of times, but it was also the best.

Notes

1. Marc Raeff, *Russia Abroad: A Cultural History of the Russian Emigration, 1919–1939.* New York: Oxford University Press, 1990.

2. Gregory L. Freeze, " 'Handmaiden of the State'? The Church in Imperial Russia Reconsidered," *Journal of Ecclesiastical History* 30, no. 1 (January 1985): 82–102; *The Parish Clergy in Nineteenth-Century Russia: Crisis, Reform, Counter-Reform.* Princeton: Princeton University Press, 1991; Robert Nichols and Theofanis Stavrou, eds., *Russian Orthodoxy Under the Old Regime.* Minneapolis: University of Minnesota Press, 1978.

3. See Nadieszda Kizenko, *A Prodigal Saint: Father John of Kronstadt and the Russian People.* University Park: Pennsylvania State University Press, 2000, especially Chapter 8, "Posthumous Legacy."

19

Post-Soviet Improvisations
Life and Work in Rural Siberia

Golfo Alexopoulos

Just weeks after the collapse of the Soviet Union, I was working in the crowded reading room of the former Central Party Archive (TsPA) in Moscow[1] when a Russian stranger approached me from behind. "Interesting," he said in a serious tone, referring to the materials on my desk. "What is your research topic?" I was thoroughly startled. Finding him intrusive and disruptive, I rudely turned my head away, but the mysterious man refused to leave my desk. He said that he could give me access to many otherwise secret archival documents of interest, and I understood that the unsavory character was looking for business. Apparently, he wanted dollars for facilitating my research in this popular archive. I repeated my reproach and the unwelcome petty operator reluctantly walked away. Such encounters were not unusual in the winter of 1992, when the archival system appeared thoroughly in flux. Old rules were being rewritten or abandoned, and the window of abuse had widened.

It was in this period of great uncertainty that I began my investigation of the Soviet disenfranchised, or *lishentsy*, a study that later formed the basis of a monograph.[2]

At the time, I was relieved to discover that the material I valued most was not available at the Central Party Archive, which was often a difficult place in which to work, given the exceptionally high demand for its newly declassified holdings. I considered myself fortunate to be primarily interested in *lishentsy* petitions, a collection of documents that were not in great demand. Many historians still viewed citizen letters as artifacts of human interest rather than reflections of Soviet power. By all indications, I was not likely to encounter difficulties locating and obtaining written appeals from the disenfranchised since these were neither Party documents nor recently declassified. However, this initial assumption proved to be wrong.

Sources Both Accessible and Inaccessible

After the collapse of the USSR, all eyes were focused on Stalin-era archival materials, and only a few researchers looked immediately at personal memoirs, petitions, and letters. My graduate advisor at the University of Chicago, Sheila Fitzpatrick, had pointed me in that direction. Of all the letters that I found in the archives, one group of narratives appeared especially interesting—the thousands from *lishentsy*, the "class enemies" of the Stalin era, seeking the restoration of their rights in the 1920s and 1930s. Access to these documents was not restricted, and had already become available to researchers in the Gorbachev years. Moreover, the abundance of *lishentsy* petitions for the reinstatement of rights seemed highly unusual and interesting. The testimonies were drafted by victims at the time of their persecution as they deluged state agents with their appeals for rights, detailed their personal biographies, and described the condition of exclusion. I hoped that these sources, which looked both easily accessible and intriguing, would constitute the cornerstone of my dissertation.

In fact, the documents I sought were far from readily obtainable. In order properly to study the Soviet disenfranchised, I needed to see the file of the Central Electoral Commission, the Kremlin agency that managed the deprivation and reinstatement of rights. After a good deal of reticence and evasion, the archivists at the State Archive of the Russian Federation (GARF) told me that this record was not in Moscow, as the archive guides had clearly indicated. Rather, the entire file—official protocols and over 100,000 individual case records—was located beyond the Urals. If I planned to write a dissertation on the Soviet disenfranchised, I would have to go to Ialutorovsk, a small town about eighty kilometers outside Tiumen in western Siberia and home to the Center for the Preservation of a Reserve Record (*Tsentr khraneniia strakhovogo fonda*, or TsKhSF). The Soviet state had built this secret storage facility in the late 1950s primarily to maintain microfilms or back-up files of important documents that resided in archives throughout the Russian republic. In addition to these microfilms, the TsKhSF facility also stored some original material, including audio recordings, motion pictures, and large files—such as the record of the Central Electoral Commission—that formerly were located in Moscow's central archives.

Access to the Ialutorovsk warehouse was no simple matter. I needed a special letter of permission from the Russian Committee on Archival Affairs (Roskomarkhiv). A powerful institution in post-Communist Russia, Roskomarkhiv was officially subordinate only to the Russian President, Boris Yeltsin. The Russian Committee on Archival Affairs, however, required a formal letter of permission from GARF, the archive that had originally held the Central Electoral Commission file. When construction of the Ialutorovsk archive was finished in the early 1960s, the entire, massive file of the Central Electoral Commission was loaded onto train cars and moved eastward. Technically, the file itself remained under the authority of GARF, but the TsKhSF archive was directly subordinate to the Russian Committee on Archival Affairs. Therefore, I needed to do two things: secure a memo from GARF which granted me access to the Central Electoral Commission file in Ialutorovsk, and take this document to the lofty offices of Roskomarkhiv to receive a formal letter of permission.

Looking back, it seems remarkable that both GARF and Roskomarkhiv gave me the necessary authorization. At the time, the acting director of GARF warned me about the conditions in Ialutorovsk; but, fortunately for me, she had been there before and had experienced firsthand the professionalism of the staff. The people at the Russian Committee on Archival Affairs were less knowledgeable and, consequently, more reluctant to grant me access. They insisted that my authorization was limited only to the documents of the Central Electoral Commission and did not give me the right to view any other material in the archive. Yet I was fortunate here, too, because the man who finally gave me the letter romanticized my trip to Ialutorovsk. He admired this foreigner's desire to leave the capital for the heartland, to see the "real" Russia, and to encounter the best of the country—the generous ordinary folk. He wished me luck and told me to be careful. It appeared at the time that he, like the acting director of GARF, considered me an innocuous graduate student who might decide not to make the long journey after all.

The Arrival of the First American

The process of conducting research in Russia often depends on personal connections, the assistance and trust of local people with inside knowledge. My work in Ialutorovsk would not have been possible without Sergei and Nastia Dubinskii, a young couple from Tiumen. Coincidentally, a colleague of mine at the University of Chicago, John McCannon, had met them just months before, so on John's advice I phoned the couple from Moscow. As soon as I introduced myself as a friend of John's, they said that they would pick me up from the Tiumen airport, house me in their apartment, and drive me to Ialutorovsk. Overwhelmed by such hospitality and generosity, I did not realize at the time that their help was simply indispensable. Throughout the months ahead, I constantly turned to them for assistance with various problems.

The first challenge consisted in simply locating the secret, closed archive of imperial and Soviet state records. Sergei, himself an historian who had spent his entire life in Tiumen, insisted that there could not be a significant warehouse of classified state records in the tiny agricultural town of Ialutorovsk as no historian in the area had ever heard of its existence. After nearly two hours in the car, avoiding potholes along a neglected two-lane road, passing through remote areas of Tiumen Province with hardly a road sign to assist us, we found Ialutorovsk. I began to share Sergei's doubts about my pioneer journey east when the address for the archive that I had located in Moscow placed us at the far end of town. A tall concrete wall topped with barbed wire and an unmarked door made no impression from the street, but Sergei noticed it and pulled over to ask someone for directions. He emerged from the building surprised to inform me that the policeman inside said we had reached our destination.

Like other towns in the former Soviet Union, Ialutorovsk possessed the usual landmarks. There was a memorial to the residents who resisted the White Army during the Civil War, a statue of Lenin in front of the administration building, a few apartment blocks, and a large dairy combine. Yet the town was hardly modern. Most residents lived in one-bedroom houses from another century and relied on wood-burning furnaces in the winter. Roaming livestock interrupted traffic on the poorly paved or unpaved roads. However, my biggest surprise consisted not in the town's peculiar mixture of old and new, but in the mysterious archive itself. I did not expect that this secret warehouse would be the largest employer in Ialutorovsk; it extended over a vast territory the size of GARF in Moscow, with several buildings and a fire station on strongly secured grounds.

I had phoned from Moscow in advance of my visit, so the director of the archive, Nelli Aleksandrovna Vakulenko, awaited my arrival that day. A poised, thoughtful, elderly woman, she greeted me warmly but wasted no time explaining her concerns to Sergei. The director knew of my plans to conduct preliminary research for one month, so she told my host frankly that her institution was wholly unprepared to accommodate a visiting scholar. This was not an archive in the proper sense. There was no reading room, and no internal inventories or *opisi*. Indeed, I later learned that the archivists themselves were not fully informed of the warehouse's contents, especially the numerous microfilm reels from important archives throughout the former Soviet Union. Except for perhaps a day, the staff had never assisted researchers on the premises, and only one small motel could actually accommodate guests. Nelli Aleksandrovna wanted to help me, but she also wanted me to understand that this was not a typical archive and to adjust my expectations accordingly.

The Vain Pursuit of Comfort and Safety

I was overwhelmed by the generous help and professional courtesy that I received from various employees of the archive—from the policeman guarding the entrance to the archivists and archive director. Most everyone at the TsKhSF earnestly tried to facilitate my work. A desk in the archivists' room was cleared for me, and a young man named Sasha, who had just completed his navy service, was designated my driver. My commute to the archive consisted of a fifteen-minute walk, and I preferred the fresh air to the chauffeur, but Nelli Aleksandrovna seemed to think that the escort was a matter of security. When I arrived at the archive every morning, the policeman at the front door would phone and have someone escort me to the room where I read my documents. Such extraordinary service (and constant oversight) made me initially uncomfortable. Used to being one of many researchers in Moscow whose presence was hardly noticed, here I was the "special guest," "the American." There simply was no way around the special attention.

Given the lack of adequate housing in Ialutorovsk, the director asked one of the archivists to accommodate me in her apartment. Liudmilla was a reserved, warm, and proper woman who was raising a four-year-old boy alone. She had a nice apartment with two rooms and a phone, both luxuries in this small town. Liuda's best friend, Marina, visited frequently to use the phone. Marina lived upstairs with her husband and two boys, and I enjoyed how she inundated me with questions about life in the States. If Liudmilla was exceedingly careful not to disturb me, the outgoing Marina wished to show me life in Ialutorovsk. A teacher at the town's high school, she invited me to the annual ceremony for the small class of 1992 graduates. I remember the young women in their elaborate prom-like dresses, and how the elders at the school repeatedly urged the graduates not to depart quickly for the bigger cities or to forget their home town. Such exhortations exposed the older generation's anxiety regarding a post-Communist trend. This dated, quiet locality witnessed a steady exodus of its energetic and resourceful youth.

At the apartment, Liudmilla and her son lived in the bedroom and gave me the living room. She kept an incredible schedule—up at six to drill Alyosha on his speech and pronunciation, then off to the day-care center before work at the archive. One morning, she showed me the impressive children's facility, whose interior was the nicest of any building I entered there. Years later, Liuda would lament that in the new Russia, where families were expected to pay for day care, she could never have supported Alyosha on her own. The Soviet welfare state, she believed, had made it possible for her to leave an alcoholic husband and to assume the responsibility of raising the boy alone. Alcohol touched nearly everyone in this small town. During my visit, the mayor of the city drank himself to death. I joined the funeral procession and spoke with Liuda and Marina about the circumstances behind the man's demise. He was a notorious drinker, but people were so used to alcoholism that they expressed genuine pity more than disdain.

Everyday life for those living in Ialutorovsk did not resemble the routine that was carefully arranged for this Western guest. Nelli Aleksandrovna insisted that Sasha pick me up every morning and drive me to the archive. The shuttle ended, however, after I simply insisted on walking, although the stroll was at times a bit uncomfortable because residents liked to watch the "foreigner." Then Liuda had the idea that a bicycle might offer the most agreeable commute, so I rode for a couple of weeks until I slipped into a huge pool of mud. I returned home looking like a soldier who had just emerged from a filthy swamp. My hosts were embarrassed and wanted Sasha to continue as chauffeur, but Liuda, sensing my discomfort, insisted that she would walk me to and from the archive. I was reminded, once again, that when I left Moscow I also left behind the privacy that comes with anonymity in a big city.

One day, Nelli Aleksandrovna announced that she was letting her staff out early to plant their potatoes for the year. Since my arrival, everyone seemed to discuss the progress and tribulations of their private gardens. The staff members had to attend to their family's potato, fruit, and vegetable supplies, so I left early along with everyone else. People often did not work entire days because the challenges of everyday life proved so great that one had to leave the office early to attend to children, crops, or essential errands. The director understood how the demands of the staff's private gardens placed unanticipated restrictions on my work time at the archive. Therefore, she agreed to let Liuda check materials out so that I could study at home. I worked as much as allowed on the archive grounds, then, after closing, selected a few items to review in the evening. In Moscow, my work at the archives and my life in the city remained distinct, and I regularly left the former behind to explore the latter. In Ialutorovsk, life and work remained inseparable.

I labored long hours in Liuda's little apartment. When she left to run errands, I often kept the door unlocked, and she gently scolded me for not securing the apartment. Someone might break in and harm me, she worried, but I dismissed her concerns as exaggeration. I felt safer here than in Moscow, however I soon realized that this was a misperception. To dispel my sense of security, Liuda reluctantly described a local news story. Two girls had been murdered following a wild graduation party weeks before, and the head of one of the murdered girls was left at the doorstep of her parents' home by the criminals. On a walk to the archive, I once saw young boys on the street brawling with steel pipes. There was unmistakable cruelty underlying the serenity of this sleepy town and my hosts tried to protect me from it.

The constant attention that I received in Ialutorovsk reflected the staff's concern for my safety, but people were also eager to learn about me and about life in the States. Moreover, they wanted to display their extraordinary hospitality, a source of local pride. One of the archivists, Valentina, generously invited me to her home for lunch almost daily. I enjoyed our simple meals together, but one afternoon, after trying some of her homemade mayonnaise, I fell deathly ill. Weeks later, I learned that I had contracted an E. coli infection. Sergei and Nastia rushed to bring me to Tiumen for convalescence, but days passed without any significant improvement. As I lay motionless, they decided to pack my things from Ialutorovsk. I insisted on having care at the American Medical Center in Moscow, so Sergei and Nastia arranged for an airline ticket on short notice, no small feat at that time.

My sudden departure from Ialutorovsk in the summer of 1992 made the director and others at the archive, especially Valentina, feel terrible. Their first American visitor—indeed, their first on-site researcher—had left writhing in pain. Kindly Russians, so concerned about being proper hosts, they felt deeply embarrassed and responsible. I repeatedly assured them that my illness was not their fault, but it was no use. If they were confused about what to do with me when I arrived, they were even more saddened by my unexpected and hasty departure. I insisted that this illness would not keep me from returning to finish my work—indeed, my dissertation depended on it.

Security, Serenity, and Surveillance

The E. coli infection came at the end of one research trip, but I returned to Russia a year later to complete my doctoral work on an IREX/Fulbright grant. During the customary orientation in Moscow, I spoke with an official from the Russian Committee on Archival Affairs. He was upset to hear about my trip to Ialutorovsk, and expressed dismay that I had been granted access to an archive he said was still closed. I thought that he might try to prohibit my next visit, but he did nothing despite his disapproval of my activities. With the Hoover Institution and the Library of Congress talking to Roskomarkhiv about various publication and microfilming projects, more significant matters demanded his attention. Fortunately, once I had gained access and made contact with the archivists, I did not need another letter of permission. But from this worrisome encounter, I deduced that the rules on archival access remained ambiguous. The original permission that I had obtained to work in Ialutorovsk was not the result of any new archival policy, but of simple chance.

I worked in the Moscow archives and libraries for several months before returning to Ialutorovsk to continue my research. I remember that during the long flight over the Urals in February 1994, in a plane full of well-dressed

Russians, I saw a sea of fur hats from my seat in the rear. I was clearly the worst dressed of the lot, having come on board with some of my belongings in a plastic bag, the classic purse for most Russians. The man who helped to secure my makeshift carry-on bag into the overhead compartment admonished me for my shameful appearance: "Did you come here off the street or something?" My trip to Tiumen, the oil capital of the new Russia, began with this unpleasant encounter with the city's elite inhabitants. Hours later, in a friendly voice that seemed less uncommon in the new Russia, the Tiumen Airlines flight attendant announced that we were approaching Tiumen and the temperature at our destination city was minus twenty-five degrees Celsius. I gasped, but noticed that those around me appeared wholly unaffected. I would later learn that Tiumen residents only described the day as "cold" when temperatures dipped to minus thirty.

Despite the new experience with Siberian winter, I was more hopeful about this second and more extended research trip to Ialutorovsk. On my last visit, I had battled with the tenacious and ubiquitous mosquitoes in Liuda's apartment and contracted a dangerous infection. Now I hoped that the bitter cold would offer improved conditions, by serving as both exterminator and refrigerator.

When I reappeared at the archive, everyone greeted me warmly and asked about my health. The archivists seemed determined to make life safer for me this time. However, the obstacles to comfort and safety were even greater now. With the post-Communist Russian economy in rapid decline, state institutions such as archives stumbled along, grossly underfunded. The heating at the Ialutorovsk archive was spotty at best. Days before my arrival, a water pipe had burst and caused a major flood, which partly shut down the archive and threatened many of its holdings. Nelli Aleksandrovna seemed to run from one crisis to another. Given the acute problems of the facility and my serious illness during the last visit, she arranged for me to work in another location. With few distractions, I labored long hours in the serenity of my new workspace.

That winter I came to conduct, among other things, a systematic sample of 500 of the over 100,000 *lishentsy* personal cases—the largest segment of documents in the Central Electoral Commission file. I was asking a lot of the archivists who would assist me. Not only did they have to find, deliver, record, and then reshelve all 500 files; I also made the task harder for them by insisting that they pull certain case files and not simply a random batch. I wanted to have a sample of the entire run of cases available from 1926–36, so they had to select particular records from among those alphabetically filed for each year. Their patience was unlimited, but not solely the result of diligence and generosity. Schooled in a Marxist tradition of social research, the archivists praised my "scientific" and "systematic" approach to historical inquiry. Their positive perception of my research method constituted a great asset, since I needed their willing cooperation in order to construct a systematic sample.

During long months of work, my health was never better. In Moscow, I would constantly catch colds from crowded subways and buses, or slip on sidewalks covered with ice. Here, I cooked my own kasha and worked without difficulty. I also had a Brita water filter that transformed the orange tap water into a drinkable liquid. The extreme cold and the intensity of my research caused me to need many hours of sleep, but I did not have to endure a lengthy commute to the archive with notebooks and computer in tow as in Moscow. To rest, I went for walks when the weather warmed up to minus ten. A thick layer of snow covered the houses and streets and made the poor town look pristine and beautiful in the winter. Often, I made tea and looked out the window at scenes of everyday life. One day I observed a road accident in which a male pedestrian was killed. It seemed like an eternity before someone was able to get help, and even longer before an ambulance came to take the man's body away. I remember watching the people who had gathered around the corpse, talking for hours. The affair dragged on all afternoon. Life was painfully slow here, even during emergencies.

Nonetheless Siberia was an ideal workplace. The only person conducting research at the archive, I promptly received documents without having to queue up or wait for even a day. Moreover, the only real distraction consisted in occasional visits with my friends in Tiumen. It didn't take long to realize that the actual distance between the provincial capital of Tiumen and the small town of Ialutorovsk was much more than eighty kilometers. The standard of living for Liuda and Marina had hardly changed in the nearly year-and-a-half since my last visit, but in Tiumen, two other women directly experienced the dollar economy of the new Russia. Not long ago, Nastia and Natasha became best friends when they had tiny adjacent apartments and shared a phone. By 1994, however, their material existence had markedly improved. Nastia and Sergei relocated to a contemporary apartment in the center of town, replete with the latest furnishings and Japanese audio-video equipment. Natasha and her husband bought the latest BMW. I spent hours in Sergei and Nastia's plush new apartment, talking, resting, and watching movie videos. On one of my weekend visits, they shared a disturbing story.

Articles about me had appeared in the Tiumen city newspaper, although no reporter had ever contacted Sergei or Nastia. The couple was clearly confused by this. How or why these articles appeared remained a mystery, but they accurately noted my university and my research topic. The latest piece made a sarcastic reference to my illness and sudden departure on a previous visit. It described a silly graduate student from the University of Chicago who got sick, refused the aid of competent local doctors, and fled to Moscow for treatment. My friends suspected that since I had not registered with the police during my visit to Tiumen, this was the authority's way of making it known that I remained under watch. In the Russian capital, an outsider was hardly noticed, but here, where people had such rare encounters with foreigners, much less with Americans, my movements generated special interest. I was a bit relieved to disappear from the gaze of people in Tiumen and Ialutorovsk when I finally departed for Moscow.

Three Years Later—The End of Secrecy

Although I had finished the 500-case sample and my dissertation research when I left Ialutorovsk in the summer of 1994, I told everyone at the archive that I would return. I was considering another research project on Soviet amnesties that would surely bring me back to this familiar facility. Moreover, in Ialutorovsk, as opposed to Moscow, it was impossible to maintain a division between life and work. The two were inseparable here, where the problems of everyday life determined research conditions in fundamental ways. As a result, I had acquired an enduring attachment to the archive staff and to others whose lives had become connected to mine during the months that I lived in this small community. Committed to preserving these special ties, I returned in the summer of 1997.

A great deal had changed during my three-year absence. Liuda still lived in her apartment with little Alyosha, but Marina's husband had been killed tragically in an industrial accident. Now it was Liuda who made frequent visits to Marina's apartment in order to help her with the two young boys. Nelli Aleksandrovna had retired and was now spending all her waking hours in the indispensable vegetable garden. In her place, a former military man had been appointed director of the TsKhSF facility. Some of the archivists disliked his "strict discipline." After my departure, apparently the authorities (no one said who exactly) had expected a steady stream of researchers to follow, but none came. Few could have been really surprised, for Ialutorovsk was hardly the workplace of choice even for a graduate student. Still, the staff at the TsKhSF archive could not hide their disappointment that their first American visitor was also their last.

As in earlier years, the institution gravely needed an infusion of funds to repair its deteriorating infrastructure and to pay its staff. The director hoped that I could help them attract other researchers and hard currency, but I reminded him that in all my visits I had been strictly limited to the Central Electoral Commission file, as specified in my permission letter from

Roskomarkhiv. If he wanted my assistance in drawing foreign scholars to the facility, I explained, he would have to tell me the contents of this enormous warehouse. The archive could no longer remain a secret, and its possessions needed to be advertised. With surprisingly little hesitation, the new director agreed.

For the first time, I was taken into the other buildings and given detailed information regarding the archive's holdings. Moving from one structure to the next, taking notes on the treasures in this remote warehouse, I understood that my tour was a remarkable occurrence. Indeed, the guides said as much. Over the years, the archivists and I had developed a special trust, but our friendly relationship never altered the fact that this was a secret facility. No one, not even a trusted researcher on site, could obtain information about or access to materials without the written permission of Roskomarkhiv in Moscow. But now the economic crisis had changed a great deal. The director and archivists believed that I could help to advertise the archive's impressive collection and attract the scholars and funds needed to modernize this neglected institution. I promised that I would publish the information they gave me on the contents of their unusual archive, and I did.[3]

Conclusion

When I began my research on the Soviet disenfranchised, openness was clearly the order of the day. Accordingly, various archival officials informed me about the existence of a remote warehouse that had been secret for over thirty years, and also gave me permission to work there. Still, I was fortunate to receive permission without major obstacles. In early 1992, there was hardly a consensus at the Russian archives regarding the boundaries of permissibility. My request to see the file of the Stalin-era Central Electoral Commission could easily have landed on another desk and languished there, unanswered. As in the late Gorbachev years, too, after the collapse of the Soviet Union possibilities of access to state and Party archives depended greatly on the director in charge, and could vary markedly from day to day and place to place. Yet such uncertainty, however frustrating, also provided definite opportunities. I kept this lesson in mind when I returned to the States to analyze my data.

When state institutions are in flux, staffed by diverse officials often with opposing dispositions and philosophies, the persistent supplicant might eventually expect a favorable reply. Faced with some chance of success, the subjects of my research, the *lishentsy*, proved relentless in their appeals to state officials for the reinstatement of their rights. Perhaps they, like me, remained persistent because a few officials in the changing bureaucracy did appear sympathetic. In my case, another factor also determined my success with archive officials. I appeared innocuous to many who viewed me as a mere female graduate student "interested in letters." Uncertainties in post-Communist Russia worked to the advantage of at least some researchers, as many overworked archivists preferred to avoid problems and grant access to visiting scholars who, like myself, appeared relatively benign and unimportant. I wondered whether some supplicants in a changing Russia decades earlier might have had similar experiences.

When the time came to write up my material, I could not deny another lesson of my experience, namely, the difficulty of generalizing across the Russian landscape. During the many months of my research in 1992–94, I experienced firsthand the asymmetries of a Russia in transition. My life in Moscow, Tiumen, and Ialutorovsk differed sharply in regard to the standard of living, degree of surveillance, presence of other foreigners, hospitality of the local population, and conditions of work. In Ialutorovsk I witnessed the profound effect of everyday life on the structure of work, the stubbornly slow pace of life even when time was of the essence, the constant effort to create comfort where there was hardly any hope of it, and the uncertainty that was so characteristic of existence. This experience surely influenced my interpretation of the data I had amassed. My historical writing describes the unevenness of social transformation in Russia, the limits of state control, and the ways in which everyday life created formidable constraints for the regime's political ambitions. Looking back, this seems hardly a coincidence.

Notes

1. Months prior to my arrival, the archive was given its current name, the Russian Center for the Preservation and Study of Documents of Recent History, or RTsKhIDNI.

2. Golfo Alexopoulos, *Stalin's Outcasts: Aliens, Citizens, and the Soviet State, 1926–1936*. Ithaca: Cornell University Press, 2002.

3. See Golfo Alexopoulos, "Voices Beyond the Urals: The Discovery of a Central State Archive," *Cahiers du Monde Russe* 40, nos. 1–2 (June 1999): 1–17.

20

Hits and Misses in the Archives of Kazakhstan

Steven A. Barnes

One Moscow evening in late 1999, I was sitting with a history graduate-student colleague having a drink and complaining about the obstacles put in the way of researchers by archivists and librarians in Moscow. My colleague made a comment that I will never forget. Comparing archivists and librarians in the United States and in Russia, he declared: "In the United States they feel that their job is to facilitate access to materials, in Russia they feel that their job is to limit access." The comment was frequently apropos in Moscow, but the truth in this statement was emphatically revealed in Almaty, the former capital of Kazakhstan.

Early 2000 brought me to Almaty for the middle portion of my IREX (International Research and Exchanges Board)-sponsored dissertation research trip. My dissertation will offer a local study of the notorious Gulag in the Karaganda region of Kazakhstan from the 1930s to the 1950s.[1] I structured my research trip in three sections, spending roughly equal amounts of time in Moscow, Almaty, and Karaganda reviewing Communist Party and Soviet state documents on central, republic, and local administration of concentration camps and internal exile. Working, or perhaps one should say attempting to work, in the archives of Almaty was a far different experience from that in Moscow. I did most of my work there in the Archive of the President of the Republic of Kazakhstan (APRK), the former archive of the Communist Party of the Republic of Kazakhstan. Everything at this archive seemed designed to cause me aggravation and to frustrate my research plans. Merely gaining access proved to be a major hassle and a trial of patience.

The archives of Kazakhstan are definitely less well-known to American scholars than those of Russia. Consequently, I arrived at APRK far less prepared than I had been for work in Moscow's archives. While a few American scholars had offered some advice about working in APRK before my departure from the United States, the lack of published archival guides, especially recent ones that would offer some insight into available materials on my subject matter, and the lack of usage of APRK by American scholars year after year left me somewhat unaware of what to expect. Upon my arrival, I met with Alma Sultangalieva, a local researcher at the Kazakh Institute of Strategic Studies (KISI). This institute, rumored to be much favored by Kazakh President Nursultan Nazarbaev, was located on the second floor of the building housing APRK. Sultangalieva made arrangements for KISI to provide me with a letter of introduction requesting access to the archive. I also secured a letter of introduction from IREX's Almaty office.

Early one morning, I arrived at the director's office of APRK armed with these letters of introduction. Failing to remove my overcoat (more on this faux pas later), I entered the office and explained who I was and what research materials I was seeking, and offered my letters of introduction. The first parry in this little game for access occurred when the director requested a letter from my home university attesting to the fact that I was a doctoral student there. Alas, this was one letter I did not have, and one difficult to obtain considering the mail service between the United States and Kazakhstan. Apparently, the two letters from local institutions—one American and one Kazakh—were not enough to provide me with access to the archive. As I tried to explain the difficult logistics involved in getting a letter from California to Almaty, I was even advised that a letter by fax would not suffice. "We have rules," the director was fond of saying, as she repeated that they would absolutely need an original letter from my university.

Frustrated, I agreed that I would get the letter from my advisor at Stanford. To avoid wasting a week waiting for the original letter to arrive by DHL, I asked my advisor, Amir Weiner, to send me both a faxed and an original letter of introduction. The next day, armed with the faxed letter, I made a second trip to the APRK director, where I repeated my faux pas and was firmly lectured. "Who did you say was your advisor again?" she asked. I gave her the name of my advisor. "Didn't your advisor ever explain to you that you should take off your overcoat when meeting the chief?"

I sat there literally stunned. Had my ignorance of a cultural norm stood in the way of my access to this archive? Had she determined to make things difficult for showing this lack of respect during my first visit to the archive? What should I do now—continue to sit here in my overcoat, or get up and walk to the outer office to remove the overcoat and then return? My forehead broke out in a sweat as I chose the latter option.

Returning to the director's office, I offered her the faxed letter from Stanford and promised the original as soon as it arrived. I was pleasantly surprised when she relented and agreed to allow me to use the archive. She asked me to leave a business card with a local phone number, and said she would have her archivists call me when I could return to begin work.

On my third visit to the archive, after having wasted half a week, I was finally allowed to enter the APRK reading room. The kindly reading-room employee, following the standard custom in most archives, asked me to read the rules and sign a statement acknowledging that I had done so. Never forgetting the archive director's mantra, "We have rules," I was amazed to discover what the rules actually stated about access: any foreign scholar was to be allowed to use the archive with a letter from their home institution or a local institution, or on their own personal declaration. So, according to those vaunted "rules," I actually needed no letter at all and should have been allowed to appear and merely declare that I was a foreign scholar needing access to the archive. The whole experience proves that the rules are often irrelevant. It is the personalities and their own individual authorities that matter in the former Soviet space. Chalking up my own little victory in this struggle, I never gave the director that original letter from Stanford.

But the difficulties of working at APRK extended far beyond the question of access. Everything at APRK seemed designed to frustrate my work. In their standard protocol, I was required to provide a one-page summary of my dissertation topic. The summary then became the defining document according to which they would determine whether the files I wished to see were related to my topic. In essence, I had to prove that every file I wanted to see contained material directly related to my research topic before I would be allowed to look at it. Given the extraordinary vagueness of file descriptions in archival indexes (and here APRK is really no different from any other Soviet-era archive), this was frequently an impossible task. Complaining to the director of the reading room, I was shown some documents in particularly poor shape and told that they could not just let researchers go flipping through documents, or they would turn to dust.

The issue of accessing materials became rather comic once I started to request documents from the year 1951. I had written my summary indicating that the chronological limits were the 1930s to 1950s. However, the reading-room staff interpreted these dates as 1930–1950. Consequently, I was grilled about why I was requesting documents outside the scope of my topic. After a great deal of convincing (following a confused double-check to ensure the accuracy of my own Russian writing), I finally gained access to documents from 1951 and later, but I was informed that they expected me to take less detailed notes on these materials.

I will never understand why archivists thought I would travel thousands of miles to waste my time reading and taking notes on materials unrelated to my dissertation. After reading a short one-page summary research plan, the archival employees acted as if they understood the boundaries of my topic better than I. In fact, from day one, the director and the reading-room staff at APRK seemed bent on pushing me out the door and on to Karaganda, my next destination, as soon as possible. I have never discovered why. The sensitivity of the Gulag as a topic could have been the problem, but I never got the feeling that this subject made anybody nervous in the year 2000. Perhaps, one might think, the archive merely had an aversion to foreigners working with their materials. This, however, seems unlikely given that other American graduate students have had notably more success working at APRK than I did.

While all the materials shown to me had been declassified, I was placed under numerous restrictions as to how I worked. I was not allowed to use a computer to take notes. I could not order photocopies. All my notes were to be taken in notebooks and left at the archive at the end of each day. After I filled a notebook, the reading-room director reviewed the notes before giving me permission to take it out of the archive. As the notes had to be read, they all had to be written in Russian, a particularly problematic restriction given that it limited my effectiveness at summarizing documents and forced me to take down more direct quotes than otherwise would have been necessary. Prior to use, the reading-room staff numbered each page in the notebook and ran a sealed string through all the pages to prevent their removal or replacement. The reading-room employee then signed and dated the notebook, attesting to the number of pages it contained.

In view of the difficulties I had already faced, the notion of the reading-room director reviewing my notebooks was a matter of much concern. I easily imagined doing a week or two of writing in a notebook only to have it taken away from me. Fortunately, this did not happen, but only after an almost surreal encounter. One day the director of the reading room called me into her office. Given my concern with providing accurate enough summaries of documents in Russian for my later use, I had adopted a practice of selectively quoting from crucial parts of documents. In the course of copying out these quotes longhand and in Russian, I made frequent use of ellipses to remind myself later where I had left out passages. These ellipses apparently evoked some notion of conspiracy for the reading-room director, as she interrogated me on whether they were in fact references to passages in some notebook that I had secreted into the archive and not shown them. Fortunately, I managed to convince her that there was no deviousness behind the ellipses and no second notebook. Ultimately, all of my notebooks were returned to me, and only one name was removed from one page of the notes.

Upon leaving the archive for good, I had one last conversation with the reading-room director. She asked me about my experience working in the

archive. I explained to her some of the differences between working conditions in Moscow and Almaty. I pointed out that in Moscow I had been allowed to take notes on a computer, that nobody had reviewed my notes, and
that I had been allowed to secure photocopies. I tried to explain to her the
particular difficulties for a foreign scholar working thousands of miles from
home and family, and trying to complete his work as efficiently as possible.
I noted how much faster I had been able to work in Moscow under fewer
restrictions. Although she promised to talk to the archive director, her response was largely one of disbelief in my descriptions of working conditions
in Moscow archives.

Ultimately, I think, the main drawback of my research experience in Almaty,
beyond the frustrations and inefficiencies, was a loss of perspective. Struggling for access to each and every file and wondering whether a local study
of the Gulag outside of Russia was going to be possible, I soon became
happy just to see any material sitting in front of me. At times, I failed to make
a proper evaluation of its value to my research. I spent just over two months
working in that archive in Almaty, and now sitting at home writing my dissertation, I realize that what I did there will likely find its way into no more
than one small section of one chapter of the finished product. While this is no
doubt attributable in part to this loss of perspective, it is also because my
next stop, Karaganda, held archival treasures.

Arriving just before the spring equinox in Karaganda (spring, alas, was a
much later arrival) was a profound difference from my earlier experiences in
the former Soviet Union. The second-largest city in Kazakhstan, Karaganda
is quite different from Moscow and Almaty. While the latter two boast robust
populations of foreign, especially American, businessmen, Karaganda is a
city in decline. The decline in coal-mining and a rapidly falling population
(largely due to the departure of German and Slavic residents for their "home"
nation-states) have led to a notable lack of vitality and an almost total absence of native or foreign wealth on display in the city streets. The only other
Americans I met in Karaganda were a few young Peace Corps volunteers
and one young couple in town to adopt a baby. The virtual absence of local
experience with Americans was a boon for me. While residents of Moscow
and Almaty frequently seemed fed up with the Americans who had entered
their cities in the past decade (and on whom they had placed blame for many
of their current problems), locals in Karaganda displayed much of the wonder, awe, and curiosity about Americans so prominent in accounts of late
Soviet and early post-Soviet visitors.

My very first days in Karaganda included an invitation to greet the gathered students and faculty of Karaganda State University during their holiday
celebration of the vernal equinox, *Nauryz*. As an "honored guest" of the his-

tory faculty, I partook in a wide array of fascinating cultural experiences. Each faculty set up its own mock traditional Kazakh community and feast. When the university rector visited the history faculty, he offered me the first slice of meat from the lamb's head—a sign of honor. After a few too many toasts in my honor with the history faculty, I entered a full-size Kazakh hut set up inside one of the university's main buildings for yet more food and drink with university deans and faculty heads.

Even everyday life was different for me in Karaganda. My decidedly non-native accent meant that nearly every visit to a shop was greeted with questions: "You're not one of ours [*ne nashe*], are you?" Soon my reluctance to reveal that I was an American—it had taken shape in Moscow—gave way to great pleasure at this opening to meet people, tell them about myself, and learn about them. On many an occasion, I was told that I was the first American that this or that person had ever met. The shops close to my apartment became a true neighborhood for me in ways I had never experienced in Moscow or Almaty.

I should note that love of Americans is by no means ubiquitous even in Karaganda. Several times, while working in the archive there, employees of the State Archive of the Karaganda Region (GAKO) invited me to lunch. The archivist who hosted these affairs—to my chagrin they frequently included vodka in the middle of a workday—had a son who was learning English. She was eager that I meet him and speak in English with him. Yet on two separate occasions, she followed a shot or two of vodka with the same question: "What do you think of the movie *Saving Private Ryan?*" This was merely the opening to a prolonged monologue, complaining that the movie did not show the "real" war. She showed a profound feeling of distaste for Americans, especially for their failure to respect and appreciate what the Soviet Union did in that war. When I tried to explain to her that American movies merely showed the American experience of war, she launched into further asides about America's lack of history, literature, and music. Mark Twain was merely a children's author, and jazz was created not by Americans but by *negry*, who were "not genuine Americans." She seemed confused and conflicted over the fact that she hated Americans but liked me.

Despite such exchanges with this one seemingly anomalous individual, life in Karaganda was refreshing. Work in the archives was similarly refreshing, especially when compared to my difficulties in Almaty. Here I found materials that will figure in virtually every page of my manuscript. In retrospect, this was nothing more than good fortune. Moving along to the regional archives of Kazakhstan, my preparation was even sketchier than it had been when I went to Almaty. In fact, I arrived in Karaganda without even knowing for certain where the materials of the local camp administration were located and whether they were accessible. Good fortune and contacts made everything work. One of the wisest things I did while in Almaty was to seek out any information I could obtain about working in Karaganda. Alma Sultangalieva arranged a meeting for me with K.S. Aldazhumanov at the Institute of History of the Kazakh Academy of Sciences. Aldazhumanov set up meetings for me with his colleagues at Karaganda State University (which led among other things to my participation in the *Nauryz* holiday already described). These colleagues arranged for me to meet long-time local history professor D.A. Shaimukhanov, a member of their faculty and author of a volume on Karlag (the main Soviet-era concentration camp in the region). Professor Shaimukhanov kindly revealed to me the location of key materials and allowed me to use his name in my first contact with local archival officials.

Karlag materials were held by the archival division of the Center for Legal Statistics and Information (TsPSI) under the Procurator of Karaganda Region. I arrived at TsPSI to meet the center's director, Viktor Goretskii, and here I got my luckiest break. Goretskii, a man of Slavic origin, is revered by his mostly female Kazakh archival employees. (Respect across this ethnic divide is frequently missing in Karaganda.) They hail Goretskii for his devotion to making the history of the camps in the Karaganda region widely known. He allowed me to see any documents held in the archive, be they administrative materials on the operation of Karlag or individual prisoner files and investigative materials on "crimes" committed in the camps. Archival materials were even more accessible here than in Moscow. The matter was a little tricky, however, because these materials had never been officially declassified. Goretskii personally authorized my use of the materials and sought to cover himself by acquiring permission from his superiors in the office of the Kazakh Procurator in Astana for me to take photocopies out of the country. With the exceptions I will describe below, my research in Karaganda was rewarding and successful. Nonetheless, the quasi-legal nature of my access to these materials does not bode well for their continued availability to scholars, particularly should there be a change in leadership at the center or at TsPSI.

While the materials I acquired at TsPSI are outstanding and will play a substantial role in my dissertation, even Goretskii's incredible openness did not mean that research in Karaganda went entirely smoothly. First, the archival materials at TsPSI are, as several of their employees told me, in an "uncivilized" condition, i.e., no archival indexes exist. My research depended in large measure upon the helpfulness of archival employees who had worked with the materials and could point me in certain directions. I also greatly benefited from a card-file index—created by previous researchers at TsPSI—of a small portion of documents in the collection. I used this index primarily to identify the different types of materials available in the archive and to direct me to their location. At times, I also resorted to the random but often successful "please bring me a few files" method of research.

As for actual working conditions, I labored in a tiny room that TsPSI rented along with file storage space from the State Archive of Karaganda Region. Cramped into the small space, most days I worked side by side with two TsPSI employees who were typically fulfilling requests from various individuals for information about their or their relatives' exile or imprisonment in the Karaganda region during the Stalin era. Periodically, local graduate students or historians would spend a few days working in the archive, but most of the time I was the only non-TsPSI researcher there.

Here I must digress to discuss language in contemporary Kazakhstan. Official government policy currently states that Kazakh is the official state language, while Russian is the official language of interethnic communication. Very few Slavic residents of Kazakhstan speak the Kazakh language. Even among the ethnic Kazakh population, it is far from universally employed. Quite frequently, Kazakh government speeches and official communications are rendered in both languages. Russian is not officially suppressed as in Uzbekistan, but the lack of knowledge of Kazakh has provoked suspicion among local Slavs of these dual-language government announcements. On more than one occasion, local Russian friends in Karaganda told me with conviction that the government was telling the Kazakh-speaking population different things than it was communicating to the rest of the population in Russian. While I have no reason to believe this was actually the case, the reasoning behind such thinking became clear to me in that tiny room at TsPSI. I do not speak Kazakh, only Russian. I worked in the room with two Kazakh women who typically spoke Russian to one another except, it seemed, when they did not want me to understand their conversation. I had always suspected this was the case. One day I overheard one of the ladies speaking on the phone in Russian about my photocopy order. When she noticed that I had looked up at the mention of my name, she abruptly shifted her conversation to Kazakh.

Many working restrictions at TsPSI were actually similar to those at Almaty. I wrote all my notes in Russian in notebooks bound and stamped by archival employees and left in the archive until archival staff had reviewed them. In marked contrast, however, I was allowed to order as many photocopies of documents as I wished. Out of approximately 1,500 pages of photocopies ordered, I was allowed to bring nearly 1,300 pages with me out of the country. This facilitated my work tremendously, allowing me to cover very large amounts of material in a very short time (and to get home to my wife on schedule some eight months after leaving).

One instructive aspect of my work in Karaganda has to do with the documents that were taken back from me. Nearly all of the photocopies that I had

ordered but were denied to me dealt with the system of internal camp surveillance. The same was true for the several pages removed from my notebooks. Sensitivity about the issue of surveillance is common to both Moscow
and Karaganda. In Moscow, all of the central Gulag administration's files
have been declassified with the exception of individual staff files and the
internal surveillance section. Furthermore, portions of the central administrative files of the Soviet internal exile system have been reclassified after
initially being available to scholars for a short period. All of the reclassified
material in this collection also deals with the system of internal surveillance.
It is easy to see why post-Soviet authorities would be cautious with materials
about informants and other especially sensitive details of concentration camp
life. Yet none of the Karaganda materials that I had requested dealt with
individuals ("agent Ivanov reports that prisoner Petrov said."), but merely
laid out the way in which the internal surveillance section of the camp worked.
While I have not been able to determine the reason for the universal reluctance to release information on this topic, one can only speculate that similar
systems of surveillance operate today inside post-Soviet places of detention.

One other document that was removed from my photocopy requests in
Karaganda was the 1939 regulation on running Soviet labor camps. This was the
most basic document governing the way that camps were to be constructed and
operated, including the rights and obligations of prisoners and camp staff. I was
told that I could not take a copy of this document out of the country with me, but
was given free rein (on my last afternoon in Karaganda, of course) to take as
many notes about this lengthy document as I wished. In a mad dash to capture as
much of it as possible in those last precious minutes of a lengthy research trip, I
wrote all my notes about the document in English to save time and on the assumption (proven true) that they would not take my notebook from me again. In
a typical case of post-Soviet irony, this sensitive document, which the archive
director seemed afraid to copy for me, has since been published in full.

The materials I gathered in Karaganda offer rich, fascinating, and sometimes tragic insights into Gulag life. The individual prisoner files, in particular, tell many tales. Many of these files draw you into a bit of an individual's
life only to crush you with a succinct death certificate advising of the com-
pass direction in which the head was pointed in its letter-coded burial place.
Over 200 pages tell of the descent into paranoia of proud Red Army veteran
Kapiton Kuznetsov, the leader of the famous Kengir camp uprising. Investigative files bespeak a certain type of resistance to Soviet authority among a
group of devoutly Orthodox believers, who refused to cooperate with Soviet
authority in any way. Their interrogation protocols all indicate their refusal
to sign any Soviet government papers. One prisoner clearly had actively resisted when they took his photograph and fingerprints. The photograph shows

him struggling and looking down, while the fingerprints are smudged. Accompanying documents note in passing that force was used to obtain both. Other files reveal prisoners trying to do more than survive, trying to live in these conditions. One young woman's file contains several eloquent love letters that had been intercepted as she threw them to her boyfriend over the wall separating a men's from a women's camp zone. All of these files reveal the complexities of an emerging Gulag society, the underlying subject of my dissertation project.

Yet one particularly important lesson about the Gulag in Karaganda came not from any archival document but from a visit to the ruins of a camp zone at Spassk in the steppe south of the city. While all the wooden buildings had either burned or been looted entirely, the stone walls of the zone's internal prison still stood, as did the zone's exterior stone walls and metal guard towers. Viewed from the floorless guard tower, the steppe in every direction is overwhelmingly flat, empty, and endless. The implications for Gulag life are many. With nowhere to hide, how was a prisoner to escape from the camp zone at Spassk? Yet even in these conditions camp authorities expended tremendous effort and resources on guards and a system of internal surveillance to prevent just such escapes.

My experiences working in Almaty and Karaganda reveal the diversity of working conditions in various post-Soviet locales just over a decade after the fall of the Soviet Union. Few generalizations can really be made. Archives are not necessarily more open the further you get from Moscow, nor are they necessarily more closed. Perhaps the unsurprising lesson of these experiences is the extreme significance for researchers of individual archive directors and archivists who serve as gatekeepers to historical sources. Whether they are erecting roadblocks that violate the official "rules" of an archive or making available documents that have never been officially declassified, the absence of significant interest at high government levels about issues of archival access leaves most practical decisions in the hands of these individual directors. Perhaps, then, the best the scholar can do when traveling to lightly researched locales is to make as many contacts as possible prior to entering an archive director's office for the first time, because the impressions and the relationship built on that first visit can potentially determine the entire course of research in an archive. Oh, and be sure to remove your overcoat.

Note

1. "Confining Soviet Society: The Gulag in the Karaganda Region of Kazakhstan, 1930s–1950s," Stanford University, forthcoming.

Index